P9-DGM-144

# Managing Technology to Meet Your Mission

Find useful tools from the book that you can manipulate and a special Webinar discount code at www.josseybass.com/go/nten.

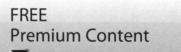

| FREE<br>Premium Content<br>▼ | JOSSEY-BASS™<br>An Imprint of<br>Ⓦ **WILEY** |
| --- | --- |
| This book includes premium content that can be accessed from our Web site when you register at **www.josseybass.com/go/nten** using the password *professional*. | |

# Managing Technology to Meet Your Mission

## A Strategic Guide for Nonprofit Leaders

HOLLY ROSS, KATRIN VERCLAS, ALISON LEVINE

### EDITORS

People Who Change the World Need the Tools to Do It
Sponsored by NTEN: The Nonprofit Technology Network

JOSSEY-BASS
A Wiley Imprint
www.josseybass.com

Copyright © 2009 by The Nonprofit Technology Network (NTEN). All rights reserved.

Published by Jossey-Bass
A Wiley Imprint
989 Market Street, San Francisco, CA 94103-1741—www.josseybass.com

No part of this publication may be reproduced, stored in a retrieval system, or transmitted in any form or by any means, electronic, mechanical, photocopying, recording, scanning, or otherwise, except as permitted under Section 107 or 108 of the 1976 United States Copyright Act, without either the prior written permission of the publisher, or authorization through payment of the appropriate per-copy fee to the Copyright Clearance Center, Inc., 222 Rosewood Drive, Danvers, MA 01923, 978-750-8400, fax 978-646-8600, or on the Web at www.copyright.com. Requests to the publisher for permission should be addressed to the Permissions Department, John Wiley & Sons, Inc., 111 River Street, Hoboken, NJ 07030, 201-748-6011, fax 201-748-6008, or online at www.wiley.com/go/permissions.

Readers should be aware that Internet Web sites offered as citations and/or sources for further information may have changed or disappeared between the time this was written and when it is read.

Limit of Liability/Disclaimer of Warranty: While the publisher and author have used their best efforts in preparing this book, they make no representations or warranties with respect to the accuracy or completeness of the contents of this book and specifically disclaim any implied warranties of merchantability or fitness for a particular purpose. No warranty may be created or extended by sales representatives or written sales materials. The advice and strategies contained herein may not be suitable for your situation. You should consult with a professional where appropriate. Neither the publisher nor author shall be liable for any loss of profit or any other commercial damages, including but not limited to special, incidental, consequential, or other damages.

Jossey-Bass books and products are available through most bookstores. To contact Jossey-Bass directly call our Customer Care Department within the U.S. at 800-956-7739, outside the U.S. at 317-572-3986, or fax 317-572-4002.

Jossey-Bass also publishes its books in a variety of electronic formats. Some content that appears in print may not be available in electronic books.

**Library of Congress Cataloging-in-Publication Data**
Managing technology to meet your mission : a strategic guide for nonprofit leaders / Holly Ross, Katrin Verclas, Alison Levine, editors.
      p. cm.
   Includes index.
   ISBN 978-0-470-34365-4 (pbk.)
   1. Nonprofit organizations—Information technology. 2. Nonprofit organizations—Effect of technological innovations on. 3. Nonprofit organizations. I. Ross, Holly. II. Verclas, Katrin. III. Levine, Alison.
   HD62.6.M366 2009
   658.4'062—dc22

                                                 2008050161

Printed in the United States of America
FIRST EDITION
*PB Printing*   10   9   8   7   6   5   4   3   2   1

# CONTENTS

PART TWO

# The Tools                                                    157

# CONTENTS OF THE WEB SITE

# ACKNOWLEDGMENTS

NTEN is a community of nonprofit technology professionals, and tight-knit communities are like families. Mostly, we support each other, we listen to each other, and we bring out the best in each other. We're better collectively than we are on our own. We also have our differences, but it's those differences, and the spaces we create to share them, that make us better.

We'd like to think that this book is a reflection of our community. Not only are all the chapter contributors NTEN members from a wide variety of backgrounds, but the book itself was born from the NTEN community. It was your queries on our discussion lists, your comments on our blog, and your hallway conversations at our annual conference that inspired us to attempt to tackle these topics. Many of our members provided feedback and ideas as we worked our way through the manuscript, and we thank you for sharing your experiences and expertise.

Along the way, numerous people helped make this book a reality. First, thank you to Alison Levine. You tackled the editing of several key chapters, provided invaluable advice on the rest, were a sounding board whenever we needed to vent. You are talented and thoughtful—a real treasure. We were very lucky to work with you.

Second, the NTEN staff and board provided the technical and emotional support one needs when wrangling eleven chapters from eleven authors. Without your advice and help, we would still be dreaming about this book.

Of course, there wouldn't be a book at all if it weren't for our talented and selfless authors. You all went above and beyond the call of duty. We are so proud of your contribution to the book and are lucky to have the opportunity to work with you.

Thank you to the editors at John Wiley & Sons in our first foray into the book-publishing world. Jesse Wiley—the young Wiley, as you are known—you know what you are doing, and you know this sector and what it needs. Thank you for seeking us out.

And most of all, we need to thank our families. There was no shortage of late nights and lost weekends while writing, reading, editing, prodding, culling, and rearranging. Thank you, Ami, John, Sam, Emma, and Lenny for love and wisdom and insights. You gave us the support and copious coffee we needed. Thank you.

**Peter Campbell** serves as director of information technology at Earthjustice, a nonprofit law firm dedicated to protecting the earth. Peter has been managing technology for nonprofits and law firms for over twenty years, and he has a broad knowledge of systems, email, and the Web. Peter's focus is on advancing communication, collaboration, and efficiency through creative use of the Web and other technology platforms. Peter is active in the nonprofit community as a member of NTEN, blogs occasionally at http://techcafeteria.com, serves as webmaster of the nonprofit technology portal at http://nptech.info, and spends as much quality time as possible with his wife, Linda, and eight-year-old son, Ethan.

**Michael Cervino** is a principal consultant and cofounder of Beaconfire Consulting (http://www.beaconfire.com), an Arlington, Virginia–based consulting firm that helps progressive and moderate nonprofit organizations build websites and online campaigns and marketing programs. For nearly two decades Michael has helped organizations create effective, results-driven online programs and integrated advocacy, fundraising, and marketing communications programs. He is an author and frequent speaker at NTC, The Bridge Conference, among other conferences. He lives with his wife, Kindra, and two sons, Mickey and Killian, in Washington, D.C., where they enjoy the cultural offerings of the city and the surrounding natural beauty of the region's campgrounds and fishing holes.

**Willow Cook** is senior editor at TechSoup.org, a project of the Tech-Soup Global Network, where she edits technology articles for an international audience of nonprofits and NGOs. With a dual background in editing and design, she has also worked on projects for organizations including Yerba Buena Center for the Arts, the World Affairs Council of Northern California, and Global Philanthropy Forum.

**Dahna Goldstein,** founder of PhilanTech LLC, develops Web-based applications for the nonprofit sector and has worked for venture philanthropies, including Ashoka and Blue Ridge Foundation New York. She has also produced interactive eLearning programs, including the award-winning "What Is a Leader?" program, for Harvard Business School Publishing and Global Education Network. Goldstein holds a bachelor of arts degree from Williams College, a master of education degree, with a concentration in technology, from Harvard University, and a master of business administration degree from New York University's Stern School of Business. She is the chair of the board of the I Do Foundation.

**Edward Granger-Happ** is the CIO at Save the Children and chairman of the board of NetHope, a consortium of top international nonprofits focused on ICT and collaboration. In 2008, he was an executive fellow and CIO in residence at the Tuck School of Business at Dartmouth, while on sabbatical from Save the Children. Save the Children is his third career; previously he was a management consultant and a Wall Street executive. In 2007, the editors of *eWEEK*, *CIO Insight*, and *Baseline* selected Mr. Granger-Happ as one of the Top 100 Most Influential People in IT and one of the Top 100 CIOs.

**Steve Heye** was most recently at the YMCA of the USA in the Technology Resource Group for ten years but has been involved in the YMCA since age twelve as a volunteer. He has a unique blend of operations, technology, communications, and training experience with a backbone of finance. Heye created resources, conferences, and training on technology for YMCAs nationwide and worked with a committee of local

YMCA staff to create a resource that helps YMCAs align their technology with the organization's strategic, business, and operations goals. He has a bachelor's degree in finance from North Central College. His blog is at http://steveheye.blogspot.com.

**Beth Kanter** is a trainer, blogger, and consultant to nonprofits and individuals in effective use of social media. Her expertise is in how to use new web tools (blogging, tagging, wikis, photo sharing, video blogging, screencasting, social networking sites, virtual worlds, and so on) to support nonprofits. She has worked on projects that include training, curriculum development, research, and evaluation. Kanter is an experienced coach to "digital immigrants" in the personal mastery of these tools. She is a professional blogger and writes about the use of social media tools in the nonprofit sector for social change.

**John Kenyon** is a nonprofit technology strategist who has worked with nonprofits for over eighteen years, providing advice, teaching seminars, and writing about technology. With Michael Stein he wrote *The eNonprofit: A Guide to ASPs, Internet Services and Online Software*. Kenyon's consulting practice concentrates on strategic uses of appropriate technologies, effective communication, and leveraging the Internet. He is an adjunct professor at the University of San Francisco and has been a featured speaker at conferences and workshops across the United States, England, and Australia and online. For updates on his work or to contact him, visit http://www.johnkenyon.org.

**Kevin Lo** is lead technology analyst at TechSoup.org, a project of the TechSoup Global Network, where he creates a variety of content—including blog posts, articles, and in-depth papers—for the TechSoup.org website. He also does research, analysis, and evaluation for TechSoup Stock, a global partnership that helps nonprofits and NGOs with technology acquisition and utilization. Lo received his master of public administration degree and master's degree in international relations at the Maxwell School of Syracuse University.

**Scott McCallum** has more than thirty years of executive experience in operations and supply management, media and public relations, marketing and development, and government relations. He served as

Wisconsin's governor, with a career spanning more than two decades in public service offices. McCallum serves as president and CEO of the Aidmatrix Foundation, a nonprofit that uses advanced information technology to create efficiencies between donors and those in need. Over $1.5 billion in aid is transacted annually over Aidmatrix solutions. McCallum earned his bachelor's degree at Macalester College and his master's degree in international studies and economics at Johns Hopkins University.

**Cassie Scarano** is the vice president and cofounder of Commongood Careers (http://www.cgcareers.org), an innovative not-for-profit search firm dedicated to supporting social entrepreneurs with recruitment and hiring at every organizational level while also addressing talent-related issues throughout the sector. She has ten years of experience in nonprofit organizations and has served as the dean of admissions at The Steppingstone Foundation, director of operations at The New Teacher Project's Massachusetts Institute for New Teachers (MINT), and director of Summerbridge Cambridge, all nonprofits dedicated to providing high-quality educational opportunities to a diversity of students. Scarano holds a master's degree in education from Boston University and a master's degree in business administration from Boston University, with a concentration in nonprofit management, as well as a bachelor's degree in sociology from Northwestern University.

**Madeline Stanionis** has been raising money, organizing, and communicating for organizations and causes for twenty years and is currently the CEO of Watershed, an online advocacy and fundraising consultancy. While at Watershed and in her previous role as president of Donordigital, Stanionis has led internet strategies for organizations including the Humane Society of the United States, Planned Parenthood Federation of America, Amnesty International, CARE, The Nation, CREDO/ Working Assets, Ocean Conservancy, Victory Fund, and NARAL Pro-Choice America. She is the author of *The Mercifully Brief, Real World Guide to Raising Thousands (If Not Tens of Thousands) of Dollars with E-Mail*, published by Emerson and Church.

**Keith R. Thode** leads daily operations for Aidmatrix, after serving in consulting and leadership roles in major technology firms Accenture, Baan Company, and i2 Technologies. He has been a founding force, contributing to Aidmatrix since its initial solution deployments in 2001. He holds a summa cum laude master's degree in industrial distribution from Texas A&M University and a bachelor of science degree in economics and organizational development from Vanderbilt University. Thode serves in advisory roles to organizations in multiple sectors. He contributes in board and officer roles with meaningful organizations such as 121 Community Church, NPower Texas, and the European Committee of Young Life International.

**James L. Weinberg** is the founder and CEO of Commongood Careers (http://www.cgcareers.org), an innovative not-for-profit search firm dedicated to supporting social entrepreneurs with recruitment and hiring at every organizational level while also addressing talent-related issues throughout the sector. Previously, he served as the development director at BELL and the executive director of the Homeless Children's Education Fund. Weinberg has a master's degree in management and public policy from Carnegie Mellon and a bachelor's degree in psychology from Tufts; he was a Coro Fellow in Public Affairs. He is the vice-chair of the Nonprofit Workforce Coalition and a board member of Emerging Practitioners in Philanthropy.

# THE EDITORS

**Holly Ross** has spent more than five years at NTEN, combing through all the technology fads and listening to the NTEN community to line up the webinars, conferences, and research that will help members use technology to make the world a better place. From ubiquitous access to technology leadership to social media trends, as executive director, She brings the wisdom of the NTEN crowd to the nonprofit sector.

Ross came to nonprofit technology after working for social change at CALPIRG and during her college days at the University of California at Berkeley. In between meetings and emailing, Holly tries to raise her three-year-old daughter and occasionally pays attention to her fabulous husband.

**Katrin Verclas** is a recognized expert in new media communications for social impact. She is the cofounder and editor of MobileActive.org, a global network of practitioners using mobile phones for social impact. She is also a principal at Calder Strategies, focusing on mobile strategy, impact evaluation, effectiveness and ROI assessment, and interactive capacity building.

Verclas has written widely on communication strategies and new media in citizen participation and civil society organizations and for development. She is a coauthor of *Wireless Technology for Social Change,* a report on trends in mobile use by NGOs with the United Nations Foundation and Vodafone Group Foundation. Her background is in IT management, IT in social change organizations, and philanthropy. She has led several nonprofit organizations, including a stint as the executive director of NTEN: The Nonprofit Technology Network, the national association of IT professionals working in the more than one million nonprofit organizations in the United States. Previously she served as a program officer at the Proteus Fund, focusing on the use of technology in civic and democratic participation, and in government transparency.

She is the author of a chapter in *Mobilizing 2.0*, a book focused on engaging young people in public life. She is a frequent speaker on communications and ICTs in civil society at national and international conferences and has published numerous articles on technology for social change in leading popular and industry publications.

**Alison Levine** has worked in the nonprofit sector for more than ten years, the last two as NTEN's Special Projects Fellow. She holds master's degrees in nonprofit administration and in science and environmental reporting. She whole-heartedly believes that technology is the most powerful tool to help nonprofits change the world. When she is not thinking about technology and nonprofits, she likes to go to the other end of the technological spectrum and get out into the wilderness where her cell phone doesn't even get reception.

# INTRODUCTION

As a nonprofit leader or manager, you probably play a number of roles: human resource manager, chief financial officer, keeper of the mission, wrangler of the board, and on occasion maybe even cleaning staff. There's one more role you need to play, even though you may not have realized that when you signed up for the job: the role of technology manager.

There is not much in your nonprofit that isn't profoundly affected by technology. From financial management to program delivery to fundraising, technology is fueling the efficiency, effectiveness, and innovations in your organization and around the sector. Nonprofit organizations are using databases to track donations, email programs to reach members with their messages, and accounting software to manage their finances. Increasingly, nonprofits are using the Web to deliver services to their clients, bringing laptops out into the field with them, and experimenting with social media like Facebook and blogging.

Yet even as technology is changing the way we live and work, many nonprofit leaders are struggling to understand how to effectively manage the technology they have and how to position themselves to leverage technology in their future work. And yes, technology in its many forms can often seem like an unruly child: full of possibilities, but sometimes tough to manage. If you are one of those leaders struggling to make sense of all this, we're here with three important messages:

It's not your fault.

You are not alone.

You can do it.

Let's start at the top: *it's not your fault.* In our conversations with nonprofit leaders around the world, we often hear about the same challenges:

- *The rate of change is accelerating.* It often feels like your technology is out of date before you get it out of the box. Get used to the feeling, because it's not going away any time soon. In fact, social scientists are throwing away their old models for predicting the rates of technology change. Some now estimate that the amount of change in the twenty-first century will be equivalent to all the change in the previous twenty thousand years.[1] That's a lot of change.

- *Language is a barrier.* Like medicine and law, the language of technology is littered with acronyms and secret meanings. RAM, ROM, and CPU are the tip of the iceberg. For the uninitiated, technology is the domain better left to experts who can navigate the zeroes and ones that make it all go. And let's be honest: working with experts isn't always easy.

- *Choosing what advances your mission is hard.* Whether you are investing time or money (and usually it's both), you are expending precious resources to get that new database up and running, redesign your website, or update your computers. Given that technology is not your core expertise and that it changes all the time, understanding how technology investments advance your organization's mission is hard.

- *Failure is scary.* You're a leader because you're successful, right? No leader wants to fail, and unless you are really comfortable with it, technology is probably one area where you will fail. Maybe more than once.

- *Managing change is not easy.* As you will see in this book, technology isn't really about technology at all; it's about change. The introduction of even the smallest technology at your organization will change how and why people do their work. And that is harder to manage than anything.

If any of those challenges sound familiar, then this book is for you. *Managing Technology to Meet Your Mission* is more than just a technology primer. It will give you the information you need to know to understand the key technologies in your nonprofit. And more important, we give you the strategies you need to manage those technologies. Because each nonprofit is unique, how and why you use technology to meet your mission will vary. You will not find hard and absolute rules here, but you will find models for making technology decisions and guiding your technology strategy. We cover a wide variety of topics in the book, from budgeting for IT to online fundraising, but there are a few key themes that appear in nearly every chapter:

- *Mission first.* As a nonprofit leader, you may find that your staff, board, and stakeholders pitch new technology ideas frequently. Well-meaning individuals sometimes develop what we like to call "shiny object syndrome." They see a new tool and are mesmerized. It may even happen to *you* from time to time. The first step in making good technology decisions at your organization is to understand which technologies matter for your mission and which don't. This will eliminate 90 percent of the technology clutter you deal with. No matter what aspect of the organization's use of technology you are addressing, you have to ask yourself first, "Will this help us meet our mission better?" If the answer is no, move on. If the answer is yes, you have some more investigative work to do.

- *People second.* Technology is always about more than the actual application or tool. If a technology is truly going to help you meet your mission, your staff, board, and stakeholders need to see that value and buy into inevitable changes. Recognizing and validating the human experiences in your organization is an essential ingredient to success. The "people" part of technology also means making sure that you have the right people providing your technology support and services.

- *Evaluate and iterate.* Regardless of size or scope, every technology undertaking should be evaluated. More than ever before, technology affords you the opportunity to measure. Although you won't want to measure everything, you should measure the impact your technologies have on your organization in time saved, money saved, new stakeholders reached, dollars raised, and, most important, meeting your mission. If your technology implementations don't advance your goals, you'll need to rethink and iterate.

This brings us to our second message: *you are not alone.* Nonprofit leaders and even the people who wrote this book encounter these challenges every day. They surface in almost every training and in the many mailing lists that NTEN runs. This is why we've created this book. We hear about these from leaders at tiny volunteer-run start-ups and at giant international organizations. We want you to know that what you're experiencing is par for the course, and that with some training and some resources you can indeed become an extraordinary leader in regard to technology.

The contributors to this book reflect the scope and diversity of the IT experience. Consultants, IT directors, and even a governor contributed chapters to this book, and each of them struggled with the issues they address before they became subject matter experts. What they'll all agree to is this: successfully managing technology is about 10 percent technology and 90 percent planning and people.

Accordingly, you'll find two parts in this book: Part One, "Planning and People," and Part Two, "The Tools."

## Planning and People

Part One addresses the softer side of technology—the things that aren't about technology specifically, but can make or break your effort. The chapters in this section address topics such as planning, staffing, and budgeting:

- *Mission First: Achieving IT Alignment.* The relationship between technology and mission isn't always clear-cut, but it's the most important part of managing technology in any organization. In this chapter, we help you understand how technology and mission relate and give you a step-by-step process for aligning technology with your mission.

- *Managing Technology Change.* Most nonprofit leaders will tell you that money and time are the two biggest barriers to technology adoption. But all the money and time in the world won't guarantee the success of a technology initiative. To introduce technology in your organization successfully, you'll need to foster the right culture in your organization. In this chapter, we discuss the finer points of learning and inclusiveness that can make or break any technology initiative.

- *Measuring the Return on Investment of Technology.* Assessing the return on investment (ROI) of technology projects is crucial to securing board support and staff buy-in. This chapter explains techniques for ROI analysis in the nonprofit context to help guide your decision making and demonstrate results.

- *How to Decide: IT Planning and Prioritizing.* Nonprofits have limited resources, which usually means that we have to make tough choices about where to spend our time and money. Here we cover best practices in planning for technology projects, providing tools to help you make smart decisions about where to invest those resources.

- *Finding and Keeping the Right People.* Having the right staff in place is crucial to success with technology. This chapter discusses different specializations within technology, how to write a good job description for IT staff, and how to match skills sets with organizational needs for maximum effect. It also discusses recruiting channels, salaries, and evaluation of applicants' skills in the hiring process.

- *Budgeting for and Funding Technology.* Setting appropriate budgets and securing resources is one of the most important jobs a leader has, and raising money for technology presents a special set of challenges. This chapter examines adequate budgeting for different types of organizations and the classification of technological expenses, including what counts toward overhead versus program expenses. We review strategies for pitching technology projects and explore the foundations that fund them.

## The Tools

Part Two gives you an overview of the common tools you will use to get your work done, communicate, evaluate, and even raise a little money.

- *The Foundation: Introduction to IT and Systems.* Fancy online fundraising strategies and a fantastic website won't matter much if your IT basics aren't working. This chapter introduces the basics of information technology and systems in nonprofits, in simple, easy-to-understand language. IT areas such as databases, websites, and back-office infrastructure are covered. You'll gain a basic understanding of the workings and uses of IT systems and tools, providing a good foundation for the chapters that follow.

- *Where Are Your Stakeholders and What Are They Doing Online?* Before you engage in any online activities, it's a good idea to find out if your audience is online and what they are doing while there. We take you through some easy to implement evaluation strategies for determining what your audience is doing online now and for evaluating your online endeavors later.

- *Effective Online Communications.* The Internet has revolutionized marketing as a field. The creation of websites, campaigns to drive traffic to those sites, email newsletters, and blogs are just a few ways that marketing has advanced. This chapter provides strategies, best practices, evaluation, and case studies about online marketing to familiarize you with the breadth of possibilities and inform your decisions about allocating your marketing budget and staff time.

- *Donate Now: Online Fundraising.* Anyone with a "Donate Now" button can tell you that online fundraising just isn't that easy. Successful online fundraising strategies take planning, flexibility, and creativity. In this chapter, we outline the basics of a successful campaign, providing case studies and benchmarks to facilitate realistic goal setting.

- *Where Will We Be Tomorrow? The Future of IT in Nonprofits.* No one can tell you exactly what technologies and tools will crop up in the coming years, but we can talk about the trends that are most likely to continue and how that will affect your organization. This chapter offers practical advice to guide your current decision making and ensure that the choices you make now will matter in the coming years.

Don't think you need to sit down right now and read this book straight through to get the most out of it. As executive directors and managers, we know that nonprofit leaders don't always have the kind of time that book reading requires. Instead, we designed the book with your typical questions (and occasional crises) in mind. If, for example, you've just installed a new database, the staff hates it, and you want to quell the mutiny before it begins, you should skip straight to Chapter Two, "Managing Technology Change." If your boss wants to you spice up your e-newsletter, head over to Chapter Nine, "Effective Online Communications." However, if you find yourself facing a whole set of technology issues and you're looking for support in developing a larger technology strategy for your organization, then the entire book will provide a nice framework for you.

We've tried to cover the most important aspects of technology management, regardless of the size or issue area of your nonprofit. As comprehensive as it is, it doesn't cover every piece of technology used by nonprofits, and it's not a how-to manual for any specific set of tools. Use this book to shape your technology strategy—that is, how you make technology decisions—not for advice about which tools or services to use.

We wrote this book to get you started on the path to expertise. We also know that you will need support along the way. Some days you will need advice; others, a place to vent. It's important that you find a community of peers that will support you on your journey. The NTEN community is designed to provide that kind of support: answering technical questions, reviewing vendors, providing new ideas, and providing you with the support and wisdom along the way. In fact, we've set up a special site for readers of this book where you can get more information from the authors and additional information we weren't able to include in the book, as well as discuss your organization and the book. Join us at http://meetyourmission.org.

Here's our third and final message for you: *you can do it.* You can lead in the realm of technology as confidently and skillfully as you lead any other part of your organization. You don't need to get special technology training, and you'll never really have to know what XML stands for. Creating real change in your community is hard—and you do it anyway. You make remarkable things happen every day. Leading your organization's use of technology will be easy for you in comparison.

We look forward to working with you!

Holly Ross
Executive Director, NTEN
holly@meetyourmission.org

Katrin Verclas
Executive Director, MobileActive
katrin@meetyourmission.org

Alison Levine
Special Projects Fellow, NTEN

## Note

1. http://www.kurzweilai.net/articles/art0563.html?printable=1.

# Managing Technology to Meet Your Mission

# Planning and People

One machine can do the work of fifty ordinary men. No machine can do the work of one extraordinary man.

  —Elbert Hubbard, *The Roycroft Dictionary and Book of Epigrams,* 1923

It may seem odd that we are opening a book about technology with discussions of planning and people. But as you've likely experienced, it's the people using the technology that control how successfully it is used.

A database can have all the reporting tools and other whiz-bang features you need to track and serve your clients, but if your staff doesn't know how to use them—or worse, doesn't want to—that database is just an expensive spreadsheet program. Your server, holding all your mission-critical files, may be the lifeblood of your organization, but if you've failed to plan for maintenance and upgrades, it will crash—becoming an expensive paperweight.

The chapters in this section of the book are designed to give you a better understanding of all those things that have nothing to do with technology directly, and everything to do with the success of your technology initiatives. The relationship between technology and your mission, change management, planning, budgeting, and staffing for technology are all covered.

After reading this section of the book, you should have the fundamentals that will allow you to navigate *any* technology situation successfully.

# CHAPTER 1

# Mission First: Achieving IT Alignment

*Steve Heye*

This book is filled with great advice about how to manage the technology in your organization, but none of it will do you one bit of good unless you remember this: mission first. As a nonprofit leader you are, in many ways, lucky in this regard. You are bombarded daily with technology news, requests for software or gadgets from staff, and advice from everyone about what technology you should use. This cyclone of technology activity can be maddening, but if you use your mission as a filter, the cyclone will become a soft breeze.

Ever since the first desktop computers made their way into the nonprofit sector, information technology (IT) has helped organizations become more efficient and more effective, while also driving nonprofit leaders a little crazy. For many leaders, technology is a necessary evil. However, if nonprofits are going to leverage technology to its fullest potential, their leaders need to change that way of thinking. They need to view technology as a partner in achieving organizational goals. In other words, they need to *align* their investments in information technology with their efforts to further their mission.

This chapter will explore the relationship between mission and technology, clearly define the concept of IT alignment, explain its many benefits, examine its different stages, and provide a clear road map for real-world implementation. Although the following information and stories were developed specifically for YMCAs by YMCAs, all of the presented principles and ideas can be applied to any organization. However, you will need to take some time to define your own situation and needs. Your staff, funding, daily operations, technical ability, mission, and organizational culture will directly impact how you adopt and employ IT alignment. Therefore the following is not a set of rigid rules; rather, it is a basic framework meant to spur ideas, questions, and concepts that can easily be applied to your own situation.

## Mission First

Why is mission the first topic of a book about technology? Because mission is what makes the nonprofit sector matter. Unlike for-profit entities, nonprofits are not accountable to a financial bottom line; rather, they are responsible for serving a social bottom line. It's true that nonprofit leaders must be good financial stewards, but that's because their organizations won't be able to keep providing services (delivering the mission) to their communities if they go out of business.

The goal of IT alignment is to use technology to support and enhance the work that you do to meet your mission. In other words, IT alignment will help you select and implement technology to achieve your mission and to avoid the trap of implementing the latest technology because it's shiny, or because someone told you to. To make the most of this chapter, then, you'll need to know what mission really means.

## Vision Versus Mission

Many organizations use the terms *vision* and *mission* interchangeably, but they are not the same.

## Vision

Your vision is the description of the world you wish to create. According to BoardSource:

Through a vision statement, a nonprofit defines its ultimate motivation, its dreams, and its image of a desired future. A vision statement describes the ideal situation if the organization could fulfill its utmost wish.[1]

Vision statements should be future-oriented and establish a standard you are trying to reach. Vision statements often look like this:

- A community where no child goes to bed hungry

- Healthy wetlands that sustain a diversity of species in our state

- Clean drinking water for all Nigerians

## Mission

Your mission, on the other hand, is what your organization does. Although your organization may want to achieve clean drinking water for all Nigerians, how you go about realizing that vision is what's articulated in your mission. You may choose to work at the policy level, or you may provide direct services in Nigerian communities by providing wells, water treatment, or other services. BoardSource defines it as follows:

The mission statement provides the basis for judging the success of an organization and its programs. It helps to verify if the organization is on the right track and making the right decisions. It provides direction when the organization must adapt to new demands.[2]

Here are some sample mission statements:

- **Mercy Corps**: Mercy Corps exists to alleviate suffering, poverty and oppression by helping people build secure, productive, and just communities.

- **A local United Way**: To inspire the people of York County to make a difference in the lives of their neighbors through financial generosity and volunteer commitment.

- **Save the Bay**: Save the Bay is committed to fostering a personal connection between people and Narragansett Bay and encouraging investment in the bay's future.

Notice that all of these examples are specific enough to tell you a little bit about how each organization plans to reach its vision (inspiring people to volunteer in their communities or connecting people to a natural resource), but they are not so specific that the organizations are locked into specific strategies or numbers (like recruiting a thousand volunteers, or connecting people to the bay only through nature walks).

## The Intersection of Technology and Mission

Ultimately, every decision you make as a nonprofit leader should be grounded in your mission. Whether it's hiring more staff or starting a new program, you do it because it will help your organization achieve its mission. It can be tough at times to draw the line between technology and mission. Many leaders think of technology in the same way that they think of office supplies: it keeps the office going, but it isn't critical to the mission.

But technology is not just another office supply. Let's say you run out of paper clips one day. You can probably still work toward your mission fairly effectively (unless your mission involves paper clips somehow). But if your computers are crashing every hour, or your staff members don't understand how to use the software they are given, your ability to meet your mission slows down drastically. The kinds of efficiencies that well-implemented technology affords can allow your organization to serve more clients, plant more trees, and so on. A recent study reported that "information technology and telecommunications hardware, software, and services turns out to be a powerful driver of growth, having an impact on worker productivity three to five times that of non-IT capital (e.g., buildings and machines)."[3] In other words, the new computer that you buy for your administrative assistant will make her three to five times more productive than practically any other investment you could make.

Of course, technology is different from your average paper clip in one other key way. Increasingly, nonprofits are using technology tools like handheld computers, smart phones, and websites not only to create efficiencies but also to become more effective. For example, online chat forums are connecting mothers of children with birth defects so that they can get the support and advice they need, regardless of the time of day or their location. In the past, this kind of service could only have been provided by expensive and time-consuming face-to-face meetings. Neighborhood associations are using smart phones to email reports of potholes, damaged lights, and other city services that need attention to city hall, rather than waiting for city hall to be open to place a report. Examples of the direct connection between technology and mission abound. You can't say that about a paper clip—or any of your other office supplies.

Knowing now how technology and mission relate, you can begin to explore the process of aligning technology with mission in your organization.

## Definition of IT Alignment

To many nonprofit leaders, technology is like a foreign language—full of buzzwords and three-letter acronyms that cause an immediate disconnect. So let's begin by defining the term *IT alignment*. At its core, IT alignment refers to the coordination of an IT strategy with the goals, strategies, and processes used to meet an organization's mission.

For example, an organization may use a database—rather than a slow and often inaccurate paper calendar—to quickly access client records and schedule new appointments. This creates efficiencies for the staff, allowing them to serve more people. Taking this example a step further, the same staff could be trained to interpret the client records and scheduling data and use it to make decisions, such as which classes should be offered more often or which classes should be dropped. That information could then be shared internally across functions and possibly with collaborating organizations. The organization could also create a website that allows clients to access their own data and schedule their own appointments any time, day or night. So with IT alignment, technology is not only allowing staff members to work faster, but also helping the organization serve more people and serve them *better*.

## Elements of an Organizational Mission

To fully comprehend this concept of IT alignment, it is important to identify and understand the three critical components of achieving an organizational mission: goals, strategies, and processes.

- **Goals** are the tactical objectives that are set based on your mission and strategic plan. Goals can be set for many areas of your organization, like operations, administration, programs, or development. For example, you may have a program goal of serving one thousand meals per week to your clients, an operations goal of reducing the amount of time spent on data entry, or an administrative goal of producing more effective financial reports for the board.

- **Strategies** are the methods that your organization is deliberately using to meet their goals. This could include raising more money, hiring staff, building an email list, or any number of other options.

- **Processes** are the steps or procedures your organization uses to get its daily work done. This includes accepting donations, paying bills, tracking clients, identifying prospects, hiring staff, communications, delivering services, and much more.

If these three elements are not clearly defined or articulated, most IT alignment efforts will fail. But when an organization's leadership and IT staff work together to understand its goals, strategies, and processes, they take the first significant step towards achieving true IT alignment.

## Benefits of IT Alignment

It's easy to focus on the costs of addressing your organization's technology, but the benefits of implementing IT alignment are numerous. There are three benefits, though, that are particularly important to nonprofit leaders: avoiding legal and financial troubles, creating efficiencies, and improving effectiveness.

### Avoid Common Legal and Financial Troubles

Technology that is aligned with the administrative goals of an organization can help prevent fraud within the organization, provide more accurate reporting information for funders and government agencies, and prevent the theft of stakeholder or client data such as sensitive health information or credit card numbers.

Although fraud and theft are rare, they do happen. According to a New York Times article, the Association of Certified Fraud Examiners reports that all organizations (for-profit and nonprofit) lose, on average, 6 percent of their revenue to fraud each year.[4] In 2006, that amounted to $40 billion in the nonprofit sector. Beyond the monetary loss, any nonprofit that loses money or data will have to face public—and possibly legal—scrutiny, costing the organization valuable time and harming its reputation. At a time when public confidence in the nonprofit sector continues to drop, you can't afford to give your stakeholders another reason to doubt your ability to effectively steward their contributions.

### Streamline Operations to Create Efficiencies

Aligning technology with the operations goals can help nonprofit leaders better understand how an organization completes work and accomplishes day-to-day tasks. You will be able to eliminate unnecessary or redundant procedures and minimize the staff time spent on data entry and systems maintenance. You will also be able to identify possibilities for enhancing services or program delivery, highlight new opportunities to serve your community, and gain a better understanding of how your organization is functioning on the whole.

A common operations problem that technology alignment can help address at nonprofits is double data entry. Every week, thousands of nonprofits around the country spend countless extra hours first entering donations into their donor database, only to have the finance staff enter the same data into the accounting software. Not only does this waste time, but the data from the two systems rarely match, and donor information is often misentered in one or both locations. Technology aligned with the operational goal of reducing double data entry can help nonprofits avoid this common problem and create more time for staff to perform mission-related work.

## Improve Effectiveness

When technology is aligned with the administrative and operational goals of your organization, you often see a savings of time and money, or improved efficiencies, as in the preceding example. When technology is part of the overall organizational strategic planning process, you can begin to see improved *effectiveness*—the types of benefits that let you not only do more, but also do it better. This is where IT alignment really starts to pay off.

The argument can be made that eliminating double data entry frees up staff time and allows your organization to then serve more clients, but the connection between technology and mission in this scenario is one step removed.

When you include technology in your organization's strategic planning, you will find that you are able to tie technology to your program goals as well, creating a direct link between technology and your mission. A great example of this connection comes from the legal services community.

Legal services agencies provide legal expertise in everything from divorce to eviction to taxes for underserved communities across the country. Many legal services agencies work with populations of migratory workers, located in remote rural areas of the states they serve. Often the lawyers have to travel by car for hours to reach their clients. Before the recent advances in technology, inevitably, during an interview, the client would pose a question that required further research. The lawyer would have to get back in her car, travel back to her office, and go online to access her legal database and find the answer. More often than not, by the time the lawyer was able to make the rounds to that part of the state again, her client would be gone. It was a waste of time for both parties, and a lost opportunity to help someone in need.

Wireless remote access has solved that problem. IT staff at several legal services offices, involved in the strategic planning process, recognized that they could help their organizations serve more clients, more effectively, if the lawyers could access the Internet—and their legal database—while they were in the field. Their organizations made the investment in laptops and cellular modems for the lawyers. Now that same lawyer can access the information she needs to successfully advise her client in minutes, not days.

These are just a few examples of the myriad benefits of IT alignment. The more that you commit to the process, the more your organization can get out of it. Now that you know what's in store for you, let's take a closer look at IT alignment.

## Stages in IT Alignment

Every organization, no matter its size or budget, can align IT with their mission for more impact. The first part of the task is to know where you are now so you can plan where you're going. Ask any nonprofit, large or small, what challenges they face with technology and you're likely to hear many scenarios that will fall into one of the following five stages:

- **Chaotic**: Chaotic organizations are struggling to keep up with a failing infrastructure, spending all their time fixing old equipment. As new staff joins the organization, member expectations change, communities grow, compliance issues arise, disaster strikes, and so on, these organizations just aren't ready. These organizations spend all of their time creating work-arounds, repairing old equipment, duplicating tasks, and missing chances to be more effective.

- **Reactive**: Reactive organizations have basic systems in place to keep workstations running, printers printing, and software updated. They budget for immediate needs, but don't plan for long-term growth or big ideas. They put fires out when they happen, rather than anticipating fires and protecting themselves.

- **Proactive**: Proactive organizations provide a stable infrastructure, solid operations software, and a good set of policies and practices. But they are also watching how their systems are used and planning for future needs. In this stage, though, organizations are still using technology primarily to build efficiencies. They are not using technology to strategically meet the mission of the organization, and IT staff are generally not involved in leadership meetings.

- **Service**: Service organizations are not only anticipating and meeting the needs of staff at an organization, but they are also involved in the strategic planning, helping to craft the future of the organization and how technology can support that work, both inside the organization and through public-facing technologies.

- **Value:** Value organizations recognize IT as an investment in mission, dedicating a percentage of each fiscal budget to technology. Existing technologies are routinely evaluated for mission and revenue impact, and new technologies are experimented with and evaluated for future use. IT systems supply critical business metrics to the organization.

Figure 1.1 illustrates the relationships between these five stages.

The arrows at the bottom of the figure represent the types of practices and services that your organization will need to address at each stage of IT alignment. For example, organizations at all stages will need to leverage tools or use hardware and software to support basic business processes. But only organizations in later stages of maturity will need to focus on planning for future technology needs in the organization or address managing IT as a business. The following section offers a more detailed explanation of these practices and services.

## Figure 1.1. The Five Stages of Managing Technology.

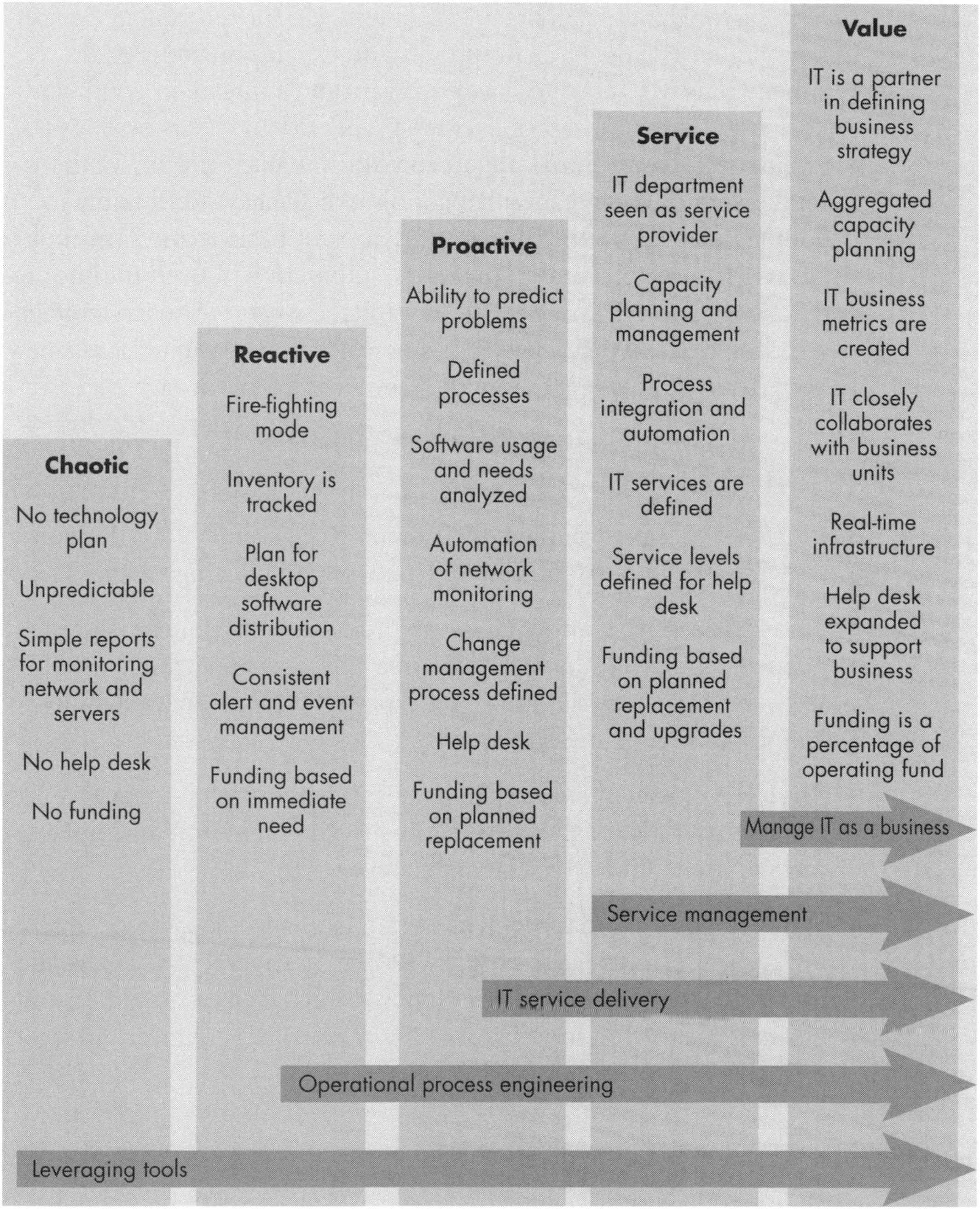

**Value**

IT is a partner in defining business strategy

Aggregated capacity planning

IT business metrics are created

IT closely collaborates with business units

Real-time infrastructure

Help desk expanded to support business

Funding is a percentage of operating fund

**Service**

IT department seen as service provider

Capacity planning and management

Process integration and automation

IT services are defined

Service levels defined for help desk

Funding based on planned replacement and upgrades

**Proactive**

Ability to predict problems

Defined processes

Software usage and needs analyzed

Automation of network monitoring

Change management process defined

Help desk

Funding based on planned replacement

**Reactive**

Fire-fighting mode

Inventory is tracked

Plan for desktop software distribution

Consistent alert and event management

Funding based on immediate need

**Chaotic**

No technology plan

Unpredictable

Simple reports for monitoring network and servers

No help desk

No funding

Manage IT as a business

Service management

IT service delivery

Operational process engineering

Leveraging tools

## Leveraging Tools

Leveraging tools means an organization uses specific technology devices to help build systems that will support and expand business processes. In other words, you need to have hardware and software in good working order so that your staff can get their work done. This is perhaps the most important aspect of IT alignment. You can't achieve any of the other levels until you are leveraging tools effectively. Additionally, you will find yourself revisiting this area often. Your basic technology tool needs will evolve constantly, and your equipment will need monitoring and maintenance. As an organization implements and learns to leverage new technologies to meet specific business needs, they can achieve a new level of maturity. Here are examples of leveraging tools at each stage:

- **Chaotic**. Back-up software and automated methods to monitor the network and servers are used.

- **Reactive**. A simple trouble-ticket system, basic IT inventory, desktop software distribution, and real-time network monitoring are provided.

- **Proactive**. A service or help desk for problem management is implemented, along with the beginning of a change-management system; software usage analysis; and server capacity, application availability, and response time measurement systems.

- **Service**. A change-management database, capacity-planning tools, and a what-if analysis—based on the measurement systems implemented in the Proactive stage—are employed.

- **Value**. IT portfolio management (systemic method to manage total infrastructure) is realized; business service management uses revenue impact analysis (tying IT services directly to changes in revenue); and business metrics are supplied via IT systems, IT governance, and legal discovery.

## Operational Process Engineering

This process includes the analysis, design, implementation, and maintenance of technology systems to support the operational needs of the business. Here are examples of operational process engineering at each stage:

- **Chaotic**. Does not exist at this level.

- **Reactive**. A simple inventory tracking of technology assets is implemented.

- **Proactive**. Configuration management for PCs and servers and full IT asset management for hardware and software are employed.

- **Service**. Service levels for technology support, capacity of what-if management, and business process alignment are defined.

- **Value**. Business process automation (improving operations through systems) and aggregated IT capacity planning (based on all branch locations) are enacted.

## IT Service Delivery

IT service delivery involves supplying staff, members, and volunteers with the services needed or demanded and ensuring a consistent, unified experience for all staff. Here are examples of IT service delivery at each stage:

- **Chaotic**. Does not exist at this level.

- **Reactive**. Does not exist at this level.

- **Proactive**. IT staff are made available to assist business, support levels begin to be defined, and a central IT command center for IT service delivery is established.

- **Service**. IT staff begin to focus on the importance of relationships with staff and customers. IT service delivery managers may become part of the leadership team.

- **Value**. The IT director participates actively in the executive decision-making process. IT is viewed as a partner for defining strategy.

## Service Management

Organizations focused on service management manage business IT systems so they are centered on the customers' perceptions and needs as they relate to the business. Here are examples of service management at each stage:

- **Chaotic**. Does not exist at this level.

- **Reactive**. Does not exist at this level.

- **Proactive**. Does not exist at this level.

- **Service**. Members of the IT team monitor and manage all IT service delivery, use capacity planning to determine future needs, and focus service management on strategic goals.

- **Value**. IT staff function as liaisons to branches and business units in support of strategic business goals.

## Managing IT as a Business

This is the stage at which business metrics and IT metrics are linked to uncover new opportunities, and IT becomes a strategic partner in the discovery and implementation of new, IT-enabled business processes. Here are examples of managing IT as a business at each stage:

- **Chaotic**. Does not exist at this level.

- **Reactive**. Does not exist at this level.

- **Proactive**. Does not exist at this level.

- **Service.** An IT fund may emerge. Some projects are tied to business needs. Methods are established for reviewing projects at an early stage.

- **Value.** An established IT fund provides long-term funding for IT and IT business processes, all IT projects are subjected to a cost-benefit analysis, and quality-of-service analytics ensure availability of business systems.

As your organization moves through the stages of IT alignment, technology systems become increasingly embedded in your organization's strategy and the value becomes increasingly apparent. As you follow this growth pattern, your organization will go through numerous changes in all areas, including how you think about and spend funds on technology.

One common misconception is that organizations at the Value stage simply have more money and staff than organizations at the Chaotic stage. This simply isn't the case. Having more money allows you to spend more on technology, but that doesn't mean that large organizations always spend that money wisely. It isn't the amount of money you can spend on technology that determines your success—it's the people and process you use to manage technology that shapes your outcomes.

It's also important to note that IT alignment is a process. Successfully aligning your technology with your mission is not the result of a single event or decision. It is an ongoing process that will take years to mature. Progress takes place along a continuum—your organization must pass through the early stages before it reaches the later ones. Trying to jump to the final step and hoping for the best can waste valuable resources of time and money. But you need to start somewhere, and the sooner you do, the better.

## Implementing IT Alignment

Now that we have established the different stages of IT alignment, let's address some steps for moving your organization from one stage to another and look at these steps in the context of both large and small organizations. Although there is no precise blueprint that will work in every situation, there are five basic steps to developing IT alignment in your own organization:

1. Know where you are.
2. Define your destination.
3. Build the buy-in.
4. Make it happen.
5. Repeat.

Although these five steps can put you well on the road to successfully aligning your technology investments with your organizational goals, please don't be afraid to try new or different tactics. When improving performance, what matters most is beginning the process.

## Know Where You Are

Your first step should be to determine what stage you are in. This will require an open and honest conversation with leadership and all levels of staff. Start by using the information shown in Table 1.1.

Review the table, then ask these questions of your own organization. Compare your answers to the indicators for each level of IT alignment on the table. This will allow you to begin to identify both your organization's current stage of IT alignment and the areas you need to work on.

Your next step is it to review the table with all levels of staff in your organization. Their IT experience may vary from your own, and their perceptions will contribute greatly to your understanding of your organization's IT alignment.

You and your colleagues may not be able to address every item in the table. If there are items that you aren't sure how to answer, note them and find a tech-savvy peer, board member, or family member who can help make it clear. The IT alignment process often includes identifying areas that are unknown to you or that are not being actively managed.

During your conversations, you will find that the table will not address all situations for every organization. Just think of it as a starting point. You should customize and add to this table based on your organization's goals and the roles that your technology team plays. You should also think through the complexity of your operations, size of your organization, and your organization's history with technology. If your organization does not have a history of supporting technology, it's not likely that you will find the internal support for any kind of change immediately. If you work at a university or an agency that works with the government, your data entry and reporting processes may be so complex that changes in those areas will require an extra amount of effort to initiate.

**Table 1.1. Determining Your Organization's Current Stage of Technology.**

| | Chaotic | Reactive | Proactive | Service | Value |
|---|---|---|---|---|---|
| *How closely is technology tied to mission?* | Information systems, if any, are used only for routine business processes. | Information systems exist but are used only for routine business processes and automating tasks. | Some technology is tied to mission objectives, but day-to-day issues often overshadow these goals. | Technology assets are seen as a mix of investments and expenses, with some elements tied to mission objectives. | Technology assets are seen as investments rather than expenses, with all elements tied to mission objectives. |
| *Is technology involved in strategic planning process and the strategic plan?* | No technology plan exists. | A limited technology plan may exist but is not linked to strategic plan. | Technology staff understand the mission. A technology plan exists but is not linked to strategic plan. | Technology staff has limited role in the strategic planning process and is directly mentioned as a tool throughout the organization's strategic plan. | Technology staff has a direct role in the strategic planning process and is integrated throughout the strategic plan. |
| *Are leadership and the board supportive of operations and technology needs?* | Leadership and the board are unaware of technology and operations needs beyond day-to-day requirements. | Leadership and the board have limited knowledge of how technology is supporting their operations. | Leadership and the board have knowledge of current technology in use, ongoing strategy, current challenges, and plans for future improvement. | Leadership supports technology strategies and works to engage the whole organization with IT. The board is aware of upcoming technology projects. | Leadership strives for full integration of IT team, with authority to act at the leadership level, and shows ongoing support of aligning IT. The board offers advice as possible and stays aware of high-impact technology projects. |

**Table 1.1. Determining Your Organization's Current Stage of Technology. (continued)**

| | Chaotic | Reactive | Proactive | Service | Value |
|---|---|---|---|---|---|
| *Are all areas of the organization actively identifying technology needs?* | The organization does not allocate any regular resources or planning for technology. | The organization is beginning to actively look for ways to use technology to support new service offerings or develop new programs. | Some departments or programs regularly engage in meetings with technology staff to identify technology needs. | All departments regularly engage in technology-enabled process improvements, with established metrics for periodic review. | The organization collaborates in regular technology-enabled process improvements tied to the strategic plan, with established metrics for periodic review. |
| *How is technology funded?* | There is no formal technology funding or budget. | Limited funds are dedicated to replacement. | Funds are dedicated to replacement, and technology is upgraded on a regular schedule. | A technology fund equal to 2 to 4 percent of the operating budget is created for technology replacement and upgrades. | A technology fund equal to 4 to 6 percent of the operating budget is created for technology replacement, upgrades, and new technology. |
| *What is the technology spending process?* | No process or forum exists to examine technology needs, nor is there a technology budget. | Processes around technology decisions and purchases are informal but have been mostly effective. | Technology replacement and upgrades are tied to department or branch requests, but there is no formal plan. | Technology is included in the operating budget and is tied to department, branch, or organization operating plans, with a formal plan to implement. | Technology is included in the operating budget and is aligned with the organization's business strategy and strategic plan. |
| *How are technology assets managed?* | Technology is generally not regarded as an asset. It requires attention only when it is broken. | Technology is regarded as an asset that requires limited attention. | There is at least one individual in the organization with the capability to assess technology needs. | There is a designated individual or committee to oversee technology issues. | There is a designated committee to oversee technology issues. |

| | | | | |
|---|---|---|---|---|
| *Are technology policies defined?* | There are no documented technology policies and procedures. | Technology policies and procedures are minimally documented. | Technology policies and procedures are in development. | Technology policies and procedures have been developed and are being implemented. | Comprehensive technology policies and procedures have been developed and are used organization-wide. |
| *How closely is technology tied to the business process?* | Business processes are not defined or supported by technology. | Some business processes are defined but are not directly tied to technology plans. | All business processes are defined, and the technology needed has been identified and planned for. | All business processes are defined and reviewed for consistency across the organization. Technology is identified and implemented to fully support the business processes. | All business processes are defined and reviewed for consistency across the organization. Technology staff, the IT steering committee, and all business units actively improve processes by upgrading the tools and technology used. |
| *Are you using current technology?* | Equipment, if existing, is outdated or is the personal property of individual employees. | Equipment is an ad hoc collection without a standard to measure it. | Equipment is up-to-date and interoperable. It meets standards set in *Healthy and Secure Computing.* | Equipment is up-to-date, integrated, and readily expanded. It exceeds all standards set in *Healthy and Secure Computing.* | Equipment is up-to-date, integrated, and readily expanded. It exceeds all standards set in *Healthy and Secure Computing* and meets industry standards. |
| *Are technology assets actively monitored?* | The technology inventory is not managed or documented. | There is some documentation of the technology inventory. | There is electronic technology inventory tracking with a replacement schedule. | The technology infrastructure is approaching real-time management. | The technology infrastructure is managed in real time. |

**Table 1.1. Determining Your Organization's Current Stage of Technology. (continued)**

| | Chaotic | Reactive | Proactive | Service | Value |
|---|---|---|---|---|---|
| *Is technology capacity monitored?* | There are simple reports for networks and management. | There is consistent alert and event management. | Network monitoring is automated. | Capacity planning is beginning. | There is aggregated capacity planning across the organization. |
| *Is technology support offered?* | Support is ad hoc or nonexistent. | Support is ad hoc or based solely on manufacturer's warranty. | There is generally someone on site or on call to respond to technology problems. | A designated individual or team of support specialists is available to users. This team offers expertise in some areas of organization operations. | A designated team of support specialists with expertise in technology and operations is available to users, with regular evaluation. |
| *Is technology-systems training offered?* | Training is provided by observation or "passed down" among volunteers or employees. | Training is provided by observation or "passed down" among volunteers or employees, but documentation exists. | Training is mostly provided by outside vendors, classes, or consultants, but is available on an as-needed basis. Documentation exists. | Super-users for major business applications have been identified in their job descriptions. Documentation exists and is regularly updated in an online resource. | Super-users for each business application are identified in their job descriptions, and a formal training plan exists. Regularly updated documentation exists in an online resource and is integrated into trainings. |
| *Is ongoing technology-systems training offered?* | There are very limited or no professional training resources available to staff. | There are limited professional training resources available to staff. | Training is included as part of a new system implementation. Follow-up training is limited to new employees when there is turnover. | Technology training is planned on a regular basis and is included in the overall technology planning process. | Technology training needs are assessed on an annual basis, then scheduled accordingly and included in the overall technology planning process. |

| | | | | | |
|---|---|---|---|---|---|
| *Is data actively managed?* | There are no clear definitions of data needs. Only minimal data is collected for billing and reporting purposes. | There are minimal definitions of data needs. Only minimal data is collected for billing and reporting purposes. | Some of the organization's data needs have been clearly defined, but they are not uniformly documented. | The organization has defined and documented its data needs across the organization in each area of service. | The organization has standardized and documented its data needs for all levels of the organization, including the board. |
| *Have data quality standards been set?* | Data is entered from a variety of sources, without defined procedures. | Data is entered from a variety of sources, with some defined procedures. | Data input documents are well defined, with some procedures for data entry and some accuracy standards set. | Data input documents are well defined, and report specification documents with written procedures for data entry have been well designed. Accuracy levels are measured for data entry. | Data input documents are well defined, and report specification documents with clearly written procedures for data entry have been well designed by cross-functional teams. Accuracy levels are measured for data entry. |
| *How is data collected and used?* | Data collection and management is not a priority for the organization. | Data collection and management is not a high priority for the organization. | The organization pays attention to data collection mainly for internal financial management. | The organization values data and is beginning to manage, collect, and use data to support better internal processes. Data is used to promote mission and advocacy. | The organization values data and prioritizes efforts to manage, collect, and use data to support better internal processes. Data is used to promote mission and advocacy, and is shared with collaborating organizations and appropriate government agencies. |

**Table 1.1. Determining Your Organization's Current Stage of Technology. (continued)**

| | Chaotic | Reactive | Proactive | Service | Value |
|---|---|---|---|---|---|
| *What are data reporting metrics?* | Reporting requirements are not well understood or met. Data is not easily accessible or accurate. | Reporting requirements are not well met. Some data is not easily accessible. Sampling is sometimes used to generate reports for which complete data is missing. | Reporting requirements for funders, government agencies, and internal management are mostly met, but with some inconsistencies. Reports are based on data samples. | The majority of reporting requirements for funders, government agencies, and internal management are met by mining data from the organization's information systems. Reports are based on complete and integrated data systems. | Reporting requirements for funders, government agencies, and internal management are met by mining data from the organization's information systems. Reports are based on complete and integrated data systems. There are established metrics to measure against. |

It's also important to note that almost no organization will exist entirely in one stage of maturity. You may be in the Proactive stage in terms of data management, but at the Reactive stage when it comes to leadership and board support. Your organization will likely hover over one or two stages in most categories. Knowing this will allow you to focus on bringing the areas at the lowest stage up to the same level as the rest of your organization.

## Large Organization Experience

The YMCAs of Metropolitan Minneapolis and Greater St. Paul, Minnesota, are unique because they operate in two cities that are very closely tied. Although they serve completely different populations, the needs of their communities are similar, and staff come from both cities as well. Because of this, they have a shared service office that delivers many administrative and operations functions for both associations, including technology. Greg Waibel serves as the chief information officer (CIO) for the organizations and is accountable to a joint task force comprising board members from both organizations and the two chief executive officers (CEOs).

Periodically the task force will ask Greg for a "state of the technology" update. They generally want to hear that staff have the equipment, software, and support they need to do their jobs well. However, Greg wanted to show the task force that technology could do more than support the work of the staff. He wanted to demonstrate the difference technology could make in meeting their mission through IT alignment. Before the next task force meeting, Greg decided to have a conversation with each of the audiences he served: leadership, IT staff, and staff from each of the organization's departments. Greg used the questions in Table 1.1 to frame the conversations he had with each area of the organization.

Based on those conversations, Greg decided that the organization was mainly in the Service stage but with some elements in the Proactive stage. For example, they already had a committee with cross-departmental representation that regularly reviewed the technology strategy against the mission (Service stage). Leadership also had a good understanding of technology, and all the staff had the core skills to use the hardware and software they needed to do their jobs (Service stage). Tech support was proactively addressing root causes of problems, like lack of training, instead of symptoms, such as specific help requests (Service stage). However, Greg and his IT staff also realized that they had some deficiencies in terms of how they monitored the network, and they lacked effective systems for managing the relationship between tech support and staff (they were in the Proactive stage in these areas).

## Small Organization Experience

Colleen Hemhauser, senior administrative director at the Ocean County YMCA in New Jersey, was a busy lady. This YMCA is a smaller agency, with no formal IT staff. Instead, the Ocean County YMCA staffed IT as many smaller nonprofits do—by asking the administrative staff to keep things running. As business administrator, Colleen handled responsibilities including IT, marketing and membership, and whatever else seemed to pop up. For years Colleen had fought to get the desktop computers in her organization replaced. Although she had a variety of responsibilities, she was spending what seemed like all of her time fighting technology fires. Computers crashed and software ran too slowly to be useful. This was keeping her from her other important work in finance, reporting, and all the jobs that kept the bills paid. When new technology was requested, her executive director's answer was always the same: "Just keep it running. We don't need anything more than we have, and we don't have the money anyway."

Colleen knew she had to do something about the situation. Using Table 1.1, Colleen was able to do a quick assessment of the current IT alignment stage of her organization. According to the information in Table 1.1, her YMCA fell into the Chaotic or Reactive stage—not the best place to be. Knowing that, Colleen now had the specific information and framework for a more productive conversation with her executive director. Subsequently she was better able to address the real need for new desktop computers.

## Define Your Destination

Knowing where you want to go can be the most difficult part of the IT alignment process. Using Table 1.1, you've taken stock of your organization and identified the stage or stages in which your organization currently resides. The next step is identifying the areas from the table that you need to address in order to move yourself into the next stage of alignment. Unfortunately, your list may be long. So start with the elements that are most critical to the daily operations of your organization, then move down the list.

It's relatively easy to identify what's not working. Deciding how to fix those problems is a different matter. Many nonprofit leaders feel the solution must be articulated in terms of the technology that will be used. But that's not the case. At this stage, don't worry about what specific technologies need to be used. You need only to articulate in broad terms what you need to accomplish. Right now you are defining the goals. You will operationalize these goals later.

For example, let's say your organization has a software problem. Most of your staff have no idea what software is on their computers. And to make things worse, copies of the software are kept all over the office, from individual cubicles to the break room. This makes installing necessary updates very difficult and may also mean that the organization is losing important and expensive software. This scenario is typical of organizations in the Chaotic stage.

So now you've identified the problem, and you realize that the solution is to implement a software inventory system. You don't need to worry about how you will conduct the inventory, or where you will store the inventory information. You simply need to identify the goal at this point: implementing a software inventory system.

## Large Organization Experience

Greg Waibel and his team knew they had some work to do. After establishing their stage of IT alignment, Greg sat down with his technology staff to review the areas where they were behind and to prioritize those needs. The team determined that the organization needed to focus on three key areas: (1) building the skills of the support staff to better serve the rest of the organization; (2) better communicating to the rest of the staff what kinds of services tech support could provide, what they couldn't do, and how best to work with tech support; and (3) increasing the speed and efficiency of their network to provide better performance for the staff.

Focusing on these key areas would help Greg and his staff demonstrate the value of technology and build stronger relationships with staff. They hoped that by focusing on these three items first, they would encourage conversations with staff about other ways in which technology could be leveraged within the organization. They also hoped that these goals would earn them the trust and support of staff for future IT implementations.

### Small Organization Experience

Colleen started with a very narrow view of her technology needs: new computers. Reflecting on the IT alignment process allowed her to see a much bigger picture and an opportunity to use technology more effectively in her organization. To move from the Chaotic to the Reactive stage, Colleen would need to do much more than buy new computers. She would have to focus on getting all of her IT infrastructure in place, documenting what she had, training her staff, and getting technology into the organization's budget.

Colleen's new IT alignment "destination" included hardware and software purchases, developing spreadsheets for tracking inventory, finding training, and lobbying the executive director for a technology line item in the budget. With these new elements in place, she knew she could spend less time fixing obsolete computers and struggling with dated software. Newer equipment would be less likely to break, and trained staff could solve more problems on their own. A line item for technology in the annual budget would give her something to work with every year as new problems arose.

## Build the Buy-In

Once you have an idea of where you want to take your organization's use of technology, the next step is making sure you have the support you need to implement your plan. One key audience is the leadership of your organization, including the board. The role of the board can vary significantly from organization to organization, but all boards have two objectives in common: stewardship of the mission and of the finances. When presenting your plan, be sure to emphasize how it will help your organization better accomplish its mission as well as improve the bottom line.

Clearly you want the support of leadership. However, many nonprofit leaders forget to include staff in the buy-in process. The board may think your ideas are the greatest thing ever, but one disgruntled staff member can easily undermine the implementation of your plan. Your staff will have to live with the disruptions and change your plan produces, so make sure they're on board before you begin. It's important to note that all technology-related projects have one thing in common: change. Chapter Two addresses the issue of change and provides specific strategies for dealing with it. But for now, just understand that you will need to be sensitive to the fears, anger, and resistance that your plans may trigger. One of the best ways to increase this sensitivity and mitigate any potential resistance is to include influential staff members in the planning and implementation process.

## Large Organization Experience

Greg and his team knew what they wanted to do. Now they had to sell it. Greg shared an overview of the assessment (the current IT alignment stage of the organization) and his plan (the hoped-for destination) with the task force. He avoided discussing the particular technologies or systems they would use. At this stage, Greg simply talked about what his plan would accomplish and how it would support the organization's mission and bottom line. Instead of asking for approval for a certain number of new computers or servers, Greg focused on agreeing to a broad strategy for moving to the next stage in IT alignment. This was the key to the ultimate acceptance of Greg's plan: he was open to the suggestions and ideas of leadership about how to implement his plan. He welcomed comments, and he asked for their support and participation.

The plan also needed the support of staff members, so Greg and his team took the plan to all departments of the organization to make sure that it met or addressed everyone's needs and concerns. When he and his team encountered resistance, they invited feedback and fostered a strong feeling of inclusion in the process.

### Small Organization Experience

Colleen knew that her executive director was focused on the bottom line. To get the support of her leaders, she would have to demonstrate how an upfront investment in technology would have long-term dividends in savings and increased productivity. She began by logging all of the service requests and emergencies that arose. She created an inventory of equipment that included information on which machines were causing delays or adversely affecting staff productivity. She then took her evidence and plan to her executive director. Based on the information she gathered, their conversation changed from one focused on asking for money to one highlighting the benefits of an investment in new technology. Her executive director approved the plan as well as an expenditure for new equipment.

## Make It Happen

With you and your organization focused on the same destination, it's time to chart a course for getting there. The next important step is identifying the resources—the time, staff, and money—you'll need to achieve your goals and create a plan and timeline to put it all into motion.

Making it happen requires great juggling skills. As often as not, as soon as you begin implementing part of your plan, a crisis will emerge that diverts precious resources. This could include staff turnover or the recent release of a new version of the tool you wanted to use. Basically, no technology implementation process runs perfectly. So stay focused on where you need to go, and recognize that you may have to change your route along the way.

The key to making it happen is having clear short- and long-term goals for your technology that are tied to your association's strategic plan; ask for the budget, get the strategy approved, and then talk to people about it.

This simple approach is true regardless of size, so I will stick with a single example. John Merritt ,the IT director at the YMCA in San Diego County, was the original example of IT alignment in YMCAs. He has successfully moved his YMCA through the stages into the service stage. He attributes his success to the "ART" of Technology. ART stands for *alignment, relationship,* and *transparency.* First establish clear goals for your technology that are aligned with the mission and goals of the organization. Then create a relationship and dialogue with all levels of staff throughout the organization. Finally, make the technology work so well that it is transparent to the people using it.

## Repeat

The simple fact is, you can't go through this process just once. As your mission, goals, strategies, and business processes evolve, so too will your technology needs. This means you should take stock of where you are and where you want to go on a regular basis to ensure that you're moving closer to IT alignment. The best way to do this is to include technology staff members in your organization's strategic planning process. This also helps identify opportunities to provide solutions that cover multiple goals, increase effectiveness, and enhance services. Technology staff members often have tools, software, or systems already available that are somehow unknown or misunderstood by the rest of the organization.

### Large Organization Experience

Once Greg and his team demonstrated the value of aligning technology with the organization's mission, goals, strategy, and business processes, they were granted greater access to strategic conversations at the leadership level. Rather than just delivering an update at task force meetings or getting the meeting minutes, they were invited to participate in larger conversations. There was a deliberate effort to allow IT to see the big picture and contribute to planning the next steps for the organization. Members of the task force now agreed on which areas in the organization's strategic plan needed technology support, and they granted the IT staff the authority to make any necessary tactical decisions for implementation.

Greg is now positioned to really move his organization to the Value stage of IT alignment. Although this initial work has not directly impacted the mission of his organization, Greg is participating in the conversations and planning that will make this possible.

## Small Organization Experience

Seeing the importance of technology in creating operational efficiency and effectiveness, Colleen's executive director asked her to become involved in budgeting. Colleen was eventually invited to become a member of the strategic planning committee. Now the executive director and Colleen have regular monthly meetings, along with weekly administrative staff and senior staff meetings. Consequently, the staff will be rewriting their new technology policies together to ensure they meet organizational goals.

Coleen's YMCA is now mostly in the Proactive stage. The organization has seen significant growth and has been able to expand its use of technology. Staff members spend less time managing older equipment; this has freed up time and allowed them to more proactively examine how well they're using their operations software. Staff are better equipped to make decisions such as canceling classes with low enrollment, identifying budget shortfalls earlier, targeting marketing to repeat participants, trending member use to determine staff needs, and reducing unnecessary steps in their operational processes.

## Conclusion

IT alignment is not about having all the newest gadgets; rather, it is the deliberate, measured process of implementing technology to meet your mission. To achieve this alignment, you'll need to first consider all of your technology investments in the context of your mission. You'll choose tools and systems that support the goals, strategies, and processes that are helping your organization meet its mission. This means nonprofit leaders need to view the IT department as a key partner in accomplishing the organizational mission, rather than just as a necessary evil or a collection of tools to be called on when a crisis emerges.

Think of your organization as a house under construction. Using this analogy, many leaders would think of technology as the hammer. It's just a tool to drive nails. Hammers are slow, though, so to improve performance the foreman buys a nail gun. This creates efficiencies. Now the carpenters can drive nails much faster. But will they build a better house because of it? Probably not.

Instead, think of technology as the foreman holding the hammer. If a foreman is going to help build a better house, she needs to see the blueprints, understand what the building will be used for, *and* have all the necessary tools (like the nail gun). Moreover, if that foreman is allowed to be involved in the early planning process, she may even suggest ways to improve the design and overall structure of the house. Now the foreman isn't simply more efficient; the foreman is more effective, building a house that better serves the needs of its occupants.

## Notes

1. http://www.boardsource.org/Knowledge.asp?ID=3.32.

2. http://www.boardsource.org/Knowledge.asp?ID=3.56.

3. Atkinson, Robert D., and McKay, Andrew S. *Digital Prosperity: Understanding the Economic Benefits of the Information Technology Revolution.* The Information Technology and Innovation Foundation, 2007.

4. http://www.nytimes.com/2008/03/29/us/29fraud.html?_r=1&sq= strompercent20light&st=nyt&adxnnl=1&oref=slogin&scp= 1&adxnnlx=1216855632-WmyA6ePI4sOruaHIxROqSQ.

# CHAPTER 2

# Managing Technology Change

*Dahna Goldstein*

Introducing or adopting a new technology in an organization necessitates change—change in a process, change in the status quo, and often change in a job description. Whether it's a new website, a different phone system, moving from index cards to a donor database, or implementing a case management system, technology implementations can create anxiety and require a learning curve that needs to be managed before, during, and after the introduction of that technology.

This chapter introduces the concept of the *adaptive organization* that is able to manage ongoing technology changes. It also introduces some of the common obstacles to successful technology initiatives and how to overcome them, describes key success factors in managing change for technology adoption, and presents a case study of a successfully managed technology adoption to highlight some best practices and lessons learned.

## Creating Conditions for Ongoing Change

There's an old joke that will illuminate one of the challenges inherent in managing change. Question: How many psychiatrists does it take to change a light bulb? Answer: Just one, but the light bulb has to really want to change.

The same can be said of organizations. Nonprofit organizations can adapt to technological change, but they have to want to change. For any initiative to be successful, the organizations—represented by the people who lead, manage, and work for them—must want to keep pace with whatever technological initiatives and tools are right for that organization.

Forming an adaptive organization—one that is positioned to absorb and engage in change on an ongoing basis rather than reacting to large disruptive changes—creates the most favorable conditions for a technology change and is likely to be, on balance, the most successful approach. The emergence of new technologies and their subsequent adoption are consistently changing internal and external environments, and organizations are wise to keep up with continuous changes rather than waiting for a large, disruptive change to be necessary. Continuous incremental change enables an organization to be flexible, allowing it to respond to its environment. If a culture of continuous adaptation is adopted by the organization, it can position itself to be proactive rather than merely reacting to changes in its environment, thereby positioning the organization to deliver better services more efficiently, improve donor communications, and facilitate board and management access to information.

Creating and maintaining a flexible and adaptive organization is a gradual process. It involves organizational and cultural change, both of which take time and care. Nonprofit leaders can start to create a culture that is comfortable with continuous change by taking these actions:

• *Challenging assumptions and encouraging questions.* Constantly questioning the status quo helps to identify opportunities for small changes. Challenging assumptions doesn't mean that the status quo isn't working or that it is wrong. It simply encourages thinking about the "why" behind a process or a system. When the answer is "Because it's always been this way," there is an opportunity to question whether a given system or process is serving the organization's needs and to potentially get ahead of a needed change, rather than waiting for a crisis to necessitate change in that system or process.

- *Encouraging experimentation.* As people in the organization are questioning assumptions, they also should be encouraged to experiment. Creating a culture that supports experimentation—and tolerates failure—will encourage people in the organization to continually strive to find new and better ways to do things. This type of experimentation can also help organizations get ahead of changes rather than initiating change as a reaction to a crisis.

- *Resisting complacency.* Organizations that remain complacent, rather than keeping a vigilant eye on their environments as well as on evolving technologies, are more likely to be faced with a large, disruptive change. Leaders should take advantage of times when the organization is doing well to encourage people to look for problems and opportunities both inside and outside the organization.

- *Decentralizing decision making.* To create a culture of change, leaders should encourage ownership of decisions throughout the organization, rather than centralizing all decision making at the top of the organization. This type of empowerment of people within the organization is equally beneficial during a change initiative and when creating a culture of continuous change.

Of course, creating an organizational culture that embraces change does not mean that every change will be easy. Technology changes, in particular, can be very disruptive, and understanding some of the barriers and success factors in technology change can help improve the odds of successfully navigating the process.

## Barriers to Technology Adoption

Technology changes are never simple. Beyond the frequent challenges surrounding the technology itself (for example, can historical data be imported? Will it work on the executive director's home computer?

Will it interface with other existing systems?), there are also human challenges that can sink any technology initiative if they are not acknowledged and handled well. Those potential barriers to technology adoption include anxiety, poor communication, and insufficient buy-in.

## Anxiety About Change

As individuals, we tend not to like change, particularly changes over which we feel we have no control. In our personal lives, change can be uncomfortable and unsettling. In our professional lives, it isn't any different. The nature of change is such that it creates uncertainty about outcomes and what those outcomes imply. In the absence of certainty, anxiety reigns. Leaving that anxiety unchecked in a technology initiative can be dangerous both to individuals and to the success of the technology implementation. But by understanding the sources of anxiety associated with change, leaders can help address and manage anxiety.

Technology change frequently requires people to think and do things in new and different ways. Depending on the nature of the technology initiative, people may suddenly be uncertain about the security of their jobs and concerned whether their jobs will change in ways they can't foresee and might not be able to deal with. People's emotions and behaviors are of critical importance to the success of any technology implementation. And understanding that those emotions are coming into play, where they are coming from, and how to help address them will position leaders for successful change management.

Although every individual will experience the change differently, there are a few common manifestations of this anxiety. Staff members may feel one or both of these reactions:

- *Can I do it?* Some people will wonder if they are capable of understanding the new technology. They will worry that the new technology will reveal some incompetence, and they experience feelings of insecurity and self-doubt.

- *Is my job in danger?* Many technologies create efficiencies by eliminating or streamlining tasks that are performed by people. Individuals whose job descriptions include these kinds of work—data entry or donation processing, for example—may fear that the new technology will make them obsolete within the organization.

Even if staff members understand that a technology change is good for the organization, it will not stop them from experiencing these feelings. Many individuals will choose to keep their feelings to themselves, but these fears can result in behaviors that change leaders can use to identify an individual's concerns:

- *Hostility.* A natural response arising from fear is anger. Many individuals involved in change at an organization will express anger toward the change leaders, and perhaps toward other staff as well. They may talk to their boss or the change leader, but they may also share their frustrations and fears with anyone who will listen.

- *Loss of motivation.* Uncertain of their future, many people simply shut down. Some staff will respond to the proposed change with an altered attitude and reduced productivity.

The natural anxiety that results from change can, in most cases, be mitigated and managed, through (1) understanding that anxiety is a natural response to change, (2) good and consistent communication, and (3) involvement and empowerment of the people whose lives and jobs are impacted by the change. The following section details what to avoid in a technology initiative.

## Poor Communication

Within some organizations, there are impediments to the good and frequent communication that is essential to a successful technology adoption. Overcoming those impediments is possible with good planning and the creation of a culture that supports change (rather than a one-off approach to a specific technology implementation) and that encourages communication. Particular communication pitfalls include the following:

- *Information hoarding.* Leaders of technology initiatives do not always see a need to share details with others in the organization. This inevitably leads to problems when people are surprised by some element of the new technology.

- *Delayed communication.* Leaders of technology initiatives can get hung up by not communicating with others in the organization early enough in the process ("I'll tell people about this before it goes live"). Early communication helps to ensure buy-in and soothe anxiety, and it enables the collection of valuable information about the technology initiative.

- *Viewing technology in isolation.* Change leaders can also get in trouble by viewing technology as an isolated function in the organization ("It's just technology, so I don't need to know about it" or "It's technology and they won't understand it, so I won't tell them about it"). Technology change initiatives frequently impact the whole organization—or at least more than just the IT staff—so not treating communication about technology changes as a broader issue invites problems down the road.

## Insufficient Buy-In

The senior leadership of the organization must be committed to a technology change and must convey that commitment throughout the organization. Insufficient buy-in from senior management will severely limit, if not doom, a technology initiative. The attitudes mentioned earlier ("It's technology and they won't understand it" or "It's just technology, so I don't need to know") can lead to technology initiatives that are poorly understood and therefore poorly embraced by the organization. Furthermore, a technology initiative without a champion who is committed to manage both up and down the chain of command will founder. In short, both a clear mandate for change tied to the organization's mission and a clear champion with influence in the organization are necessary for success.

## Key Success Factors for Managing Change

There are a number of key success factors that can help leaders successfully manage a technology change initiative, despite the potential obstacles. Forethought, good management, and some (learnable) skills can help change leaders avoid those pitfalls and achieve the organization's goals.

## Get Ahead of the Change

Crisis breeds change. More often than not, nonprofits institute a backup *after* they have lost all their data, or find a more reliable web host *after* their website goes offline. But managers and leaders can create an environment that fosters change before a crisis occurs and without resorting to crisis tactics. Planning for a new technology initiative and knowing how various people will be involved and how the technology plan will be communicated, and creating a clear understanding of the need and benefits before the initiative is undertaken—and as it is being undertaken—all will help support the success of the technology initiative.

## Create Context

Even when staff members know a change is coming, they'll want to know why. Tying the need for the technology to the organization's mission and work and to the reason for the change—whether it is an internal or an external driver—can help foster an understanding of why action is necessary. With that understanding, people will be more motivated to accept and adapt to the new technology.

The leader of the change initiative needs to clearly convey to everyone involved the vision for the outcome of the technology adoption and how the new technology will help the organization better achieve its mission and goals. This vision must be clearly communicated throughout all levels of the organization. Conversation about the change is healthy and should be encouraged. It can help people understand how changes in technology will affect them, and it can help them feel more comfortable.

## Communicate Early and Often

Good communication is always essential, whether or not the organization is in the midst of changing technologies, but communication is of particular importance to an organization undergoing change. Communication must be ongoing and consistent and flow in all directions. It is insufficient for communication to be solely top-down; people at the bottom of the organization chart need to be able to communicate among themselves, as well as with their managers and with the top management of the organization. This bottom-up and horizontal communication accomplishes several things. It enables people to mitigate their own anxiety by asking questions about the implications of the new technology and how it affects them. Good communication also allows line staff to give feedback to top management about their perception of the technology initiative's feasibility and impact. This both mitigates anxiety and improves the initiative's chances of success by generating buy-in and eliciting feedback.

Specifically, the leaders of the technology initiative should provide opportunities for conversation and encourage people to voice their emotions and offer input about the impending technology adoption. The change leaders should also create opportunities for the voices of people at all levels in the organization to be heard. When problems are voiced, they need to be addressed. Some problems or challenges can be anticipated, and the leaders of the technology initiative should communicate information about anticipated problems or challenges before they are voiced by someone else in the organization. This proactive approach helps to defuse stress before it starts.

## Tip from the Field

Starting a conversation with staff about technology change can be difficult. Here are a few questions that may be useful for sparking a dialogue that can lead to a more successful implementation:

- What are you looking forward to about this project?

- How do you think this project may help your work?

- What other opportunities do you think this project creates for your department or the organization?

- What difficulties do you think this project may cause you?

- What problems might this project cause for your department or the organization?

- If you were leading this initiative, what do you think would be the most important success factors?

Frequency and consistency of communication are vital to managing some of the anxiety associated with change. If messages about the change aren't consistent, people will find nothing they can feel comfortable about. Good and frequent communication should explain the need for the new technology, how it supports and furthers the organization's mission and goals, how it will impact the organization as a whole as well as its staff and stakeholders, and what concrete actions and resources are required and available.

Communications about change should honestly assess any impact on staff, such as a change in job requirements, the need for ongoing training on a new tool, or any down time required while information is transferred from an old system into a new one. Even if there is bad news, it is better to avoid fear and uncertainty by sharing it up front than to have it come as a surprise later.

Change leaders also must know their audience. The message of the communication should be framed in a way that makes sense to the people who will be reading or hearing it. It has to demonstrate that the leaders of the technology initiative (and the organization) are taking into account the feelings of people who will be affected by the new technology, while keeping a focus on the purpose and goals of the initiative. In an ideal situation, everyone who will be affected by the change initiative will have some involvement in it. But technology initiatives can also have ripple effects in an organization, and it is essential to be aware of the scope of the potential impact of any change and to tailor messages to the people who are likely to be affected in any way.

## Involve and Empower Staff

The people who make up the organization are the best resources in addressing change in general and new technology in particular. Taking staff involvement to another level can yield even better results. Getting staff involved at the beginning of the process enables them to feel they really have a say. For example, a nonprofit selecting a new content management system (CMS) for its website could form a CMS selection committee consisting of staff from senior management, IT, and also marketing, development, and program staff—anyone who will be responsible for maintaining the CMS, and also anyone whose job or day-to-day responsibilities would be impacted (this includes responsibilities such as fundraising, communicating with service recipients who visit the site, and creating the organization's brand and presence on the web).

Involvement can range from sitting on a cross-functional selection committee to attending specific input meetings. The degree of involvement that is appropriate will vary from organization to organization and will depend on the scope and scale of the technology, but some degree of structured involvement for people in the organization who will be affected increases the odds of successful implementation and adoption.

Another benefit of inclusion is a sense of responsibility for—and ownership of—the project. That shared sense of responsibility and ownership across the organization helps to support and ensure the success of a new technology implementation. Those who are involved in the decision making can then be internal champions in their departments or with their coworkers—helping to get buy-in and commitment even from those who have not been as actively involved.

There are several elements leaders should consider when creating a plan to involve and empower staff.

## Who Is Involved

Who will be affected by the technology? Communication about the initiative, as mentioned earlier, should be tailored to people who will be both directly and indirectly impacted by the change. People who will be most directly affected should be involved more heavily.

## When and How to Solicit Input

Where are the key decision points at which getting input would be helpful and valuable? Not everyone in the organization can or should be involved in every step of the process, but there are likely a few key points in the process that require input and information sharing.

## Change Champions

Every technology change needs a champion—a change leader who will bring others along, communicating throughout the organization what is happening and why, and helping to involve others in the organization. It is important for that champion to have authority within the organization; a person who is a dedicated cheerleader for a change initiative but has no influence will be an ineffective champion. The leaders and champions of the technology change (who may be different people) should be clearly identified to the organization so that people know who to approach with concerns and from whom to expect communication about the initiative.

## The Organization's Key Influencers

Who are the influencers in the organization? Involving key influencers early in the process can be an efficient way to generate buy-in across the organization. When people see that a key influencer has bought into the change and is involved, they are more likely to be amenable to getting on board themselves. The more a sense of shared responsibility and buy-in spreads throughout the organization, the better the chances of a successful technology adoption. Influencers can also be recruited to help communicate information about an impending change throughout the organization. They can even help get feedback and input into the process, thereby efficiently bringing others in the organization into the decision-making process.

## Acknowledge Input and Explain Decisions

Not everyone involved in a search and selection process—or any other technology planning or implementation initiative—will necessarily always be happy with the decision or outcome. Other factors—cost, contract terms, more pressing needs in one department than another, to name a few—can result in a decision that differs from what one or more staff members may have preferred. Although this situation is difficult to avoid, it can be managed by acknowledging the input of those staff members and by clearly explaining how their input was taken into account, all the factors that influenced the decision, and how the decision supports the mission and goals of the organization. Staff will generally get on board with a new technology if they feel their concerns have been heard and addressed to the greatest degree possible. Although technology initiatives that lack organization-wide buy-in may meet with initial success, such buy-in is necessary for long-term sustainable success.

## Mitigate Anxiety

Anxiety is a natural part of any change. Nonprofit leaders can help their organizations and their staff members manage the anxiety that accompanies the introduction of a new technology by first acknowledging that it is okay to feel anxious. Leaders may even choose to share the experience of their own anxiety from a similar situation in the past. For example, a leader might say, "I know how you feel. I felt the same way when I worked in development at a different organization. The new database was unfamiliar to me, and I thought it was going to be hard to learn and a lot more work to use it. But I learned it, and it ultimately helped make the organization's fundraising more efficient." The formula outlined in this example ("I know how you feel . . . I felt the same way . . . I found that . . .") helps people feel that their anxiety is understandable, normal, and manageable.

Once a decision about a new technology has been made, nonprofit leaders should create opportunities to ensure that people feel their concerns and anxiety are heard—and they should directly address those anxieties. The first step is to help people understand what impact the technology will have on their work lives.

## Tip from the Field

Addressing an individual's anxieties can go a long way toward resolving his or her issues. But since anxiety and fear can provoke hostility, it's important to frame the conversation carefully, acknowledging and supporting the individual's feelings. Use this formula when talking to an individual experiencing anxiety:

- I know how you feel . . .
- I felt the same way . . .
- I found that . . .

Most important, remember to listen more and talk less.

Second, and most important, staff need to feel confident that they have the skill set and knowledge to be able to incorporate the new technology into their work—knowing how it will impact their day-to-day lives and what training, support, and transition processes the organization will provide. As the technology is being implemented, training should also be provided to help people get comfortable with the new technology as quickly as possible. Where possible, it is helpful to provide "sandbox" opportunities for people to experiment with and use the technology in nonthreatening ways that enable them to learn and get comfortable with it (for example, a test database, or updating pages in a content management system and previewing them without publishing them). Some people may require more training and support than others.

After a new technology has been implemented, providing options for ongoing training and support—such as user manuals, cheat sheets with instructions for using the new technology, optional refresher courses at regular intervals, and on-demand web-based tutorials (if resources are available to create and support them)—can help people get comfortable with the new technology and stay comfortable with it.

It's important to recognize that some people may not acknowledge their need for support. Some may feel that they should understand the new technology and not want to admit that they don't, either out of embarrassment or possibly out of fear that such an admission might be harmful to their job or role in the organization. To address this, it may be helpful to provide a high-comfort, low-profile way for those in need to get extra help. For example, two people who are comfortable with the technology could make themselves available to help those who aren't and ensure that those who request help will be afforded privacy. Additionally, frequent check-ins—particularly soon after the new technology adoption—provide opportunities to offer additional support without calling attention to those who may be having a difficult time adjusting.

Finally, ongoing opportunities for feedback about the new technology, in both structured ways (such as checking in as an agenda item in a staff meeting) and unstructured ways (such as an open-door policy for people to talk about the technology), provide people with an enduring sense that their input and concerns matter. Creating opportunities for anonymous feedback, such as with a suggestion box, can also help determine whether people are still feeling anxious as well as identify potential needs for additional support and training.

## Conclusion

Change is hard. Organizations often resist change. However, a rapidly changing environment and, more important, an ongoing need and desire to deliver needed services efficiently and effectively means that nonprofits cannot stand still. This is especially true for technology initiatives. One important thing to remember in all technology implementations is the people factor, which is critical to the success of any technology change initiative, regardless of how large or small, how simple or complicated the technology is.

There are many obstacles to successful technology initiatives, but they can be overcome with good management that includes a clear mandate for change tied to the organization's mission, good and frequent communication, buy-in across the organization, and understanding and mitigation of the anxiety inherent in any change.

Top-down change initiatives that seem handed down by fiat rather than through good communication and mission alignment raise the risk of alienating people in the organization who are critical to the success of an initiative.

Nonprofit leaders should also be open to changes that originate elsewhere in the organization. Frequently, staff members who are on the organization's front lines—serving constituents and donors, and delivering the organization's key services—will be very aware of needed or beneficial technology changes and will have great ideas. Leaders who are open to technology changes that originate throughout the organization can often stay ahead of the technology change game and learn quickly from evolving constituent needs.

Finally, nonprofit leaders should strive to create a culture of continuous improvement in their organizations, one in which frequent small changes—prompted by asking questions, challenging assumptions, and decentralizing decision making—help to both reduce the need for large, disruptive changes and better position the organization to handle large technology changes when they are needed to help further the organization's mission and goals.

Development Executives Roundtable (DER) is a San Francisco–based membership organization dedicated to providing accessible training and support to Bay Area fundraisers at all stages of their careers to help build thriving organizations and communities. It was founded in 1968 by Hank Rosso, and it served as an informal networking and support group for fundraisers until 2006, when the board saw a need to change. DER incorporated, and the board realized that it was facing a business driver, prompted by outside pressures. To become a sustainable, growing, and competitive organization, it needed to change its "business as usual" practices. DER had no web presence, and it was handling registration for its monthly luncheons by email, which not only was time consuming but also frequently deferred revenue from the events until after the events actually took place. The organization needed to increase awareness, grow its membership (and its annual budget), and find a more efficient process for managing its event registration.

DER formed a working committee to evaluate website and membership database alternatives. DER is an entirely volunteer-run organization, and the committee consisted of four members of the board, one of whom became the website coordinator and project leader. Guided by consultant Robert Weiner, the committee defined requirements for the new system and started to evaluate alternatives.

Using an evaluation framework provided by the consultant, the working committee conducted conference calls and webinars with each of the vendors to evaluate the systems and brought information back to the board.

The committee solicited input from the board at specific stages in the process. Although not all of the board members had comparable levels of understanding of the technology and its specific benefits, they all understood that DER needed some means to increase its presence, recruit new members, and handle event registration more efficiently. The board chair at the time was a strong supporter of the initiative, helping the committee to follow up with individual board members for input and setting the tone to prioritize the committee's work. Having the committee take ownership of the process, solicit input about specific elements, listen to and address concerns, and then present findings to the board worked well. In that way, the committee was able to get buy-in—and enthusiastic support—from the board. The committee ultimately recommended Memberclicks membership management software, and the board approved.

Prior to implementation, the board proactively communicated with DER members that a technology change was in the works. They sent postcards and flyers to members and announced at the beginning and end of monthly luncheons—the organization's main events—that DER would be launching a new website and event registration process. When the new website launched, the board sent an email to members with site and login information.

The web project manager took the lead in the implementation process. She worked closely with the vendor and served as a liaison between the vendor and the organization's board members. Once the website was ready for launch, the vendor sales staff conducted an online training session for the working committee. The committee, in turn, trained other members of the board who would be involved with the website. The web project manager provided additional one-on-one training sessions to some board members who either were not as comfortable with technology as others or would be responsible for updating some sections of the website. For those board members and organization members who needed additional support, the web project manager created cheat sheets with instructions for common website functions and answers to common questions and provided one-on-one hand-holding. She continues to provide additional support when needed.

In addition to doubling its membership, creating a web presence, and making events registration more efficient by reducing the time spent by volunteers on registration for the events and collecting event fees prior to the events, DER learned some valuable lessons about managing technology change initiatives. They learned that it is critical to get input and buy-in early in the process by ensuring that people understand the objective of the initiative and how it supports the organization's mission and goals—and the internal or external driver catalyzing the change. For any initiative, getting clear support from leadership (in this case, the board chair) helps garner support. Communicating clearly before, during, and after the implementation of the new technology, as well as providing multiple opportunities for ongoing support, helps mitigate anxiety and provide the skills and comfort necessary to get people on board with a new technology.

## Recommended Reading

Abrahamson, Eric. "Change Without Pain." *Harvard Business Review* 78, no. 4 (July-August 2000).

Beer, Michael, and Nitin Nohria. "Cracking the Code of Change." *Harvard Business Review* 78, no. 3 (May-June 2000).

———. "Resolving the Tension Between Theories E and O of Change." In *Breaking the Code of Change*. Boston: Harvard Business School Press, 2000.

Beer, Michael, Russell A. Eisenstat, and Bert A. Spector. "Why Change Programs Don't Produce Change." In *Attacking Change from All Angles*. Boston: Harvard Business School Press, 2002.

Bennis, Warren. "Leadership of Change." In *Breaking the Code of Change*, edited by Michael Beer and Nitin Nohria. Boston: Harvard Business School Press, 2000.

Burnes, Bernard. *Managing Change: A Strategic Approach to Organizational Dynamics*. Essex, England: Pearson Education, 2000.

Duck, Jeanie Daniel. "Managing Change: The Art of Balancing." *Harvard Business Review* 78, no. 6 (November-December 2000).

*Harvard Business Essentials: Managing Change and Transition*. Boston: Harvard Business School Press, 2003.

Hayes, John. The Theory and Practice of Change Management. New York: Palgrave, 2002.

Hirschhorn, Larry. "Campaigning for Change." In *Attacking Change from All Angles*. Boston: Harvard Business School Press, 2002.

————. "Changing Structure Is Not Enough: The Moral Meaning of Organizational Design." In *Breaking the Code of Change*, edited by Michael Beer and Nitin Nohria. Boston: Harvard Business School Press, 2000.

Kotter, John F. "Leading Change: Why Transformation Efforts Fail." In *Attacking Change from All Angles*. Boston: Harvard Business School Press, 2002.

————. *Leading Change.* Boston: Harvard Business School Press, 1996.

Markedes, Constantinos C. *All the Right Moves: A Guide to Crafting Breakthrough Strategy.* Boston: Harvard Business School Press, 2000.

# CHAPTER 3

# Measuring the Return on Investment of Technology

*Beth Kanter*

To optimize technology within an organization, you have to find a way to measure whether these investments will bring value to the organization. It is important for a decision maker to understand the concept of *return on investment* (ROI). This chapter will help nonprofit technology leaders answer the question, "How will a technology investment pay off and contribute to the organization's mission?" It will help demystify the concept of ROI and illustrate how nonprofit decision makers can effectively use ROI processes, techniques, and formulas to help their organizations make better technology decisions. The chapter outlines how to calculate and quantify the benefits of a technology purchase, looks at how and where to incorporate qualitative information in a useful way, and covers techniques to communicate the case for support to people in the organization.

## What Is ROI? Getting Beyond the Magic Spreadsheet

When most of us hear the term *ROI*, we immediately envision a magic spreadsheet or calculator that illustrates whether or not the investment in question will "pay for itself." That's not surprising, if we think about the origins of ROI: as a way to measure overall company performance in the commercial sector. The ROI accounting process, created in the 1920s, was a financial measure developed by DuPont and used by Alfred Sloan to make General Motors manageable.[1] It is a flow chart that calculates business performance, taking into account not only whether the company had a profit but also whether that profit was good enough relative to the assets it took to generate it. Since that time the process has been polished and refined and is now deeply embedded in business thinking as a means of measuring business performance.

Although financial calculations are a building block for the ROI process, for our purposes ROI is defined as a pre- or post-evaluation process and analysis of three factors: benefits, costs, and value of a specific technology purchase over time.

## Why Thinking About Returns on Investment Is Important

Considering a purchase with an eye toward the return on the investment has two benefits: it can prevent technology purchases that would turn out to be a huge mistake, and conversely it helps avoid *not* making a purchase when the technology could be beneficial. The following are a few scenarios in which using an ROI approach can be useful.

### Stop Focusing on the Hammer

There are often situations in which technologists or other people on staff get seduced by a technology tool and do not focus on how it will be used. Says one executive director, "It's like thinking about the tools to build the house—the hammer and nails—and we don't give enough thought to who will be living in the house." Many nonprofit techies admit to falling into this trap. And this kind of thinking isn't limited just to the techies. Managers and program staff can fall victim to it as well.

When we let our fascination with the tools drive our technology investment decisions, we often end up with unused systems or failed strategies. Says one nonprofit technology staff person, "Six months ago, my executive director was out to lunch with some board members who were all using high-end cell phones. He came back to the office and wanted to buy them for everyone on staff. If we had done that without a thorough ROI process, it would have been a disaster because we only had two program staff members who worked in the field. What they really needed were laptops and wireless cards to get their work done."

## Costs but No Benefit

Techies often speak in terms of cost for a technology purchase, but decision makers need to consider benefit as well. Describing the technology features and comparing the features and prices to those of other similar tools is not enough, because it does not consider concretely how the tool may help staff to be more efficient or more effective in delivery of services. A cost-only approach fails to translate these benefits into monetary value.

Says one technology staff person at a legal services organization:

> I work with large spreadsheets and have many windows open. A thirty-inch monitor would eliminate a lot of scrolling and wasted time. There were others in the organization with the same problem. So I put together a proposal for our executive director, but it was a price comparison of different brands of monitors. The executive director rejected it. Later, we had some team meetings in which staff members talked about how much more effective they would be if they had the larger monitors, and I found some benchmarking studies that showed how many minutes could be saved from not having to scroll based on the size of the monitor. I put together a case for support that translated the value of the saved time. The executive director approved a pilot purchase of one monitor. I gave it to his assistant. She started to rave about it and he observed first-hand how much more efficient it was. A few months later, we had large monitors for almost everyone on staff who needed one.

## Getting Buy-In

When a technology project proposal is designed and researched by one person—such as the organization's techie—there is no buy-in if there is no feedback from those who will actually use the technology. The case for support may not be much more than budget and description of the technology used. There may be no data collected or research undertaken, and the financials do not consider the cost of alternative investments or of not making the investment.

Says one executive director:

> Our agency invested in a video conferencing system to connect staff with other staff or clients from our offices around the state. If I had written a proposal without an ROI process and it was based on the cost alone, it would have been rejected. We really had to look at how the system would improve our service delivery and effectiveness of staff—and translate that into dollar amounts. The way we did that was to analyze how much it would cost us if we didn't invest. We had to talk to everyone and get staff involved. There was initially a lot of resistance to the video conferencing system because we could have hired more staff instead. We had to address that as part of the ROI process or we wouldn't have gotten past it. Using ROI thinking can help you effect change.

## Unpacking ROI

What are the qualities of an ROI process for a nonprofit that wants to use it for making technology decisions? Let's take a look.

## It Goes Beyond Asking "How Much Does It Cost?"

The financial analysis in an ROI process is more than subtracting expenses from projected income and saying, "It breaks even or pays for itself." Although an ROI process does include financial calculations, they are but one component of a measurement and evaluation process that key concept

Using an ROI process to assess technology investments is useful because:

- It quantifies the technology's benefit to your organization's mission by forcing you to quantify the benefits into a monetary value.

- It provides you with important data; for example, how much time it takes to complete a task.

- It helps start a discussion about change needed in the organization before the technology is purchased. This can be valuable in increasing the likelihood of successful technology adoption if it occurs as part of the decision-making process and not after the fact. Although the cost of change cannot be easily converted into a dollar value, understanding the adoption issues can certainly pave the way to a more successful project implementation.

- It helps set priorities for your investments. Most nonprofits have limited staff and time and are managing multiple projects and programs. Resources are often limited. So it's very helpful to have a method for determining when a technology purchase simply won't deliver promises of saved time or effectiveness. Also, an ROI process is a good reality check for those who may seduced by the latest technology tools—even if you are one of them. It helps decision makers focus on benefits, not features.

- It helps with forecasting staffing patterns and allocating available resources. At the heart of many technology investments is the desire to free staff from work processes that are inefficient, frustrating, or nonessential. By quantifying these, the organization can more accurately understand how the technology purchase might affect staffing needs and weigh that against available resources.

- Finally, it alters management and program staff perceptions of technology. A good ROI case for support will address any negative perceptions of the technology and help turn those around. It vividly paints a picture of how the technology will save time or expenses, make staff more effective, or impact outcomes. This can change technology skeptics to technology advocates.

looks at the benefits, costs, and value of a technology investment over time. If you approach ROI as a financial analysis only, you will miss out on the full benefits of using the approach. As you identify and unpack the benefits—efficiency and effectiveness—you need to translate these into dollar amounts or value. Some benefits can be easily translated into dollar amounts; others cannot. You may be tempted to ignore the latter, but often these are extremely important to include in your case for support to illustrate the quantitative information. Although numbers are essential to building your case, it is often the stories and intangibles that really help convince people. The point is, you need both—one won't work without the other.

## It Is Simple and Streamlined

Although an ROI process will involve some data collection, it should not take you more time to implement than the technology project itself. Many ROI processes go wrong when management or technology staff get too obsessed with the data collection itself. Remember, the data collection should not be a burden. Avoid excessive surveying or overly complicated spreadsheets.

## A Data Collection Example

A community health center wanted to purchase laptop computers with wireless Internet access for staff to do health screenings of migrant workers in the field. The ROI study needed to identify the approximate number of hours it would take to accomplish the task without the benefit of the technology tools, and the number of trips back and forth to the office. The organization developed a very simple task analysis form and asked the program staff person to complete it for a typical case—not for every single client, which would have been a data collection burden. The ROI process also usually results in a written report or business case that shares the numbers, anecdotes that illustrate benefits, and a description of the technology. The business case can be as simple as an internal memo.

## It Is Credible

The process for data collection and financial calculations needs to be credible. The numbers presented must be clear, concise, understandable, and believable to everyone in the organization. The data collection process will include both internal information gathering—for example, looking at previous year's budgets and actual performance—and outside research. It is important to keep an eye out for published studies from credible sources that provide acceptable benchmarks about the efficiency or effectiveness of a particular technology. It is also useful to gather information from other nonprofits that have implemented similar technology programs. Nonprofit technology conferences and industry email discussion lists are useful for finding out who has implemented a similar project and how they made the business case for a technology purchase. Doing some homework will make the case for a technology investment more credible.

## It Is Detailed—but Not Too Detailed

The ROI process often gets down to understanding the details of how staff does their work—the nitty-gritty of task analysis. This can be difficult because you may be doing this analysis for a core system that could impact your entire organization—like a client management system, intranet, or document automation system. For that you need to take an in-depth look at how these systems improve efficiency—which means taking a granular look at how the technology improves effectiveness in the delivery of your program or service to clients and how the technology saves time or costs. However, this micro view of how work gets done should not get bogged down with excessive data collection and should keep the bigger picture in mind. The ultimate question ought to be, How are we improving efficiency or effectiveness?

## When Is ROI Used?

Among nonprofit organizations, an ROI process is most commonly used before the organization makes a technology investment, to help in making the decision whether to invest. However, nonprofit organizations can also use an ROI process after implementing a small pilot project to determine the full ROI implications.

## Anticipating the Future

ROI analysis is commonly used prospectively, especially for larger purchases for which a smaller proof of concept is not possible. Results from the analysis inform an IT purchase. Typically, cost and performance estimates are based on assumptions about the future that may involve considerable uncertainty. Sometimes an ROI analysis is used to pave the way for organizational change.

The organization we mentioned earlier used an ROI process prospectively to make the decision about investing in a video conference system to facilitate communication, training, and program delivery between regional offices. The organization's executive director says, "It was a large upfront investment, over $100,000. We analyzed the staff cost of travel time and gas against the cost of the system over a three-year period. We also estimated the income that could be generated if the 'saved staff time' were applied to direct program work versus travel time."

He also notes that the ROI process looked at some of the intangible benefits of being able to do more trainings between offices. He says, "We do a lot of staff mentoring, and the video conference system allowed us to assign mentors based on expertise versus geographic location. That would help us improve the effectiveness of our staff, but it was nearly impossible to measure." The ROI process gathered anecdotal evidence. For example, if a client came into the office with a Medicaid issue, but the person with expertise was in an office an hour away, the client would have had to wait to schedule an appointment or drive over. With the video conference system, staff are able to serve the client sooner.

Finally, the organization analyzed the cost of the video conference system and asked what the impact would be if they spent this money on something else. For the conference system, they compared the cost/benefit of investing in more staff, for example. The additional staff would not have yielded the same cost savings in travel time or helped facilitate internal mentoring.

## Learning from the Past

Sometimes organizations use ROI to learn from the past or after a purchase has been made. It is commonly used for a small pilot project and based on actual performance data.

The legal services organization introduced earlier had quite a few program staff who work with clients in the field rather than having clients come to the office, because the clients do not have a permanent residence—for example, some were migrant farm workers. The technology committee had discussed getting laptops and cell phone cards for all staff who work outside of the office, but they did not have the upfront information on time and cost savings. Rather than make the investment for all program staff, they decided to run a small pilot with two staff members who worked with migrant farm workers.

They interviewed the attorneys about their current work flow before using the laptops and wireless Internet card. They asked a lot of questions about how and when having Internet access and a laptop would improve the efficiency and effectiveness of their work. The committee learned that these staff members would be in the field and the client's question or situation would require Internet or other electronic research to resolve. Typically, the staff person would have to drive back to the office, do the research, and then schedule a second trip to meet with the client. Because the farm workers did not have phones, it would be difficult for the staff person to complete the service or it would require several trips. In addition, staff members would have to work late back at the office, entering their client case notes into the client management system. It took multiple steps to complete the work, and frequently cases could not be closed because it was difficult to reach migrant workers to reschedule.

During the pilot phase, staff members kept time diaries and trip logs for each client. "If our staff was standing in the middle of a tomato field and the client asked a hard question, they could answer it on the spot without having drive back to the office. All the attorney had to do is get on the laptop and connect to Lexis. Or they could enter the case notes into the system while all the details were fresh, without having to transcribe notes back at the office. This one-stop service, made possible by the technology investment, made our staff far more effective." At the end of the pilot period, they had collected enough data to conduct an ROI analysis using the following formulas:

- Analyze the cost of travel time and mileage from monthly time sheets
- Analyze what they could be doing with that time (for example, what other billable work could be done)
- Translate that time into an hourly billable rate
- Estimate how many trips it takes the attorneys to complete the work with a single client without a laptop (two or three) and how many it would take with a laptop (just one)
- Compared travel costs and time with the cost of the laptop and wireless Internet access

According to the organization, the ROI analysis helped decision makers in the organization understand that the use of laptops and wireless Internet access was far more efficient and effective than doing remote legal work without them. They were able to use pilot information to do an analysis of investing in laptops and wireless Internet for all program staff who work with clients outside of the office. Notes the executive director, "A small pilot to learn how to calculate the ROI of a larger rollout can be really valuable."

Having gained an understanding of when an ROI process is used and how to approach it simply, it is now time to explore the process.

## ROI: The Building Blocks

There are four basic building blocks to using ROI: benefits, metrics, value, and financial formulas.

### Benefits

When considering technology investments for a nonprofit organization, the key is to ask, how does this technology investment improve

## In What Situations Should You Consider Using an ROI Method?

It is not necessary to use an ROI process for every single technology purchase your organization may be considering. However, it is definitely recommended for projects that

- Have a long life cycle

- Are essential to meeting the organization's mission and linked to strategic goals

- Are very expensive

- Are highly visible or controversial

- Have a large target audience

our staff's ability to do their work or improve our clients' situation? The benefits building block of ROI covers how the technology is expected to enhance programs, or improve services, or increase efficiency through reduced costs or increased revenue. When your technology committee starts to think about benefits, they need to include all benefits, whether they are *tangible* or *intangible*.

Tangibles are those benefits we can easily measure and convert. Intangibles are those benefits or detriments directly linked to the IT project that cannot or should not be converted to monetary units but that may be quantifiable.

Intangibles may truly make a difference in the success of the project and enhancement of the organization. These benefits include staff effectiveness, morale, customer satisfaction, business relationships, and others. Some of these are clearly more quantifiable than others, but all are important to consider in an ROI analysis. Intangible measures are often noted in the upfront proposal and tracked as part of project implementation.

## Differentiating Tangible Benefits from Intangible Benefits

Tangible benefits are typically those that are required for organizational operations; they are readily visible, rigorously quantified, and presented as a line item on a budget. Tangible benefits can be described as

- Objective

- Easy to quantify

- Easy to assign a monetary value

- Measurable in common measures such as dollars, time units (minutes, hours), and the like

- Credible with leadership

For example, an organization wants to invest in an online registration system that is linked to its customer database. This is fairly easy to quantify because the organization can take a look at how much time is spent doing manual and redundant data entry and multiply this by the staff person's hourly wage. The time that is no longer spent on manual and redundant data entry could be spent doing another task, and if that task contributes to bringing in income or improving client services, that could be also be quantified.

Intangible benefits are key to organizational effectiveness, but, again, may be difficult to quantify and are not tracked through budgeting or accounting procedures. They can be described as

- Subjective

- Difficult to measure and quantify

- Difficult to assign monetary value to

- Less credible as a performance measure

- Usually behaviorally oriented

Consider the earlier example of the organization seeking to invest in an online registration system linked to its customer database. Perhaps the intangible benefit of being relieved of a lot of manual and redundant data entry may improve morale in the organization and reduce employee frustration. Further, this may lead to a lower rate of staff turnover.

Improved morale is an important benefit but not as easily quantified as time savings.

### Some Typical Intangible Benefits

The following benefits are often presented as intangibles. For each, there may be exceptions for which the organization can convert the data to monetary value. Additional data collection may be required in order to make this conversion (we'll discuss the conversion process shortly).

## Intangible Benefits

- Job Satisfaction
- Productivity
- Job commitment
- Work environment
- Morale
- Employee retention
- Innovation
- Competencies
- Leadership
- Teamwork
- Cooperation
- Decision making
- Communication
- Client satisfaction
- Client complaints
- Client response time

key concept

The first step in identifying benefits of both kinds is to have a brainstorming session with your technology committee in which you'll ask the following questions to determine the *efficiency* and *effectiveness* gains anticipated from the technology.

# Determining Efficiency and Effectiveness

**Efficiency**

• How much time or money can we save?

• What are the work processes and estimated costs for the project?

**Effectiveness**

• How will this investment contribute to program goals and results?

• How will this investment contribute to the effectiveness of staff to serve clients?

It is important to note that efficiency and effectiveness go hand and hand. Let's look at some examples.

## Efficiency: Time or Cost Savings

Looking at efficiency—time or cost savings—is easier than considering effectiveness, because time and cost savings are concrete and measurable (tangible). Whatever the technology investment you're analyzing, look at how the technology makes staff members' jobs easier and less frustrating, removes redundant tasks, saves time, saves the need for travel, or reduces other operating costs. Table 3.1 presents some examples.

## Effectiveness: Better Use of Time to Serve Clients or Improve Quality of Work

Effectiveness improvements from technology are a little more difficult to make concrete (intangible). But a good exercise is to ask what staff might do with the time or cost savings. Says one technology staff person, "We don't just look at how many hours are spent on a particular task—we look at the task itself and the results. If our program staff members are spending twenty hours on referrals, we want to make sure that the twenty hours are being spent on delivering high-quality expertise. We don't want ten of those hours being spent on formatting documents or trying to arrange a consult with another office or rebooting computers because the system crashes." Table 3.2 presents some examples of effectiveness improvements to be gained from technology.

## Table 3.1. Examples of Time and Cost Savings from Technology.

| Benefit | Example |
| --- | --- |
| Improves the ability to maintain a system | A content management system allows a legal services organization to more efficiently maintain its website content. |
| Eliminates duplicate systems | A wide area network (WAN) allows satellite offices to more easily share information and avoid having to maintain separate systems.<br><br>A client management system eliminates the need for copying data from email or other sources into spreadsheets. |
| Accommodates increases in workload or demand without additional costs | An intranet provides a final repository for all the case-handling procedures, latest statistics on performance, health insurance manuals, personnel manuals—all so they do not need to be copied when hopelessly out of date and endlessly clogging book shelves. |
| Reduces manual operations | A case management system replaces a system that had multiple data entry. |
| Increases the number of people served | Case management statistics can create "profiles" of productivity and let staff know of their achievements.<br><br>Software-based TDD aids clients who are hearing-impaired or deaf.<br><br>Enables staff members to work with deaf or hearing-impaired clients from their desktops rather than having to move to a TDD phone line to a different location. |
| Reduces travel cost and time | Legal staff are provided with laptops and wireless Internet access and able to complete work in remote locations or during trial down time.<br><br>Video conferencing system eliminates the need for staff travel time and expenses for training. |

## Table 3.2. Examples of Effectiveness
## Improvements from Technology.

| Benefit | Example |
|---|---|
| Improves ability to deliver | Legal staff who work in multiple field locations use laptops with wireless Internet access, which allows them to respond to client requests more quickly and complete work while in the field. |
| | Hotline software decreases wait time for clients so they are less frustrated and less likely to drop off the call and not get served. |
| Improves access to services | Hotline increases the number of people who can access the organization's staff for advice or screening or referral. |
| Improves access to information | Video tutorials on the legal services website help clients find the information they need and understand how to use it. |
| Improves accuracy | The document automation system improves accuracy by reducing both the need for manual creation of standard documents and the incidence of data entry errors. This may also improve productivity and reduce operating costs by reducing time spent on error correction. |
| Improves effectiveness of information delivered | Instant messaging is a tool to get quick answers from supervisors who are not in the room with the client— or even in the same city. |
| | Video conference systems allows clients coming into one office to instantly access staff expertise from a remote location. |

After collecting your data, once you have identified any intangible benefits, you should spend time on a *conversion test*. Sit down with your technology team and ask these questions:

1. Is there an acceptable, standard monetary value for the measure?
2. Is there a method that can be used to convert the measure to money?
3. Can the conversion be accomplished with minimum resources?
4. Can the conversion process be described to an executive director so as to secure their buy-in in two minutes?

Although executive directors love tangibles—benefits that can be confidently asserted in a statement such as "This technology investment will reduce our staff costs by 15 percent"—intangibles are still critical to an ROI process and need to be included in your final report. Also, with some degree of additional data collection or thought, they can possibly be quantified.

One strategy is to present the intangibles as anecdotal evidence coupled with tangible measures. The best way to identify intangibles is to observe how staff and clients are using the technology. Consider setting up a "benefits, metrics, and values discovery" brainstorming session with a small group of people who are knowledgeable about the areas or programs that will experience the largest impacts. Another approach is to look for the published tangible evidence from studies or reports from other nonprofits (for example, *Making Technology Investments Profitable* by Jack Keen and Bonnie Digrius). These insights can be valuable because they add credibility to the analysis. Again, it is really useful to know what others in your field or discipline have done.

Sometimes it is hard to claim that investments in IT alone resulted in the improved client service or other benefit. One solution is to identify all possible connections that might lead to the benefit or improvement. This requires conversation with others or staff—not only to gather the data necessary to establish the chain but also to obtain their agreement on the technology's contribution to the business improvement. It is essential to ask questions like "Is there anything else over and above the technology itself that could have contributed to the results we're seeing?"

Finally, if you are seeking to quantify intangibles, it is extremely important to obtain consensus among the key decision makers about what constitutes a meaningful measurement.

## Metrics and Value

Metrics and value are another integral part of the ROI process, to be addressed once you have identified the benefits. Metrics are a unit of measure. Value is the process of quantifying the benefits with a metric and, if possible, translating it into dollars. Dollars are not the only metric of value; the best metric will align the investment with its intended objective.

Data collection will be part of the ROI process, particularly if you need to convert intangible benefits to tangible equivalents. Here are some of the kinds of data you may need to collect:

- Staff surveys
- Staff interviews
- Client surveys
- Clients interviews
- Data from system
- Task analysis
- Time sheet analysis
- Articles
- Field research
- Observation
- Secondary research reports
- Benchmark studies
- Budget and financial analysis

## Converting Intangibles to Tangibles: ROI Financial Formulas

The traditional ROI calculations that are undertaken by corporate IT departments—such as the benefit/cost ratio and ROI formula—are not always appropriate for nonprofits, because they are designed to answer these questions: "How much does it cost? How much revenue will it generate? Will it pay for itself?"

Many nonprofit techies say there is no magic formula or spreadsheet. What works for one organization may not be appropriate for other organizations. After you have identified benefits, metrics, and values, it is time for the financial calculations that answer these questions:

- What is the direct cost of the technology investment?
- What is the value of any expense or staff time savings?
- What is the value of intangible benefits?
- What is the cost of alternatives or not investing?

In the next section, we take a look at three different nonprofit organizations and how they used the building blocks of ROI to help guide their technology investment decisions.

### Example: Telecommunications Device for the Deaf (TDD)

A legal services organization recently switched from analog telecommunications device for the deaf (TDD) machines that had to be maintained on an old-style analog phone line. They looked at the benefits of moving to a software solution that would enable staff to access the TDD from their desktops. They calculated the cost of keeping the analog phone lines and the staff time that was wasted running around the office to use the TDD machine at $75,000. They compared that with the cost of software licenses and one digital phone line ($45,000). They also identified a few intangibles, like improved service to clients and improved staff productivity—it was a better use of their time to work with the client than to keep running back and forth in the office to use the TDD machine.

## Example: Centralized Intake System

The legal services organization had invested in a centralized intake system several years earlier that ultimately decreased costs and improved services to clients. At first, however, the service was so successful that they saw a major increase in calls—so much so that clients were being put on hold for too long a time. Complaints soared.

They analyzed their complaint log to determine the nature of the complaints: the fact that clients had to wait on the phone on hold for twenty to thirty minutes or more until they got served.

The team then researched software solutions that allowed the client to push a button and hold their place in the line, then receive a call back, as well as how many additional screeners would be required to reduce waiting time to an acceptable level.

The cost of the software solution was a $35,000 one-time expenditure. The team compared it to the cost of hiring additional staff to reduce the wait time. That cost was $70,000 annually. Clearly, investing in the software solution was a better investment decision.

Table 3.3 presents some of the possibilities.

**Table 3.3. ROI Analysis of a Centralized Intake System Solution.**

| Benefits | Metrics | Values | Cost |
|---|---|---|---|
| Improved delivery of referral service to clients | Complaints reduced | Clients don't feel frustrated | Software option: $35,000 one-time investment in software, support, and so on |
| | Reduced turnover rate of screeners | Improved word of mouth | |
| | Reduced unproductive waiting time for clients | Less stress for the screener, who doesn't have to deal with angry people on the phone | Human option: $70,000 recurring cost |
| | Number of clients served increases; fewer people hang up and don't get a referral | | |

# Example: Justifying an Intranet

This legal services organization does not have an intranet. As a result, attorneys, paralegals, and administrative staff use—or rather, overuse—the organization's aging photocopier. Given excessive use, it frequently runs out of toner or breaks down. The photocopier's malfunctioning impacts major court deadlines. Staff complain a lot about the photocopier, because making copies is now a task that can't be easily automated. Many times staff members try to do without making copies—and this prevents the sharing of information with other people on staff and causes many communications issues.

Because the organization is using paper-based systems, key internal documents are not as up-to-date as they should be. For example, new attorneys on staff can't quickly get up to speed on case handling procedures because the informational binders have not been updated. There are many, many other examples of why not having an intranet impairs internal communication.

The legal services technology staff member convenes the organization's technology committee, composed of program staff people, to do an ROI analysis. Over the course of several meetings, they do the following:

- Brainstorm and discuss how an intranet might save money and time through the following benefits:

  - Reduced costs from paper, toner, and photocopier repairs.

  - Saved staff time that would have been spent waiting to use the photocopier or waiting for it to be fixed.

  - Saved staff time that would have been spent manually updating binders.

- Design a work diary form and ask a couple of key staff members to fill it out so they can use it to quantify the time savings. Specifically, they ask how they might be spending their time if they were not waiting for the photocopier.

- Conduct interviews with key staff to better understand how technology might improve staff effectiveness. They hear a lot of complaints and suggestions that they also let the executive director know this in a staff meeting scheduled to discuss the topic. Staff suggest that technology improvements could

- Improve staff morale.
- Improve collaboration on staff.
- Get new staff members up to speed on procedures faster.
- Ensure that staff reviews are done in a more timely manner, thereby improving job performance.

• Research the Internet for published studies that show how an intranet can improve staff productivity and efficiency. These are provided to staff interviewed and saved to use in a written memo or ROI case report for the executive director.

• Ask the HR director/green activist to research whether they can reduce their carbon footprint by using less paper in the office.

• Put the intranet discussion on the agenda for full staff meetings that are attended and led by the executive director.

• Brainstorm, as a committee, about the content of the ROI memo for the executive director. They decide to include the following:

- Because the executive director of the legal services organization has an MBA and did his graduate work in team management and leadership, they describe the key benefit of an intranet as a way to improve teamwork.

- They decide to tell the story of one staff person and how much time they would save with an intranet. They present some vignettes about how more timely reviews, up-to-date procedures, and so on would improve work performance.

- They integrate highlights of research.

- They include a cost/benefit analysis converting the benefits into dollar amounts.

## Communicating Results

The ROI process is more than data collection and number crunching; it also consists of an organizational conversation and storytelling. Your organization may have conducted an excellent ROI process—identifying benefits, quantifying the value, identifying metrics, and doing financial calculations—but you can't stop there. The way you communicate your findings can make or break your success, particularly if you need to use your ROI process as a change process. If you already have a formal team or committee that is responsible for IT planning in your organization, this is the ideal group to champion the ROI process. The group should consist of a balance of technical and nontechnical people and represent people who will be impacted by the technology purchase.

It is also important to keep in mind that you will need to produce a written product from your ROI process. It can be an informal memo or a full-blown report, depending on the style and culture of your organization. A good, credible ROI process incorporates storytelling techniques.

### ROI Storytelling Techniques

The business case presents the key issues and facts while spotlighting the investment's contribution to the organization's mission. It may come as no surprise that good business cases are calculated based on numbers, but they are *approved* based on stories. ROI numbers, no matter how compelling, won't speak for themselves. It's up to you to explain what they mean to the enterprise's visions and goals.

Successful ROI storytelling techniques include a number of components. It is important to include a well-prepared business case that incorporates both the numbers and nonfinancial factors in a concise and informative presentation. Remember, the key purpose is to sell the value of the proposed project.

Clever storytelling is one of the quickest and most effective ways to gain executive director understanding, buy-in, and funding. It also helps attract support and cooperation from reluctant users during project implementation and operation.

Creating effective stories is not hard, provided you clearly understand who these decision influencers are, know well what they most care about, and understand where to place stories for the most impact.

## What Happens If ROI Is Negative?

What if the upfront cost is huge and the benefits are all intangible and can't be quantified? This prospect strikes terror into the hearts of not just the technology staff, but also of program staff and executive directors. The project may waste resources that could be used in some other area with better results, like hiring more staff. If you have followed all the steps, your analysis provides an opportunity for learning and change. Here are some tips:

- Use your research to identify a "proof of concept" project that is less of a risk, then use that to get a better handle on the costs/benefits and, if possible, convert the intangibles into tangibles.

- Manage expectations through discussion.

- Use your information to drive change. Focus on the cost to your client service or staff of *not* implementing.

Keep in mind that a negative ROI should be seen not as the ending, but as an opportunity for organizational change.

## Conclusion

There is no single "right" way to conduct a return on investment analysis. Nor are there standardized ROI analysis processes or benchmark calculations for nonprofit technology. The best advice is to focus on connecting the analysis to the organization's goals and business processes. This focus will help guide decisions about the resources and methods to use to conduct a sound and valuable ROI analysis. Here's how to do it:

- Focus on benefits, not features.

- Don't ignore intangibles.

- Present more than just the numbers.
- Compare costs of alternatives, cost/benefit, and the cost of doing nothing.
- Use pilot projects to get credible numbers.
- Collect the data you need.
- Get buy-in by using a committee.
- Use ROI to drive change, if needed.

This focus will help guide decisions about the resources and methods to use to conduct a sound and valuable ROI analysis.

## Note

1. http://en.wikipedia.org/wiki/Alfred_Sloan.

# CHAPTER 4

# How to Decide: IT Planning and Prioritizing

*Peter Campbell*

To many of us, the world of technology feels like a circus, with high wires to be crossed and far too many lions to be tamed. We know—because every report that we read and consultant we meet tells us so—that there is value in investing in the Web, databases, mobile phones, and all of this shiny 2.0 stuff. But contrary to the popular story about running off to join the circus, you don't just show up at the tent door and fly with the greatest of ease. Making technology work in the world of nonprofits is like juggling a ball, a balloon, and a chainsaw. We have to know which items have to be caught, which can hang in the air, and what will wow the crowds. The goal of this chapter is to make you the ringmaster, not the clown, and to suggest a strategic planning framework that can allow a cash-strapped, mission-focused organization to select technology that furthers the cause.

## Building a Culture That Frames Technology Planning

Consider that, although computer technology is much like traditional infrastructure—the buildings, lights, and photocopiers that you use every day—it differs in its ability to streamline and propel processes. It's faster and far less expensive to send mass emails than mass mailings. Self-service benefits portals reduce the workloads of strained HR staff. Integrated donor management and financial systems cut down on repetitive data entry tasks. If we account for technology by simply counting heads and allocating computers, we miss out on the opportunity to realize the greatest benefits of information systems: streamlining wasteful activities, enhancing our ability to understand and use our data, and propelling our messages to the world. Technology investments should be weighed against the efficiencies and expense reductions they can enable. And this takes planning.

## Strategic Planning

One of the circus-like aspects of technology is the fast-paced rate of change. Systems get more powerful, software gains capabilities, new tools replace standard tools. Sometimes it makes no sense—things that look like good solid ideas prove to be short-lived fads; silly-sounding startups like Google and Yahoo! become critical business systems. In the face of all of the instability, the idea of long-term planning seems futile—why build a wooden house when your neighbor is inventing the brick, and his neighbor has an idea for something called aluminum siding? Although technology is a swiftly evolving field, you can't just wait for it to slow down; at some point you need to make the leap. Of course, you can't move forward confidently if you don't know where you're going. Or, more accurately, you *can*, but you're leaving it to the wind to push you there, and the wind might be going in a poor direction. In technology planning, the end does generally justify the means, and the art of technology planning is to focus on the ends and play the means like the stock market. In five years, we're still going to be fundraising. We're still going to be practicing our mission-related services, in one form or another. And we'll still have finance and human resources.

Our buildings might become a bit more virtual, and we'll probably make fewer trips to the post office. But we may employ twice as many staff. We may double our fundraising goal. As long as we're focusing on what it is that we want to accomplish, we can identify what broad things our technology systems need to do in order to support it. Without a plan, it's all a gamble.

## Organizational Planning

Technology planning is a piece of a larger, organizational strategic planning process. A *unified strategic plan* ties together the

- Strategic plan

- Business plans

- Budget

by using *balanced scorecards* and *business process maps* to strictly tie actions and expenses to mission-serving strategies.

Developing a technology plan without first having a strategic plan for your organization is a bit like doing the lion tamer bit without a chair and whip. You want to have a plan, but it must be tied to the larger organizational picture.

A *strategic plan* articulates the key strategies to be employed in delivering your organization's mission. If your goal is to keep children from using illegal drugs, then a strategy might be education, or it might be to work with law enforcement to eliminate the market for the drugs. If your mission is to provide food to undernourished communities, a strategy might be partnering with the charitable arms of established food vendors. A strategic plan outlines these strategies, often for a five- or ten-year period. Because some strategies don't prove effective, and new strategic opportunities can arise as conditions change, a good strategic plan is a living document that is subject to regular review and revision.

A *business plan* is a short-term outline of the steps that will be taken to support the strategies, usually done annually. If the strategy is to increase funding by increasing the number of online donors, then the plan might include improving the website and identifying new online prospects.

The *budget*, of course, is the estimated allocation of the funds available to accomplish the business plan.

## Unified Planning

Maintaining a tight relationship between strategic planning, business planning, and budgeting can be an effective first step in ensuring that all of your planning—technology-related and otherwise—accomplishes what your plan calls for.

A *unified plan* ties business plan objectives and budget items directly to the strategies in the plan. Although some of this process can seem a bit strained (yes, those RAM upgrades do support the strategy to develop business data reporting in order to better articulate outcomes, but you're going to buy them regardless), it accomplishes a few things, one of them being a better alignment of spending to goals. A by-product, of particular use to IT and administrative staff, is how the unified plan amplifies the ways in which somewhat conventional tasks support the mission.

Upfront planning not only will increase your effectiveness at whatever service you perform but will also simplify and democratize the budgeting process. Budgeting is often a very political exercise, with resource allocation determined more by who shouted loudest than where the investment offered the best return. Tying each budget item to an articulated organizational strategy, then identifying exactly whom it will serve, what the projected return is, and how it will be measured via the balanced scorecard, will allow you to weigh issues on their merits. As this becomes an annual process, it will become easier to do and the measurements will gain in accuracy.

## Balanced Scorecards

Alternatively, or in addition to the unified plan, a balanced scorecard[1] approach can also focus planning and spending in ways that maximize effectiveness. This can be layered onto the planning process so that, as you're tying business objectives and investments to mission, you're concurrently identifying the stakeholders that the investments will serve. The balanced scorecard identifies four areas that your strategic plan should address: financial, constituent (or customer), internal business processes, and employee learning and growth.

Each strategy identified in the plan should be associated with one of the four areas in the balanced scorecard, and the overall plan should show advancement in all four areas. For each strategy proposed in the plan, objectives, measurements, targets, and initiatives, are identified. Table 4.1 presents a single strategy, in this case for the constituent area, with the supporting criteria.

### Table 4.1. Example of a Strategy with Supporting Criteria.

| Strategy | Area | Objectives | Measures | Targets | Initiatives |
|---|---|---|---|---|---|
| Increase constituent awareness of our accomplishments by distributing a monthly email newsletter | Constituents | Increase mission awareness<br><br>Increase donations<br><br>Improve communication | eCRM Statistics<br><br>Donations increases | 5% increase in new prospects<br><br>7% increase in donations | Start monthly newsletter as of 1/15; Add subscribe link to web site; publicize in NP Times. |

*Financial* strategies might include increasing donations by aggressively seeking new donor prospects; selling an asset, such as a piece of land; or renegotiating a group of support contracts with a goal of paying less.

*Constituent* strategies might include starting a newsletter to inform and engage constituents; or most program-related services, such as offering classes to job seekers or providing counseling to abuse victims.

*Internal business process* strategies might include replacing analog phones with a Voice over Internet Protocol (VoIP) system or instituting a new purchase order process.

*Employee training and growth* strategies includes employee bonuses, internal training, and mentoring and coaching programs.

## Making Planning Part of the Routine

Of course, a strategic planning schedule should not be so intensive that it paralyzes your ability to provide the services that you're planning for. Planning sessions should be scheduled in ways that allow for steady progress but don't interrupt the business flow. It's best to make strategic discussions, planning, and evaluations an ongoing activity, so that the practice of strategic thinking—which can differ greatly from the process of performing your business-driven duties—is an easier thing to adapt to. Just as high-wire artists practice their balancing act daily even when they're on vacation, you should be regularly reviewing your plan in order to stay on top of your game.

## Technology Planning

It's true that the state of technology changes rapidly, and perfectly good ideas become yesterday's news pretty fast, sometimes. You don't want to be writing your donor thank-you notes on a typewriter. But you don't want to jump on every trend, either—neither your budget nor your sanity would survive that. Sticking to a plan based on obsolesced technological standards would be self-defeating. But there are at least two reasons why having a long-term plan and a big-picture vision for technology is critical:

1. *You can't budget effectively on a year-to-year basis unless you know what you are budgeting for.* Long-term planning allows you to spread out recurring costs and space out large projects in ways that even out the expense. For example, few nonprofits can afford to replace all their computers or printers in a single year, but failing to have a long-term plan can put you at risk for this kind of big, unaffordable budget hit.

2. *Developing a road map for major system upgrades and replacements will smooth and foster adoption.* Large projects, such as email system upgrades or changing databases, can be planned in ways that will ease the pain for everyone involved. If staff are used to a reasonable level of technology updating and change, they are going to

be far more receptive to it than they will be to a sudden, complete overhaul every six years or so, after the systems have become so old and unsuitable that the organization is in a crisis state.

Certainly, if, in 2002, your plan had been to develop a new Access database to manage donations by 2007, you might have wanted to revisit that at some point and take a look at one of the many available CRM systems that are far more capable. A five-year plan identifies a destination—you don't change where you are going, but you may find new and better ways to get there. The key to the five-year plan is to recognize it as a direction, not cast in stone, and to hold truer to the overarching strategy than the specific details. The true art of technology planning lies in having both the foresight to understand where your technology should be in five years and the agility to flow with the changes and recognize the innovations that might jumpstart or improve on your plan.

## Guidance for GuideStar

The particular nonprofit balancing act that has to be mastered is that of making long-term investments without inflating short-term spending. Overhead—the cost of operating, as opposed to the cost of providing service—needs to be kept to a drastic minimum. Given that Charity Navigator and GuideStar publish 990 forms and rate organizations largely by what percentage of a dollar goes toward the mission, nonprofits must operate lean and keep expenses tight. Higher overhead and fundraising costs can have a negative impact on funding. But the cost savings that can be realized by strategic technology implementations require investment in hardware, software, and consulting.

When an organization is planning for and preparing budgets, projects that are clearly identified as adding equipment and new applications to the network must be separated out as capital investments. From a management perspective, this can also help determine the required resources, with a clear outline of what is recurring work and what's new.

Nonprofits operate under a level of scrutiny that demands a lean approach to operating. Money is tight and staffing is light. So to expect a nonprofit organization to operate like a fully staffed for-profit business is unrealistic, at best. Nonprofits have far more in common with marginal, cash-strapped small businesses than with your typical corporation. Given that real limitation, the worst mistake that an organization can make is to simply spend less. Living within constrained means is a strategic initiative that requires analysis and planning. To do otherwise is simply to live with the limitations and underperform.

## Elements of the Plan

A thorough technology plan should have at least three components: strategy, support, and actions (not necessarily in that order).

## Key Concept

Technology plans should have at least three components:

* Strategy

* Support

* Actions

The plan, of course, is going to discuss the key upcoming goals and projects, such as replacing the email system or donor database, adding or upgrading servers, and updating office suites. These might be laid out in a timeline, which stands as the action plan. A common mistake, however, is to lay out the plan without considering the how and the why. As useful as it is for a technology plan to articulate the IT priorities, the plan is more than just an announcement. A strong plan also ties planning to broader objectives and prepares the organization for the technology changes. A good plan will answer these questions:

* How will the actions laid out in the plan support the mission and organizational strategic plan?

* How will staff be resourced to use the technology?

* Does the organization have a coherent strategy for application support and training?

In addition to these broad questions, a solid technology plan will also articulate a data management strategy and present an IT staffing plan.

As database applications are purchased and upgraded, it is critical to understand how they will integrate (if at all) and what roles they will play. Here's a common scenario: You get a new job at a nonprofit. They have a finance system. They have a donor database. They have a case management system. They may have an HR system, or maybe HR just has a ridiculous number of spreadsheets. Donation data is entered into the donor system, then re-entered into Finance. Payroll data is printed out by HR and handed to Finance for entry into the payroll module of the finance system. Client data is exported to Excel and manipulated in order to report on outcomes. Mistakes are made—often. Names are misspelled in different systems. The donation totals, as summed by finance, don't match with the donor database reports. And there is no metric expressing the organization's effectiveness, from a financial or service standpoint.

The first thing to do is understand how things are getting done; how they could be done; and how much time, effort, and money could be saved if things were done more efficiently. In business lingo, this is called business process management (BPM); unlike most trendy acronyms, this one is pretty compelling. By managing the process, we can tie our activities more directly to our outcomes and create new efficiencies. In most environments, our work processes are dictated by individual styles, habit, and, in many cases, technology. We do things the way our software applications expect us to. The problem is that all software makes assumptions about how we work. The more popular the software is, the more generic the assumptions. But nonprofits operate under different assumptions than for-profit businesses, and each nonprofit and mission has its own unique attributes. One key to successfully deploying systems is to get them to enhance your processes, as opposed to bending your processes to meet their assumptions. There is always some give and take here, but all too often systems are deployed without this analysis, and the case for planning is the case for having our day-to-day systems support our outcomes, not inhibit them.

## Business Process Mapping

When striving to make technology affordable and worth the investment, one key approach is business process mapping. Many processes are performed at your organization, such as hiring and orienting a new employee; receiving, acknowledging, and processing an online donation; and generating a monthly board report. Each of these processes involves a mix of human and system interactions. To map a process, such as the receiving of an online donation, you can use a flowcharting application or a program with drawing capabilities. Figure 4.1 illustrates how to map your current process.

In many cases, a person reviewing incoming gifts, as opposed to an automated process, makes the "$100 or more" determination. Entry into donor and financial systems is manual. The $100 amount could trigger an email to inform a development officer that a personal letter is required. The letter-writing process is an additional process that might be reviewed. And of course, as you buy new eCRM (electronic constituent relationship management) and donor database systems, you'll want to include either compatibility or integration options to allow gift data to flow from the initial point of giving to all systems that store the information.

Understanding your processes and how they could be improved is a prerequisite for deploying any major technology system, in particular those with heavy data-entry functions, like HR, CRM, and case management.

## Planning the Technology Show

Properly planning for a resource-strapped organization requires a thorough, shared understanding of your systems and their role in serving your mission. The trick is really in knowing which systems are critical and which can be given a lower priority or be more creatively deployed. If you are a small, community-based nonprofit with a constituency that lives in the same neighborhood as your offices, then you probably don't need the most expensive or reliable phone system. This

## Figure 4.1. A Business Process Map.

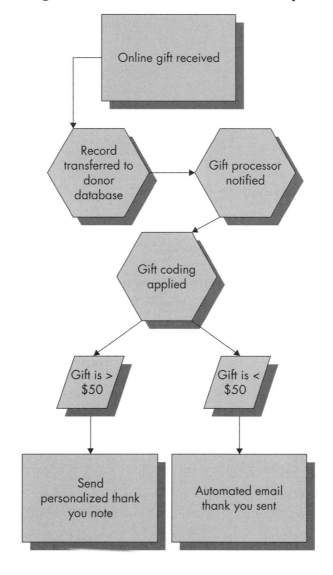

is something that you can save on by buying something used or refurbished and doing without a maintenance contract or expensive battery backup. Putting additional money into wireless access and handheld computing might give you a strategic communications advantage that balances the weak investment in voice.

## Key Concept

Critical technology investments require comprehensive evaluation:

- SWOT analyses
- Technical and end-user assessments of options
- Clear understanding of business needs versus software assumptions
- Creativity

## Identifying the Headline Acts

From a strictly IT perspective, "identifying the headline acts" means understanding when you have to put in the time, money, and project planning to ensure a successful outcome—as might be necessary for deploying a new donor management system—and when you can get away with recycled computers and a quick-and-dirty rollout, as might be appropriate for putting some kiosk systems in an area where employees would like Internet and email access, but these don't have to function as reliably as your more critical systems.

## SWOT Analyses

The granddaddy of strategic planning tools is the SWOT analysis of four areas: strengths, weaknesses, opportunities, and threats. Usually, a particular initiative or investment is identified for analysis, and a chart is developed with four quadrants, one for each area. The key organizational leaders and strategic thinkers involved in the subject get together and submit items in each area.

For technology planning purposes, you can create or obtain a list of the areas that you currently invest in or may invest in, then perform a basic SWOT analysis on each one. Gathering the items to analyze can be done both by assessing your current systems and by using tools like the interactive Technology Plan builder at http://techatlas.org to identify areas that you might invest in. Sample items include a CRM/donor database, email, telephony, website, intranet, and smartphones or PDAs.

For each one, evaluate the strengths and opportunities in investing heavily in the resource, and the risks of not having the item or enough multiples of it. The end product of the exercise will be a road map indicating where you should be making technology investments and where you can get away with not making the type of investment that a for-profit business might.

For example, if you are a small, community-based workforce development agency, engaging local youth in training, mentoring, and job placement support, you might perform a SWOT on the value of buying smartphones for all counselors (see Table 4.2). Depending on how much work is done outside of the office, this might be a worthwhile investment or a waste of money. If the key use is client visits supporting distance learning, a pool of laptops with mobile access cards might be much more useful or effective. The exercise helps frame the value of the investment.

The SWOT analyses should result in a list of both critical and noncritical systems and functions, and some initial guidance into what you have to plan and budget heavily for and what you've got room to play with. It's

**Table 4.2. SWOT Analysis Example: Investing in Smartphones.**

| Strengths | Weaknesses |
|---|---|
| Keeps staff in regular voice or email communication, at work and in field | Cost of phones and plans |
| Supports regular access to calendar info and schedules | Difficulty in managing billing, work versus personal use |
| | Training required |
| Opportunities | Threats |
| Additional resources to support onsite distance learning visits | Loss, theft |
| Could replace traditional phones, costs for voicemail, and other services | |
| Handheld mapping (Google maps, GPS) useful for travel | |

the room-to-play items that require the imaginative approaches—this is where you can save time and money.

There are some broad strategies for reducing technology costs. Unfortunately, none of this is spelled out—a good idea for one application might be disaster for another. Here are some options to consider:

## Hosted Services

Having someone else run the hardware can save staff time and expense. For example, a current popular trend is to move to web-based HR and payroll systems. The two key questions to ask before making this move are the fundamental "Does this application meet my needs?" and "Are the hosting fees a savings over the in-house support costs?" The answer to the first question is beyond the scope of this chapter, but ample resources are out there for evaluating data products. Look to Idealware (http://www.idealware.org) and NTEN's report on evaluating data products (http://www.nten.org/research). For the second question, estimate the IT time and hardware purchase/maintenance costs for keeping the HR system in-house. Although there are other considerations here, the web-based options for HR do tend to be less expensive, and the applications are getting richer all the time.

## Open Source

Acknowledging that open source software—which is not sold, but freely shared—is not necessarily free, there are certainly cases in which it will prove more cost-effective than closed-source software. There are more and more simple open source applications that can plug some expensive holes. For instance, if your staff needs a more robust graphics manipulation application than the Microsoft Paint application that comes with the Windows operating system, but the cost and complexity of Adobe Photoshop is more than you want to invest in, there's lots of middle ground in the open source world.

For a company intranet, you might price out a web development tool or use Microsoft's SharePoint Services, which comes free with Windows Server. But consider that an open source content management system will be much easier to manage than a website created from scratch in a page-based application, and it will be easier to allow people without full network licenses access to an open source intranet than a SharePoint intranet, which requires a Windows Server license in order to log on.

### Homegrown

Even assuming you have someone on staff with the skills and willingness to design their own applications, it's still a very risky business. There is great value to having a commercial program with tech support or an established open source application with strong community support. Homegrown applications are supported only by the people who write them, and if those folks run away to join a different circus. . . . That said, in some cases it will make sense to go the homegrown route—for example, if you'll have to so extensively customize a commercial application to meet your needs that it will be just as unique as a homegrown solution, or if there is no commercial application that can do what you need.

Under these conditions—a demonstrated need and a programmer available who knows how to do it—you can take advantage of a custom application to support and streamline key processes in ways that no commercial applications can. And as needs change, the application can change with you. An example of how and where this might work is in the Goodwill case study later in this chapter.

## Look Before You Leap

One of the most important things that a nonprofit can do to insure that technology investments are realized is to formalize and invest in the software evaluation process. Buying software is not like buying toilet paper, particularly when it's a key database, web development project, or anything directly involved in mission delivery. And these choices are far too important to leave solely in or entirely out of the hands of the IT staff.

## Setting the Stage

If you were building a house, would you hire separate contractors to build the bedroom, bathrooms, living room, and kitchen? Then why is it so common to do so with a technology platform? Applications aren't isolated. They interact; they share data; they contribute to the same business processes. Or they should! But, far too often, software choices are left to individual departments: finance picks the accounting system, development picks the donor database, marketing chooses the web content management system, and HR picks the HR system. And when the need to integrate accrual-basis donations with cash-based finance comes up, or the website donors need to be integrated into the donor database, or the HR recruitment module has to work with the website, there's a complex technical challenge on the schedule that could have been eased or avoided by a careful, inclusive evaluation at the time the software was purchased.

Software evaluations have to be made by both the technologists and the end users, and those decisions have to be vetted from the top. Technologists are organization-wide service providers and therefore advocates for the different departments. They will know the impact that the donor database selection has on marketing and finance. They're also the owners and protectors of the technology platform. They'll know whether the database design and reporting capabilities of a web-based application are going to lock the organization out of future integrations. And they'll know whether the additional costs for servers and bandwidth are incremental or astronomical.

On the other end of the spectrum, the worst mistake that techies make is in thinking that they know what the organization's technical needs are. If IT is choosing the donor database for development, that's a cause for panic. Technical staff don't generally understand donor engagement and management strategies. They tend to focus more on the platform and data integration features of a database than the basic functionality, like how many clicks it takes to turn a donor into a major giving prospect. The dangers of having IT determine the application requirements for a department are just as dire as the dangers of leaving IT out.

Finally, senior management—EDs, CEOs, and COOs have to understand what's being installed and who and what purpose it serves, and to support and speak for the process. Agency-wide CRM will not be adopted if the CEO is an uninterested party.

## If You Build It, They Won't Come

It's this simple: if the users don't know what the application will do for them, it's not worth buying. Whatever the articulated and perceived need—whether it comes from the CEO, the board, the IT director or the data entry clerk—it's a waste of money to implement something that the intended users don't know that they want. To ensure that software investments are realized, the best practices are to have an articulated and adhered-to standard for computer literacy in your organization. Staff should understand what technology does for them, why they use it, and how they use it in their functions. They don't have to be geeks, but they do have to be competent. And software evaluation should be a heavily attended function. A request for proposals should be developed for any major purchase, and three to ten systems should be evaluated. Those evaluations should include onsite (or, as a second choice, web-based) demonstrations with broad attendance. The demos are not just opportunities to see what the software does and how it does it; they're also opportunities to educate the staff as to what the software might do for them. And the better staff envision their use of the application before the first dollar is spent, the better the chance that the dollars will be returned.

## The Goodwill Case Study

Goodwill Industries of San Francisco, San Mateo, and Marin counties (SF Goodwill) is an autonomous social enterprise dedicated to creating solutions to poverty through workforce creation and environmental stewardship. SF Goodwill is one of approximately two hundred separately incorporated Goodwills, all loosely affiliated. The work associated with this case study covered the years 2002 and 2003, and work was primarily funded by the operation of SF Goodwill thrift stores, many of which employ the clients that they serve. In 2002 the vendor providing SF Goodwill with the technology used for sales in the thrift stores informed them that there were no longer computers slow enough to run their application! It was critical that these systems be replaced.

An initial SWOT analysis identified some strengths and many threats, weaknesses, and opportunities. Strengths were represented mainly in a smart, capable staff who were all committed to the process and project. A major weakness was limited funding for a project of this magnitude. Opportunities were plentiful: improved processes to make things easier and more efficient; dramatic increases in the amount of strategic sales data; and an upgrade to scanners and other modern technology. The primary threat was the obsolescence of the current system.

From a balanced scorecard perspective, the project could support increased sales, serving financial needs; customer service would be improved by faster lines at the register; internal processes could be streamlined and simplified; and the clients—who worked in the stores and production facilities—would learn relevant skills using modern retail technology.

SF Goodwill needed a high-quality solution not just for the point of sale (POS) system, but also for managing the sorting, pricing, and sale of donated goods and reporting on the sales and results. Early evaluations suggested that just the POS hardware and software that would meet the organization's minimum needs would cost, at a minimum, $600,000 to deploy; more realistically $1 million. Given the fact that SF Goodwill's entire annual capital budget was $600,000, there had to be a way to bring the costs down. SF Goodwill had another asset that helped to offset the limited budget: technical staff that could, if warranted, develop customized reports.

As a first step, SF Goodwill needed to evaluate its business processes to ensure that any new system provided the means to streamline the work that needed to be done. When donated items arrived to be processed, the staff would note the value and price of each item on a paper form, which would be hand entered into an Excel spreadsheet at the end of each day. The keyboards of the point of sale system in the stores were riddled with color-coded keys, and training was complex. The staff, who were largely made up of the population that SF Goodwill was serving, were learning outdated skills, which meant that their workforce-creation mission was not being effectively accomplished. Each night, point of sale reports were printed and faxed to the main office. The next day, the finance staff would input the faxed reports and publish a fifty-page, 11- by 17-inch report in 8-point type. This report was highly inaccurate and difficult to read. Clearly, the systems in place were cumbersome and inefficient.

After establishing the needs of the organization, it was important for management to understand that this project went far beyond just replacing the point-of-sale computers—it was a project to deploy an entire retail management system. Staff members from retail, finance, security, and administration (including the CEO) were included in the RFP and demonstration process to review eight mid-ranged POS products in order to educate them about the scope of the project and receive their input on implementation. Ultimately, SF Goodwill went with a vendor that had installed the package at another Goodwill and was therefore pretty familiar with the model—and, as a nonprofit-focused vendor, offered excellent pricing. The software they had pitched was far from the most sophisticated package reviewed, and it had inadequate internal reporting and multistore capabilities. But these were limitations that SF Goodwill was in a position to supplement with a homegrown reporting and management system.

This was a risky choice, and not one that most organizations could— or would—make. The key risk was in trusting the IT staff to be able to write the reporting software.

Of course, even the best-laid plans hit snags. The proposed plan required that the intake process in place would have to be dramatically revamped. Some key staff, including the director of operations and two of the sales managers, didn't believe that these changes could be made. To resolve the situation, the VP of Retail took his whole team to Seattle to see the system in action. This did the trick: the whole team was sold on the same project and goals.

Once the new system was implemented, clients received better job training, hours of staff time were saved, and retail management and analysts could perform trend analyses that could be exported to an Excel spreadsheet. The new reporting capabilities included item-level detail that allowed SF Goodwill to become the first—and for those two years, the only—Goodwill that dynamically tailored shipments to each store based on analysis of their individual sales.

The entire project came in at $350,000 to $400,000, depending on cost allocation assumptions. Spread out over two fiscal years, SF Goodwill was able to stay well within budget. Over the following two years, two stores were closed and three donation sites were lost, occurrences that should have been serious impediments to revenue. But thanks to the improved sales from the individually tailored shipments and increased staff efficiency, revenue went up 10 percent each year.

From a planning and budgeting perspective, this project demonstrates how taking a creative approach can succeed, and how homegrown development may be far more effective than commercial alternatives. By blending a custom backend management and reporting system with an inexpensive commercial application, SF Goodwill saved hundreds of thousands of dollars. Working as a multidisciplinary team that understood that technology improvements were only one facet of the project was crucial to identifying a system that clearly met their needs and garnered spectacular results. Some of this success was enabled by the size of the organization and the resources on hand, but that's the IT planning challenge—understanding who you are, what you have, what you need, and how you can deploy the right technology to support it.

## Sample Technology Plan Worksheet

So what does a technology plan look like? Here's one sample structure that assumes that elements of the unified plan described earlier in this chapter are in place (see Exhibit 4.1). This should be a three- to five-year plan that serves three overall purposes: to discuss the role of technology development and support in the organization; to describe the current state of systems and outline broad priorities; and to itemize the key actions that will be taken over the life of the plan. It's generally a good idea to articulate that these are the plan purposes in the introductory section. It's also important to include a prominent disclaimer that anything presented in the plan is subject to change, given the rapid changes in the broader technological landscape.

## Exhibit 4.1. Sample Technology Plan Worksheet.

1. Title

2. Table of Contents

3. *IT department mission* (optional). Assuming you have an IT staff of two or more, the department might have its own mission. More to the point, the plan should incorporate the views and buy-in of the IT staff. Selling the organization will never happen if your staff members aren't bought-in to the plan.

4. *Section 1: The State of Technology*

   a. *Introduction.* This should be a narrative assessment of current technology, not an itemized list. Here is where you discuss the strengths and weaknesses of the current platform, with topics such as interoperability between databases (is your donor database integrated with your online system?), support for remote computing, and overall security. A plan takes you from one place to another, so we start by discussing where we are.

   b. *Current IT staffing roles and responsibilities.* Discuss how your staff is currently structured, and provide an honest assessment as to how suited the team is to supporting the current technology. If there is a technology committee, discuss their role and the planning process.

   c. *The role of technology in the organization.* We're past the days when anything technical could be delegated to IT to deal with. Computers are too widely used to make it that simple. A good technology plan will articulate what IT believes they are responsible for and what they expect other staff to handle. This will vary from organization to organization, but the goal here is for IT and the rest of the staff to share a consistent expectation of what IT can and should accomplish.

5. *Section 2: Methodology and Strategic Objectives*

   a. *Plan sources.* Identify the sources for technology planning: organizational strategic plan and related work; key documents; staff from whom you've sought input; and outside influences, like NTEN. Make clear that this document is based on research and staff and management input, as well as best practices from the outside community—not just a best guess.

   b. *Key strategies.* This is a series of bullet points discussing broad strategies, such as greening the technology or establishing a data integration platform. It should be less about applications and more about what organizational goals the application selection will support.

6. *Section 3: The Project Plan.* Section 3 is a timeline outlining the actual IT plans, such as upgrading to the latest version of Microsoft Office in September of this year or moving to a Voice over IP phone system in July of the next. Estimated budget information is a welcome addition to these items.

7. *GANTT chart.* Use Microsoft Project or another suitable tool to create a visual representation of the project plan.

8. *Attachments and addenda.* Include only documents relevant to topics discussed in the plan, such as IT staff org. charts and support policies.

## Conclusion: The Nonprofit Planning Framework

Strategically planning and budgeting for technology at a nonprofit organization is a juggling act, and all involved—particularly the juggler—must keep their eyes on the objects in the air. To plan effectively in a resource-strapped environment, where the goal is not to have the best systems but to have the systems that will best support the mission, you need to plan far ahead. Develop long-term strategies, tie them to short-term objectives, frame them as mission-focused objectives. Develop a unified plan—a balanced plan with shared vision and accountability.

Good planning requires that you understand who you are, what technology must do well for you, and where you can get away with it by doing things more creatively, or, perhaps, not quite as elegantly as a for-profit organization might. Don't let anyone tell you that your organization is just like a business, and don't let them tell you it *isn't* a business. Know who you are and how you're going to keep the dollars focused on the mission without sacrificing the power and potential of the platform.

Work with your peers, the ones who aren't techies. Value their input as much as—or more than—your own. Make software evaluation a recurring group activity. Refuse to install anything that won't be used. The most effective way to save money on technology is to not waste money on applications that don't get used. Techies don't operate like everyone else, and it's everyone else who uses the platform, so design it to meet the needs of the people who use the software—but on the platforms that the techs recommend.

Good planning requires you to be agile and flexibly staffed. Plan, but constantly review your plan, and take opportunities as they present themselves.

Technology planning is dynamic. Practicing it at a nonprofit is an art.

## Note

1. For in-depth explanations of the balanced scorecard approach, visit the Balanced Scorecard Institute at http://www.balancedscore card.org. For a quick explanation, Six Sigma has a good article at http://www.isixsigma.com/library/content/c011008a.asp.

# CHAPTER 5

# Finding and Keeping the Right People

*James L. Weinberg*
*Cassie Scarano*

These days, technology is no longer a luxury for the nonprofit sector. It is an essential component of serving your mission and getting your work done efficiently and effectively. Often, however, these efforts need to be led by highly skilled and well-compensated people—the kind of people who can be difficult to attract. Additionally, many of the same characteristics that go into developing a great IT professional can also make it hard for them to fit in with a mission-driven organization that has a highly collaborative environment. Most nonprofits operate under resource-constraints, so it can also be challenging to determine how and when to fill technology positions—and which candidates to choose. Lack of technical expertise and financial resources can make it difficult to fill IT roles with people who will fit, perform, and stay with the organization.

Regardless of the challenges, we know that having the right staff in the right place at the right time is crucial to success with technology. This chapter explores how to find and hire the right IT staff, and how to develop and retain that talent. Topics include specifics such as scoping IT positions, tapping into recruiting channels, setting and benchmarking salary levels, evaluating candidates, hiring based on core competencies, building career ladders, and supporting professional development. By the end of this chapter, we hope that you will be armed with all the information needed to confidently build and manage the IT staff in your organization.

## Deciding to Hire

When undertaking any new endeavor, creating a solid game plan is always the best place to start. There are four basic steps that you can take to help determine if, when, and to what extent you need to hire IT staffers:

1. Determine the overall technological needs of the organization, both immediately and over the next several years.

2. Map these needs across functional roles, identifying individual responsibilities and the means by which performance will be evaluated.

3. Develop competency-based models to help define roles and identify required skills and experiences.

4. Consider which roles can be delegated to existing staff and volunteers, which ones may be best suited for outsourcing firms and consultants, and finally which tasks will require the hiring of new employees.

This four-step approach holds true whether it is going to be your first designated hire in this department or you are growing an existing department through additional hires. In this section, we explore each of these steps in detail.

### Step One: Determining Your Organization's Technology Needs

The first step in deciding who to hire and in what roles requires conducting a technology needs assessment. Convene organizational managers and ask questions such as these:

- What hardware, software, communications, and technology-driven systems do we need to function across all of our programs and departments?

- What ongoing training and support systems are required to maximize the efficient use of these systems?

- What IT functions and infrastructure currently exist in our organization?

- What strategic changes are likely to occur over the next several months and years, and how will those changes impact our IT needs?

- What capacity gaps can be observed between our current resources and both our immediate needs and our projected future needs?

If you are concerned that you may not have sufficient IT-specific knowledge on staff to complete a thorough needs assessment, there are some resources to which you can turn. The TechSoup Learning Center has a great resource designed to help nonprofits conduct needs assessments, which can be found at http://www.techsoup.org/learningcenter/tech plan/page4902.cfm. Groups such as NTEN, CompuMentor, NPower, and your regional nonprofit association may also be able to provide resources and guidance. Many nonprofits are able to enlist the help of IT-savvy board members, or to have board members who are leaders at large corporations ask their IT teams to dedicate some pro bono time to assist you with planning.

## Step Two: Mapping Your Technology Needs to Specific Functional Roles

To take the next step of turning your organization's IT needs into a strategic staffing plan of one hire or many, start by grouping the myriad of responsibilities according to the ones you think might be handled by single individuals. Ask yourself questions such as these:

- In what areas do you need expertise in development versus maintenance versus user support and training?

- Which tasks are so intertwined that they really could only be performed by one person?

- During an average week, how many hours will be required by each task? Are part-time or full-time roles developing?

- In terms of variations in timing, are there peaks and valleys in the amount of time required for these tasks? This could be a predictable seasonality in organizational usage (say, slow summers) or large-scale efforts that are required up front to develop a project that ultimately will require more modest amounts of time to maintain.

- What can I expect from a single individual at any given time?

- What specific forms of expertise will I need in each of these areas?

## Step Three: Using a Competency-Based Approach

When beginning to scope out individual roles, it is useful to use a "core competency" model. Core competencies refer to two aspects of an individual's qualifications: (1) their skills, knowledge, and technical qualifications, as well as (2) their behavioral characteristics, personality attributes, and individual aptitudes. Whereas traditional hiring has focused primarily on evaluating a candidate's skills and technical qualifications, a competency-based approach adds an analysis of a candidate's personal traits. This is particularly useful for nonprofits, which generally value employee cultural fit above all other factors, as well as for hiring IT professionals, with whom cultural fit can be one of the hardest elements to find.

It is important to develop core competency models early in the process, as this approach will help frame your decisions around how to delegate responsibilities and who to hire into new roles, if any. Creating realistic models along these lines can be especially tricky with nonprofit IT positions, as it is for the sector with any highly analytical or technical role. This is because so many of the factors that lead people to pursue and excel at these professions can be opposites of the elements that make up the social fabric of most nonprofits.

For example, many people who are good with numbers and technology are not as strong with interpersonal relationships and communications. These people may make great web developers but fall short as "Help Desk" staff members, a role that requires a high level of end-user

## Types of IT Roles

*General information technology.* The most common category of IT staff, and generally included as part of the operations team, individuals in these roles are responsible for internal systems and network administration as well as user support. They oversee infrastructure decisions and maintenance in areas such as email, servers, security, and connectivity. In smaller organizations, one or two employees may play both administrator and support roles simultaneously.

*Web design and development.* Web designers manage the public face seen on your organization's website—colors, images, fonts, photos, and so on. Web developers, on the other hand, do the actual coding to create and maintain the website. This involves managing the site's architecture and infrastructure, including databases or other applications that run behind the scenes.

*Database management.* Today's nonprofits use many different databases to help manage a variety of functions, from operations and development to finance and human resources. As a result, organizations will often need to have at least one database-savvy person in each department, as well as someone helping to coordinate all of those applications. To the extent that these systems need to be customized, configured, or developed, highly skilled project managers may be required to ensure success.

*Project management and business analysis.* These staff members bridge the gap between end users and technology developers by scoping out new projects, analyzing departmental business needs, and considering how technical solutions can enhance efficiency and effectiveness across the organization. These roles are most commonly filled by strong managers who have technical knowledge and can lead planning processes but who may not be the ones executing those plans.

*Program delivery.* At the end of the technology staffing chain are the users who will employ your systems, software, and hardware to pursue the organization's mission, deliver services to constituents, and make the organization run. Because almost everyone in the organization is a user, this group forms the largest technology-related staffing unit. It is therefore essential to remember user perspectives and responsibilities throughout the planning process.

definition

interaction. If you determine that a functional role will require high levels of both technical skill and interpersonal capacity, recognize how rare that combination can be and consider dividing up a role, working harder to retain someone with both skills sets whom you already have on staff, or just prepare yourself for a potentially long and difficult search process.

To determine what competencies are required for a particular position, ask the people who know the position best what they see as the top three to five characteristics and traits that will make someone successful in the role. If your organization doesn't have the internal knowledge to identify required competencies, ask knowledgeable partner organizations, board members, or industry professionals for their advice. Once you have identified the required competencies for a particular role, ensure that those competencies inform every step of the hiring process, from scoping the role to writing the job posting, screening candidates, and making a hire.

## Step Four: Review Staffing Options

Once you know what you need, you have to determine where you are going to get it. Be patient in hiring new staff. Hiring can be a difficult, time-consuming, expensive, and potentially risky process, not to mention one that will result in a full-time salary and benefits package being added to your ongoing expenses indefinitely.

So begin by looking around your organization to consider whether there are already people on the team who can take on part or all of the responsibilities that you identified through your organizational needs assessment and role mapping processes.

Looking beyond current staff capacity, especially in the technology field, nonprofits have many alternatives to hiring full-time permanent IT staff. For project-based needs, individual consultants with strong nonprofit experience can be an excellent solution. These projects may include developing a strategic IT plan, selecting and installing a new server and network, or customizing a new database system. For longer, ongoing technical support needs, consider outsourcing your entire technology management system to a dedicated vendor. Finally, nonprofits are just starting to follow their private sector colleagues in looking oversees to outsource IT-specific functions. Especially if your work requires substantial amounts of data entry and manipulation, technology user support, digital and phone outreach, or other similar tasks, you may be able to look to professionals and firms in countries like India to support your IT needs.

In many and perhaps even most cases, organizations will find that there is nobody on staff to fill a specific role and that neither consultants nor outsourced vendors seem like a good fit or provide the levels of dedicated services that they seek. In this case, it is time to move forward with the hiring process.

## Writing Compelling and Useful Job Descriptions

Based on your needs assessment, job scoping, and analysis of required core competencies, it is now time to develop both *job descriptions* and *job postings*. It is important to distinguish between these two different but related documents. A job description is an internal HR tool that exhaustively describes a position's duties and responsibilities, as well as all specific organizational and legal considerations, such as the position's reporting structure, salary range, overtime exemption status, and so on. This document may be shared with a finalist or new hire at a later stage in the process.

A job posting, on the other hand, is an external marketing tool that will be used to attract candidates to apply for your position. You should never intentionally misrepresent your hiring opportunity, but the content in a job posting should be significantly more refined and may even have a different job title than its corresponding job description.

There are at least eight key elements to a good job posting. All of this content should ideally be included in a one-page document, two pages maximum. Anything longer than that is a job description, not a posting. Here are the elements:

1. *Job Title.* A good job title should be short, easily understood by a diverse audience, highly appealing to the right kinds of candidates,

and descriptive of the true nature of the role. For example, although the position may be internally titled as "Employee IT Support Technician," it may be more effective to publicize the job as "Help Desk Manager." Additionally, because many candidates will try to advance their careers by applying for jobs that are a stretch for their experience, you may wish to make the title senior-leaning if you have the flexibility to do so.

2. *Organizational overview.* At the beginning of the job posting, provide one simple, well-written paragraph introducing your organization. This should include an overview of your mission and programs, focusing on key achievements and metrics. Highlight any interesting elements of your growth plans, and really work to describe and sell your organization's work culture. Don't forget to include a link to your website for those who want further information.

3. *Position overview.* Include one paragraph describing the overall function of the position. Focus on communicating the core nature of the role and the strategic elements that will make it exciting. If the position reports to a senior leader in the organization, VP level or higher, you may wish to include that information as well. Remember, this paragraph is your one best chance to sell prospects on applying for the role.

4. *Responsibilities detail.* This section should include approximately five or six bullet points that use compelling language to describe major areas of responsibility and focus on all possible leadership opportunities. Especially with highly technical roles, try not to focus on the minutiae; but rather stay focused on the essential elements of the function. Similarly, try to communicate the business need behind the technical role in order to better connect the job with the mission-related needs of the organization. For example, "performing data entry using Salesforce.com" may not be very compelling, but you may get better results with something along the lines of "overseeing the donor management system, suggesting enhancements where appropriate, so that we can secure the resources needed to pursue our mission."

5. *Qualifications section.* In crafting your qualifications, you have to make a fundamental decision between: (a) using the job posting as a first screen to weed out unsuitable candidates; or (b) using it as a net to bring in as many candidates as possible, and then relying on the screening techniques described in a subsequent section to sort out qualified from unqualified candidates. The first scenario is more appropriate for organizations with limited staff capacity for search management. The second scenario will require more screening time, but it will also bring a greater volume and diversity of candidates, allowing you to see more "outside the box" contenders. In this model, your qualifications should be minimized as much as possible, replacing elements such as "MCSA certified, with ten years developing integrated SQL-based data management systems" with descriptors such as "several years of experience managing database systems." Using either strategy, make sure to include required personality traits drawn from your core competency model. When hiring for IT roles in the nonprofit sector, it is essential to convey the importance of elements such as being collaborative, functioning as part of a team, having strong interpersonal skills and communication abilities, and, above all else, demonstrating a passion for your mission and programming.

6. *Compensation declaration.* For most organizations, it is not recommended to list specific compensation information. Omitting that information will allow more flexibility in the negotiation process and keep your organization's general compensation levels confidential. Many people opt here for a statement such as "compensation commensurate with experience." However, if your organization has a robust and competitive benefits package, you may want to highlight that in order to attract great candidates.

7. *Application instructions.* In closing, provide clear direction to candidates about how to submit an application, included to whom it should be addressed, what should be included, and what file formats are acceptable. For IT hiring in the for-profit sector, cover letters are less commonly used because candidates are able to communicate all of their key technical skills and experiences in

their résumés. In the nonprofit sector, however, you should insist on a thoughtful cover letter to ensure that a candidate has a passion for the mission and will be a good fit with the organizational culture. Even with this request, don't be surprised if many applicants fail to include a cover letter. For viable candidates, you can follow up with a specific request.

8. *Equal opportunity statement.* In most organizations, it is good policy to close a job posting with a statement such as "XYZ Agency is an equal opportunity employer and encourages candidates from a diversity of backgrounds to apply for this role." Make sure that the organization has an equal opportunity employer policy to support this statement. If possible, talk to a lawyer about developing such a policy, but if those resources are not available to you, look for templates available online.

## Sample Job Posting

**Position:** Help Desk Manager

**Organization:** ABC Nonprofit

**Location:** Our Town, USA

**Organization Overview:** The mission of ABC is to help children and families to fulfill their potential and be the best that they can be. ABC provides mentoring and tutoring to children, as well as coaching and parenting classes. These programs have produced outstanding results, including a 62 percent increase in children's achievement rates, which won ABC the coveted award of "Best Nonprofit of the Year." ABC has ambitious growth plans to add new programs focused on family values and plans to replicate its programming in five new cities around the country over the next two years. ABC has an entrepreneurial culture and a collaborative work environment in which enthusiasm and initiative are valued. Please visit http://www.abc.org for more information.

**Position Overview:** The Help Desk Manager will play a vital role in ABC's technology department as we strive to ensure proper IT infrastruc-

*tip from the field*

ture and operation, help IT users to be most effective in their business tasks, and enable our students to achieve their full potential. ABC is in the midst of a major systems improvement effort that will build the foundation for substantial scaling of our program. The Help Desk Manager is responsible for ensuring the stable operation of in-house computer systems, network connections, and other organizational IT assets. The Help Desk Manager will identify the causes of problems in order to best direct corrective measures and reduce the likelihood of problem recurrence and will provide individualized, hands-on, and in-person support at the desktop level to ensure that end users are given appropriate assistance and training.

**Responsibilities**

- Coordinate and manage user services for staff members, including providing help desk and technical support to ensure courteous, timely, and effective resolution of issues

- Coordinate and perform hands-on fixes at the desktop level, including installing and upgrading software, installing hardware, implementing backups, and configuring systems and applications

- Monitor and test solutions to ensure that problems have been adequately resolved

- Access software updates, drivers, knowledge bases, and frequently asked questions to aid in problem resolution

- Perform root cause analysis on IT and user support issues and develop appropriate technical or training solutions

- Build and maintain user systems, ensuring compliance with established policies, standards, licensing agreements, and configuration guidelines

**Qualifications**

- Several years of professional experience in a deadline-driven, dynamic, technology-based environment, with a strong knowledge of trends in technology and applicable data privacy practices and laws

- Proven experience in coordinating and managing user services including help desk and technical support, with a very strong customer service orientation

tip from the field

- Detailed knowledge of Microsoft Windows and Office and familiarity with technologies such as Active Directory, Terminal Services, Remote Desktop, Windows Server 2003, SharePoint Portal Server 2003, and SQL Server 2005.

- Excellent written, oral, interpersonal, and presentational skills, with the ability to present ideas effectively in business-friendly and user-friendly language, combined with strong listening and questioning skills

- Demonstrated analytical and problem-solving abilities and keen attention to detail, as well as being highly self-motivated and directed, with experience working in a team-oriented, collaborative environment

**To Apply:** Please email a résumé and thoughtful cover letter, outlining how your skills and experience meet the qualifications of the position and stating how you heard about this opportunity (both in Microsoft Word format), to Joe Nonprofit at careers@abc.org, subject line "Help Desk Manager." Applications will be reviewed on a rolling basis.

**Please Note:** ABC is an equal opportunity employer and encourages candidates from all backgrounds to apply for this position.

## Determining Appropriate and Competitive Compensation

The majority of competition that nonprofits face in hiring IT staff comes from for-profit corporations. These companies generally offer significantly better salaries, professional development, and career ladder opportunities within larger departments. Moreover, with the rise of corporate social responsibility and eco-friendly business operations, many companies are finding that they can attract and retain even those socially conscious professionals who might have gone to the nonprofit sector just a few years ago.

Organizational leaders must recognize, however, that they are also competing with other nonprofits. Those few IT professionals of high quality with experience in the sector are in great demand and will be sought after, especially by larger nonprofits with dedicated recruiting functions and strong brand name appeal. Institutions of higher education and health care, for example, will connect with the majority of good candidates before the average-sized nonprofit can.

Finally, there is little recognition of the degree to which nonprofits are also competing with government agencies. The public sector generally offers better benefits, professional development, and job security than most nonprofits, and in many cases can also offer an opportunity for candidates to make a difference in the world by working for health, human services, or environmental agencies.

To compete in this marketplace, you need to define your competitive advantages and your *employer brand*. Separate from your organization's overall brand, your employer brand is what defines you publicly as a hiring and employing organization. To define these elements, ask yourself questions such as these:

- Why is it better to work here than in a higher-paying private company or public agency?

- What sets us apart from other similar nonprofit organizations?

- What kinds of incentives can we offer, including financial, nonfinancial, and intangible?

- What makes us a great place to work? What do people love about working here?

- What do people not like about working here, and how can we remedy or downplay those facts?

Remember that techies want to advance their skills, stay current with new technologies, work on interesting projects, and be appreciated for the unique and powerful knowledge that they possess. Do everything you can to provide such opportunities. Specifically, focus on benefits of working in your organization, such as the opportunity to work on a wide range of strategic projects, greater decision-making power, accelerated career paths, collaborative work environments, laid-back cultures, like-minded colleagues, and mission-driven work. To the extent that these are true, they will help sell your organization to prospective employees, as well as help retain your current staff members.

## Making Compensation Competitive

When it comes to IT professionals, the stiff competition means that you will have to pay proportionately for the level of talent and experience that you need (see Table 5.1). Many nonprofits have developed narrow salary bands for different levels of seniority that cut horizontally across their entire organization. But many organizations are coming to realize that it is almost impossible to apply the same salary models to certain departments, such as development and IT. To stay competitive without introducing an out-of-line base salary, many organizations are using compensation systems developed in the private sector, such as signing bonuses and performance-based bonuses.

More and more, nonprofits IT salaries have been driven up by demand across sectors. It is not unusual to find associate-level staff making $40,000 to $60,000, managers making $60,000 to $80,000, and senior directors making $80,000 to $100,000 plus. And at this level, it can often be true that "you get what you pay for." Hiring lower-wage technology professionals can represent a significant trade-off in quality and performance.

**Table 5.1. NTEN's "IT Salaries by
Title Chart from Budgets, Salaries,
Training, and Planning Report."**

| Position | Average Annual Salary ($) |
|---|---|
| Chief Technology Officer/Chief Information Officer | 71,500 |
| Online Communications Manager | 52,500 |
| IT Director/Technology Director | 52,500 |
| Project Manager/Technical Specialist | 51,000 |
| Systems or Network Administrator | 50,000 |
| Webmaster or Web Developer | 47,500 |
| Database Manager | 39,000 |
| PC Technician or IT Support Staff | 37,500 |

It is important to look at compensation holistically, not limiting the conversation to just salary. *Total compensation* refers to the full picture of how an organization demonstrates the value of its employees, including benefits and perks. Employers who think about what is important to their employees and make decisions accordingly will usually command a competitive advantage. Of course, this includes a great benefits package and selling the mission-connection of working in a nonprofit, but it can also mean much more.

For example, IT professionals may value a flexible schedule, which can allow them to work on systems in the evenings, during down time for other staff members. This after hours work can be offset by taking half days or full days off in exchange. Working from home may also be a valued perk for IT professionals, especially those with young families. Communication technologies have increasingly provided the opportunity to be fully wired from anywhere in the world. For those IT staff craving professional development opportunities, you may be able to connect them with more senior mentors in other organizations or invest in online training and development opportunities, most of which are operated at fairly low costs.

## Benchmarking to Ensure Competitiveness

When trying to determine levels of financial compensation for a particular role, do your homework, but make sure you are comparing apples to apples. Research benchmarks for similar positions at other organizations. Remember that salary is determined by many factors, including an individual's education level, years and nature of experience, skills, and job function. Organization-specific factors, such as mission, size, budget, and location, also play a role in determining appropriate benchmarks.

To figure out what is happening in the external environment, it is important to use published sources of aggregated data as well as to conduct primary research within your particular context. For example, talk with your colleagues to trade information. How are they structuring compensation packages for their IT staff? How do they gauge appropriate salary ranges? What would they like to be able to offer their best IT staff members, if resources weren't constrained?

*tip from the field*

## Salary Resources

To dig deeper into specific salary benchmarks, we recommend the following resources:

- *NTEN* (http://www.nten.org/research), the Nonprofit Technology Network, has produced two recent reports on nonprofit IT staffing: *Staffing Levels, Recruiting, Retention,* and *Outsourcing and Budgets, Salaries, Training, and Planning.*

- *GuideStar* (http://www.guidestar.org) is a free searchable database of over 1.5 million nonprofit organizations. It includes Form 990 tax return data that documents salary information for the highest paid positions at each filing organization. Guidestar also offers a nonprofit compensation report and salary search tool.

- *The NonProfit Times* (http://www.nptimes.com/Feb05/NPT_TopExec 2005.pdf) produces an annual survey as a special report for publication in *The NonProfit Times*. The report provides benchmarks primarily for senior-to-executive management positions.

- *Professionals for NonProfits* (http://www.nonprofitstaffing.com) produces an annual salary survey for both New York City and Washington, D.C., nonprofits, providing salary ranges in management, finance, fundraising, marketing, programs, and IT.

- *DICE* (http://www.dice.com) provides a variety of salary resources for IT professionals and those hiring them. Although this data is based almost exclusively on the for-profit sector, it provides interesting insight into the competition.

## Recruiting Talent Early and Often

Recruiting is essentially a marketing function that can and should be leveraged broadly. Done well, it not only will yield great candidates for all of your hiring needs, but also will increase your brand awareness and lead to new volunteers, community partners, board members, and donors.

## Year-Round Generalized Recruiting

Some of the most successful nonprofits, whether they have five or five hundred employees, conduct recruiting on a proactive, year-round basis. These groups continually build "talent pipelines" to targeted groups like graduate schools, professional associations, affinity groups, and cultural communities. They attend local career fairs when possible and have their employees maintain contact with robust peer groups through social networking tools like LinkedIn. They have an engaging point person dedicated to conducting year-round informational interviews, and they use a database or other contact management system that is specifically designated for tracking interactions with talented individuals. As a result, they fill the majority of positions with candidates already in their network or through word-of-mouth connections. These ongoing recruiting techniques are particularly important for recruiting IT professionals, as the competition is strong and organizations must be opportunistic about their hiring. In addition, many IT staff working in nonprofits are drawn to the sector because they have friends or colleagues who have made the shift, so make sure your current IT staff and friends are out there talking to their colleagues at every opportunity.

In these efforts, it is particularly important to communicate your employer brand, discussed earlier in this chapter. Engage any marketing expertise at your disposal in this process, whether it be in-house staff, support from a pro bono or paid agency, the marketing team at a board member's company, or just your development department. Whatever your resources or capacity, ensure that all job posting templates and recruiting-related collateral materials are reflective of your brand. For recruiting IT specific roles, it can be helpful to include a highly specific overview of your technological infrastructure and resources, as well as where you hope that your technical capacity will develop over the next few years as a way to attract top candidates.

## Job-Specific Recruiting

Start your outreach efforts by mapping your network, which is creating a list of all key contacts and possible connectors. Send an email, ideally from a senior executive, which is personalized and communicates excitement about bringing great new people on board to help pursue the organization's opportunities. Attach the job postings for any open positions and include a short overview of the role in the text of the email. Search the Internet for related listservs and blast your opportunities out wherever possible.

For technology positions in particular, it is important to use online social networking sites and Web 2.0 technology as much as possible. Don't be intimidated; explore a few of the sites that interest you and experiment with trying to find friends and colleagues through them. Popular professional networking sites include LinkedIn, Ecademy, and Ryze. A few social networking sites that serve individuals interested in the social sector include Rethos, Care2, and Change.org. Personal networking sites include Facebook, Friendster, and MySpace. If possible, have staff blog to their favorite sites. Ask the most technically savvy people in your office about any other opportunities with which they may be familiar.

In addition to networking through both email and online sites, don't forget about the tried-and-true strategy of posting your positions to online job boards. In this day and age, especially for IT positions, it no longer makes any sense to take out ads in printed newspapers and periodicals, as many of the largest news companies now have online job boards that are more affordable and connect with a larger audience. Although many sources are free of charge, most of the more effective sources do charge a fee that can vary from $50 to $500.

It is important to gather as much information as you can about potential posting sources and their audiences and fees to determine the best strategy. Some sources will be nonprofit-specific, like Idealist; some will be IT-specific, like DICE; and others will be geographically specific, like BostonWorks or the equivalent in your community. Also remember to contact universities to connect with both current students and alumni, two groups that are generally managed through separate offices and listservs. Remember that on many sites opportunities are listed chronologically by their posting date, so you may need to repost or refresh frequently to stay at the top of the list.

tip from the field

## IT-Specific Recruiting Resources

Here are some suggested IT-specific job boards and listservs:

- DICE.com
- TechSoup
- NTEN
- Nonprofit_Tech_Jobs@yahoogroups.com
- NPO-Techies
- Developers.net
- Information_systems_forum@yahoogroups.com
- Computerwork.com
- Justtechjobs.com

## Ensuring Strong Applicant Flow

Having followed the preceding suggestions, you should have a great flow of candidates throughout the hiring process. Sometimes, however, the applications may be slow to a trickle or may not represent the quality that you want. To jumpstart applicant flow, try some of the following techniques:

- Make sure that your posting has a clear title and is attracting the right level of candidate. If this isn't happening, consider changing the advertised level of the position from associate to manager or the other way around, depending on what you are seeing in the pool.

- Make sure that your posting is written in a compelling way and change the text as needed to really sell the role.

- Refresh your postings and invest in new sources that you might not have included in the first round of advertising.

- Tap back into your networks through another email blast or online social networking outreach.

- If all else fails, pull down all postings for a few weeks and then try again with a slightly different job posting.

If you feel that you do not have the capacity to conduct a robust recruiting effort internally, or if you have tried unsuccessfully for several months and want to bring in additional resources, you may consider working with a professional recruiter. Retained search firms are always an option, but for technology jobs there is also a fairly large network of contingent placement firms. Search online for local and national recruiters, but make sure that they have a strong track record of working with nonprofits. Many social sector organizations find that for-profit recruiters never really understand their culture or what they want in a hire.

## Interviewing Candidates

Once you have a pool of candidates, it is time to figure out which one has the greatest likelihood for success in the role. It is best to review candidates on a rolling basis as they come in. This is because the IT sector moves so quickly that if you wait three to four weeks to get back to a good candidate, they are likely to have already found another position.

As you are planning your screening and interview processes, remember to focus on core competencies, those elements that encompass both types of qualifications: skills, knowledge, and technical qualifications, as well as behavioral characteristics, personality attributes, and individual aptitudes. Also remember that to have a legally compliant hiring process, you must take into consideration only those criteria that are directly related to a person's ability to perform the job and succeed in that position. (See the accompanying box on legal issues.)

## Key Concept: Legal Issues

Federal legislation addressing discrimination includes the following:

- The Civil Rights Act of 1964 forbids employment discrimination based on a person's race, gender, national origin, ethnicity, or religion.
- The Age Discrimination in Employment Act prohibits workplace discrimination against persons aged forty years and older.
- The Pregnancy Discrimination Act of 1978 (amending the Civil Rights Act of 1964) forbids workplace discrimination on the basis of pregnancy or a related medical problem.

- The Americans with Disabilities Act of 1990 forbids discrimination against physically and mentally disabled people.

- The Immigration Reform and Control Act of 1986 forbids discrimination against individuals based on national origin and citizenship.

- The Equal Pay Act of 1963 protects men and women who perform substantially equal work in the same establishment from sex-based wage discrimination.

Visit the U.S. Equal Employment Opportunity Commission's website to learn more about preventing discriminatory hiring practices: http://www.eeoc.gov/abouteeo/overview_laws.html. To learn more about the laws governing your state, visit http://www.shrm.org/hrresources/stresources.

Also, in terms of what kinds of questions you are legally allowed to ask, the following examples may be helpful:

You may *not* ask questions such as these:

- Are you married? What does your husband/wife do for a living?

- How old are you? When did you graduate from high school/college?

- What race are you? What is your religion?

- Where are you or your parents from?

- Do you have any disabilities?

- Do you have a history of substance abuse?

If it is based on a *bona fide occupational qualification* (BFOQ), you *may* ask questions like these:

- This position requires working at a computer for substantial periods of time. Will you be able to meet that requirement?

- As you know, this job requires some overnight travel. Would that be a problem for you?

- This position requires work on Saturday and Sunday. Will you be able to meet that requirement?

- Are you eligible to work in the United States? If hired, will you be able to provide proof of that eligibility?

A typical screening process will potentially include the following steps for each candidate (of course, not all candidates will make it through all six steps):

1. Résumé screen

2. Phone screen

3. Initial in-person interview

4. One or more follow-up interviews

5. Reference and background checks

6. Offer negotiation and hiring

The entire process and each step should be planned in advance to ensure consistency and equity across candidates. In addition, each stage in the process should incorporate the legal requirements of the process, particularly in case a disgruntled candidate or employee tries to take action against you for your hiring decisions. Overall, you should focus on consistently working through a well-thought-out process, treating every candidate equally and carefully, and maintaining appropriate records in regard to information collected and decisions made.

## Résumé Screening

Before the first application for the job is considered, you should develop an evaluation rubric that can be used to quantitatively assess each candidate along equal terms. Start with the job description and the position's core competencies to develop a list of related criteria that can be assessed simply from a candidate's résumé and cover letter. When assessing IT candidates, a screening rubric can provide an essential checklist of required technical skills and experiences.

IT résumés can be hard to evaluate for those who are not knowledgeable about the field. Of course, you may not recognize many of the technical skills outlined in the résumé, but in addition, the way IT careers progress may be unusual to you. For example, contract positions often offer great benefits and flexibility for IT professionals, but seeing a series of apparently disconnected positions on a résumé may concern an employer who is not familiar with the industry. In Washington, D.C., many help desk professionals have a successful career moving from contract to contract within government agencies. Talk to IT professionals and those who have hired IT professionals to better understand the market in your area so that you are able to accurately evaluate an application.

## Phone Screening

A phone screen is a highly effective method for determining whether an in-person interview is warranted. It saves both the candidate and the interviewer the time and effort involved in jumping to an in-person interview immediately after the résumé screen. From the phone screen, the interviewer can gain insight into the candidate's energy level, interest, and competencies. In addition, because salary can be a barrier for many nonprofits hiring IT staff, initial salary discussions can happen during a phone interview to ensure that there is not a large disconnect between what the candidate is seeking and what the organization can offer.

For technology positions, the phone screen stage can be enormously important and informative. More so here than in other functional areas, candidates mass-apply for opportunities and may not take the time to fully explore the roles for which they are applying.

Finally, the phone screen is your first opportunity to interact directly with a candidate, and you will be able to tell a lot from the nature of the candidate's voice and reactions to your questions. That said, speaking over the phone removes many of the nonverbal forms of communication that are so essential to adequately getting to know a person. Although it is important to trust your instincts when evaluating a candidate, it is also important to not jump to conclusions. For example, IT professionals can often be weaker than many other professionals at verbal communication, because it is generally not required as part of their core job. If you are ambivalent about pursuing a candidate after a phone screen, you may want to suspend your judgment and bring them in for an in-person meeting.

## In-Person Interviewing

As you are planning your interview process, you should develop an interview structure that can be kept consistent across all candidates.

As much as possible, standardize the questions, environment, and interviewers involved so that you can really compare apples to apples when it comes down to a few finalists. Also, know what you want to see from great candidates before the first interview starts. Ideally, candidates should be selected for roles, rather than roles being created or crafted to fit around candidates.

In selecting your interview format, you have several options. A one-on-one meeting is more likely to put a candidate at ease and facilitate a conversational relationship, but it does not provide the objectivity gained by having two or more interviewers involved. In the latter case, make sure that each participant's role is distinct and mutually understood. For example, have one person focus on employment experience, another on skills requirements, and a third on personality fit with organizational culture. Good interview questions should meet most of the following criteria:

- *Relevant:* centered on the required core competencies without requiring any "unknowable" or organization-specific information

- *Behaviorally based:* asking candidates to describe past experiences in which they successfully demonstrated specific competencies

- *Open-ended:* allowing insight into a candidate's thought processes without "leading" the answers you want or giving a candidate an opportunity for a yes or no response

- *Probing:* avoiding "cliché" interview questions and working to stimulate a candidate's capacity for critical thinking

To delve deeply into the candidate's technical competencies, ask questions along the following lines for each of the essential skill areas for the role. (The following examples are based on assessing web design skills.)

- This role requires exceptional skills around web design. How do you think that your peers or former managers would describe your abilities along these lines?

- Tell me about a time in your professional experience when your web design skills were really put to the test. What was the nature of the challenge and how did you approach it?

- How did you learn to do web design? Was there any formal education or training involved?

- What aspects of your web design skills are you still hoping to learn and develop? How would you see pursuing those learning experiences?

- What web design–specific aspects of the role do you think will be most challenging or give you the greatest amount of concern?

Creating evaluation tools, such as checklists or scales, in advance can help you easily determine a candidate's fit with the technical requirements of the position. A checklist that lists information by topic, such as email servers or databases, and then delves further into each topic, such as depth of experience or number of users supported, will help even a nontechnical interviewer assess whether a candidate meets the requirements of a position. All of the information to collect on a checklist should be measured against the requirements in the original job description.

In evaluating candidate responses to questions around technical skills, consider whether or not the candidate truly understood the nature of the skill requirement and was able to provide an honest assessment of his or her strengths and weaknesses along these lines. Probe into examples of past experiences to determine whether a candidate has really done the work or is just claiming knowledge of how to do something.

## Assessment Tools

Some organizations find it useful to incorporate a "skills assessment" into their hiring process. Requesting a writing sample is a common type of skills assessment, but probably will not be applicable to most IT positions. For these positions, it might make sense to set up an exercise through which candidates can demonstrate their proficiency with particular software, provide user support in a real-life environment, or troubleshoot a network problem. If you are considering incorporating a skills assessment of some kind, make sure that you develop the particular exercise with the end result in mind: this is one more opportunity for the candidates to demonstrate their competency in a particular area. It should not be a "test" designed to trip up candidates, but should allow them to learn about the systems you use and exhibit proficiency.

# Interview Questions

**Sample Phone Screening Questions**

- Please provide a brief overview of your professional experience.

- What in particular draws you to this organization and to this role?

- Why do you think that you would be a good fit for this organization and role?

- This role requires XYZ skills; can you tell me about a time in your experience when you demonstrated those skills?

- Why are you leaving your current job, or why did you leave your last job?

- What was your most recent salary level, and what are you hoping for in terms of salary for this role?

- If an offer was extended for this role, how soon would you be available to start work?

**Sample Follow-Up In-Person Interview Questions**

- Please describe the experience you have in helping a growing organization develop and execute on an IT strategy.

- Please describe an example of a time when you identified a business need and then implemented an effective IT solution. What challenges did you have in managing this project? What were the measurable results?

- Tell me about a project in which you were responsible for collecting, organizing, and analyzing a large volume of data. What technology solutions have you used for this purpose?

- When presented with a technology question that you can't answer, how do you go about finding a solution? What resources do you use and how do you evaluate possible solutions?

- Describe the IT environment in your last position(s). For what aspects of IT did you have primary responsibility?

- What role have you played in ensuring that an organization's data systems allow for efficient access, use, and evaluation of critical data?

- What role have you played in presenting new software applications to users who have little skill or experience in a technical background?

- Describe the most challenging IT problem that you have had to tackle. What did you learn from that experience, and what would you do differently in the future?

*tip from the field*

Other organizations use personality assessment tools like the Myers-Briggs test to inform their hiring decisions. Again, it is important to understand what the assessment is designed to measure, how the analysis is completed, and what it means for your organization. With highly technical roles, although it is important to consider cultural fit, it is generally not as important to go deeply into a candidate's personality as it is to thoroughly assess their skills. Also remember that the candidates are judging your organization throughout the entire interview process. Make sure that you are not sending the wrong message by asking candidates to take numerous tests that are not necessarily applicable to their work.

## Managing and Developing Employees

You never get a second chance to make a first impression or to position new employees for success from the first time they enter your office. Effective employee "on-boarding" serves three interrelated purposes. First, it ensures that the new hire feels welcomed, comfortable, prepared, and supported. As has already been discussed, this can be a challenge for technology professionals working in highly social nonprofit cultures and so should be addressed early. Second, it leads to the new hire's ability to perform well and make a positive impact within the organization, both immediately and over time. Third, employee success leads to satisfaction and retention, which allows the organization to continue to meet its mission. Investing time and energy in employee on-boarding can be essential to integrating IT staff into the organization, given that their department is traditionally segregated from core programs and operations in most nonprofits.

### On-Boarding During the First Week

Start by developing an agenda for the first week on the job. As part of the agenda, schedule times for the new hire to meet with key staff members. Make sure that new employees meet with any people they will be managing, any people who will be managing them, and leaders from across the different departments in the organization. Create a comfortable workstation for the new hire. Stock it with the tools needed for the new person to hit the ground running, such as paper, pens, computer, phone, keys, and business cards. Make sure that voice-mail and email accounts are set up. For IT professionals in particular, make sure they have immediate access to any software or hardware systems with which they will be working.

## Performance Management and Evaluation

Organizations should have or develop a formal method for evaluating the performance of all staff members. Such systems help to enhance the relationship between individual and organizational performance, create an established basis for promotion and compensation, facilitate professional development, and increase overall employee satisfaction.

Together, the IT professional and the manager should work together to lay out quarterly objectives, metrics, and goals that clearly tie into the technology needs of the organization discovered during the needs assessment discussed earlier in this chapter. Regularly evaluating performance and providing feedback against shared goals will ensure that your IT staff members are focused on organizational outcomes. In addition, effectively setting quarterly goals will support your staff retention, as individual employees will face new and interesting challenges and will continue to learn and grow as professionals. Specifically, a good performance evaluation will include the following components (see Exhibit 5.1):

- Four to six key performance objectives that directly support the organization's overall IT goals

- Specific metrics that can be used to evaluate relative success along these lines

- Goals within each metric for what would constitute substandard, acceptable, and exceptional performance levels

- Outlines of strategies that will be used to meet or exceed the goals

- Forms of support that will be needed from the manager or others to meet or exceed goals

**Exhibit 5.1. Sample Performance Evaluation Form.**

**Position:** Director of IT  
**Period:** Q4, 2008  
**Date Goals Set:** September 3, 2008  
**Manager:** Catherine R.  
**Employee:** John T.

| Key Performance Objective | Metrics | Exceptional Performance | Acceptable Performance | Substandard Performance | Action Plan | Manager Support Required |
|---|---|---|---|---|---|---|
| Integrate three existing databases into one cross-functional system | Percentage of interim action steps completed on time | >90% of identified action steps are completed on time, per strategic plan | 70%–90% of action steps are completed on time | <70% of action steps are completed on time | Develop business needs map; build system; migrate data; manage training | Coordinate department heads to participate in planning and training |
| Ensure security of all data systems | Time to implement security system and security breaches | Security system is complete by Oct 15 and encounters 0 security breaches | Security system is complete by Oct 15 and encounters no more than 2 security breaches | Security system is not complete by Oct 15 or encounters more than 2 security breaches | Price several security options; work with selected vendor to complete system; monitor system for performance | Review options and assist with decision making |
| Ensure timely technical support for users | Response time to user requests for technical support | >80% of requests are responded to within 2 hours | 60%–80% of requests are responded to within 2 hours | <60% of requests are responded to within 2 hours | Develop and implement Tech Support Request Form; track response time and results | Review system and evaluate results |
| Engage in personal and/or professional development | Whether or not MCSE certification is pursued and received | Preparation for and completion of MCSE exam occurs in Q4 | MCSE preparation happens in Q4; exam is not taken | No preparation happens and certification is not received | Get study guide; register for exam date; schedule study preparation time | Approval to take ½ day each month to study |

It is also important to take an interest in the professional and personal development of your employees. At least one of the employee's key performance objectives should relate to professional development. Ask your IT staff about the skills and abilities that they would like to improve, then develop a plan for making sure that happens. Perhaps staffers want to learn about a new type of hardware or software, but it's just as likely they want to work on their management skills or interpersonal communication abilities. Find local groups or lone communities and resources such as NTEN, TechSoup.org, Aspirationtech.org, and DICE to help IT professionals stay connected to their field, and encourage them to bring new ideas back to your organization. Whatever the focus, helping your IT professionals continue along a lifelong learning path is one of the keys to retaining great people.

## Developing Career Ladders

One of the most important aspects of employee retention is creating career ladders so that employees can continue to grow within your organization. It is difficult to create career ladders for IT staff in nonprofits, so you may need to think creatively. For example, a career ladder may involve the development of additional responsibilities and more senior titles without involving a direct promotion from one role to another. Having the best understanding of their own work, the IT staff members themselves can be effective in helping to think through these possibilities. For example, a web coder may aspire to be an architect or a tech support person may want to become a network administrator. To help retain staff, make sure that all of your IT employees have a plan for the next one, three, and five years within your organization. Then work with them to provide the resources and opportunities to make those plans achievable.

If you cannot offer any forms of professional growth or career paths, be prepared for turnover of staff members once they are ready to grow and move on. It can be helpful for employee relations and general employer branding if you are willing and able to help these professionals move on to more senior roles at other organizations. Such outplacement work may involve helping them prepare their résumés, writing letters of recommendation, and introducing them to friends and colleagues.

## Creating Opportunities for Professional Development

To help your IT employees progress along their career paths within your organization, provide them with multiple opportunities for professional development. There are many high-quality programs available online and through local educational institutions for technical training and development. Some of these programs are more expensive than others, but many of the most powerful forms of professional development are actually free! If you invest in growing and cultivating your employees, you will produce highly satisfied high-performers who propel your organization forward and stay on as enthusiastic members of your team for years to come.

## Conclusion

Attracting, hiring, and retaining a high-quality IT staff is imperative for any employer today, but is especially critical to the success of nonprofit organizations, which rely on technology innovations to increase efficiency and leverage limited resources. Effectively staffing an IT function requires a comprehensive technology needs assessment, continuous and active recruiting, strong and consistent interviewing, and a commitment to ongoing professional development and support for IT staff. To compete for the best talent, nonprofits have to think creatively about their recruiting practices and compensation packages while maintaining effective interviewing, hiring, and staff development processes.

# CHAPTER 6

# Budgeting for and Funding Technology

*Scott McCallum*
*Keith R. Thode*

This is why you came to lead a mission-driven organization—the years of serving your time, investments in advanced degrees, the forgoing of commercial salary pay scales and expense accounts—all so you could be on the front lines, making great decisions that affect the social good of our society. Decisions like this one: "Uh, Camille, Daniel from Accounting called and wanted to know, do we book the invoice from Prendergast Technology Solutions under 'administration,' 'programs,' or 'fundraising'?"

It may seem trivial at the time, but securing resources, setting appropriate budgets, and ensuring that expenses are properly classified are all important parts of running an organization. This chapter examines adequate technology budgeting for different types of organizations and the classification of technological expenses, including what counts towards overhead versus program expenses. Strategies for pitching technology projects and engaging the corporate sector are also reviewed.

## Organizational Budgeting: Getting It Right

How much should you invest in the shelter program versus the rehabilitation program? Do you invest in a new bulk mail fundraising campaign or hire a development intern? Or should you just put that money in the bank, because next year's cash flow projections are tenuous, and you don't want to risk not being able to make payroll?

An important part of leadership is making sure that organizational resource investments have maximum impact on your mission today while balancing the need for appropriate resources in the future. Technology is a particularly difficult area for which to divine the best course of action and determine an investment level and mix providing high ROI—return on investment.

First, we examine some basic metrics and other guidelines around determining your overall technology budget; we then move on to some specific budgeting and investment strategies that can help your IT investments achieve their objectives.

## The Lay of the Land

A typical first step in determining an appropriate overall IT budget is to review some benchmark data and develop a strong understanding of what total IT spending looks like at organizations with similar structures and budget sizes. In 2008 the Nonprofit Technology Network (NTEN) published its first release of its comprehensive study analyzing IT investments for the sector, *Nonprofit IT Staffing: Staffing Levels, Recruiting, Retention, and Outsourcing.*[1] The report found that smaller organizations tended to invest a greater percentage of their budgets on hardware, whereas the larger organizations focused more on software and value-added services. The dollar value of IT investments at nonprofit organizations varies widely, and it does not scale as one might expect. Investments by smaller organizations were, of course, found to be smaller than IT investments made by their larger counterparts. What is surprising, however, is that this same investment disparity existed on a *per employee* basis as well—with larger organizations actually spending more per staff member on IT.

There was significant variance in the responses; on average, organizations reported spending between $1,250 and $1,517 per employee. Although this average may serve as one benchmark for your evaluation, be cautious; remember that a statistician could have her head in an oven and her feet in ice and still tell you, "On average, I feel fine."

## Your Analysis Parameters: The View from the Top

As a senior nonprofit executive, you hope that you will come out from the corner office with great confidence in your budget figures. But if you feel more like you had to consult your Magic 8-Ball, you are not alone. A few tips can help you avoid an "Outlook not so good" response and instead be able to deliver a reasonable financial plan with "Signs point to yes" for a successful budget submittal ahead of the next board meeting.

The following sections address how to facilitate detailed information-gathering from your staff. But first we're going to take a good look at the top-down portion of budget derivation. Nonprofit organizations by nature are very collaborative and consensus driven, and this factor often plays out in the budgeting process. However, effective leadership in this area requires a good grasp of the big picture as well as the general goals and limitations of the organization.

## Finding Your Place on the Technology Curve

One primary question is to determine where your organization ought to be on the technology curve. Although the whole concept of being on a technology curve at all may sound fraught with peril, the fact of the matter is you're on it, whether you mean to be or not. Jumping at the latest technologies or being on the "bleeding edge of the curve" can be as dangerous as the expression implies (the people trying to talk you into these projects will call it "early adoption"). But the reverse—languishing with the Luddites—carries its own set of threats to your mission and sustainability.

There are advantages and disadvantages to working on the "bleeding edge." You will likely experience a higher cost, in terms of both time and money, and run higher risks than more conservative organizations will. But you may benefit from greater and earlier returns as part of your just rewards for taking that risk. Many factors will influence your comfort level with risky technology projects, including the size of your organization. Smaller organizations probably cannot afford to take risks that would be acceptable to a larger organization. But dedicated funding from a technology provider may help level the playing field and make innovative projects more palatable for organizations of any size.

Although your organization has an overall positioning on the technology curve, you may have a desire to sit on different points of the curve with respect to different types of technologies and areas of your operation. For example, you may invest in world-class solutions for your program delivery (say, remote scanners for a humanitarian aid organization), but adopt technologies further back from the edge for administrative staff who probably don't need the latest PC with the fastest processor and beta versions of the latest operating system.

You can gain significant advantage for your organization just by realizing (1) there is such a thing as a technology curve; (2) there are different places you may want to be on the curve, based on the technology and the area of your organization the technology is supporting; and (3) you ought to have a good level of comfort about where your organization generally should be with respect to the curve.

## Creating the Standards of Measurement

Benchmarking is another critical (and comforting) component of developing a technology budget. Although this in itself can be an arduous task, there are some methods to help you quickly gather information to impart to your support team. Benchmarking provides some guidance and reassurance on where you will end up from a general technology investment perspective.

The first method of benchmarking is one of the most valuable: "getting by with a little help from your friends." Nonprofit leaders familiar with grant-requesting processes and donor transparency obligations should already be comfortable with explaining their financials to a diverse set of audiences. Meeting with executives from other nonprofits to share perspectives, data, and the like can provide a greater comfort level as you approach the task at hand. As you communicate with your peers, ask questions and make observations about them that you have been making about yourself—where they are on the technology learning curve, how their investments align with their mission objectives, and so on. This will help you process the financial data and other information they share. People in your professional network can help you identify other good partners for dialogue. If your network in this arena is a little thin, you should look into the local Center for Nonprofit Management, if there is one in your area. For example, the Center for Nonprofit Management in Dallas, Texas, serves as a leader in the community, providing resources, conferences, and networking opportunities among a community of nonprofits with a demonstrated commitment to operational excellence.

These informal approaches to benchmarking provide many additional benefits—anecdotal information on technology projects and vendors can be shared, commonly planned investments can be identified, and the pursuit of joint projects with shared costs can be explored. Nonprofits should take advantage of the fact that similar organizations can save time and money by sharing information and working together. Technology is one of those "intellectual property" areas for which this partnering benefit can be most significant.

Leveraging relational opportunities to gain information and confidence can be extremely effective, but of course it also requires a lot of face-to-face interaction. For those on the technology side, having to relate to other people has its own set of stresses—so for the comfort of the introverted, we'll return to discussing methods of benchmarking and information sharing that require less human interaction.

## Putting Research to Work

Earlier in the chapter we mentioned an NTEN study that can prove helpful. Part of the value of such resources is that the research and publication effort is led by people rooted in the nonprofit world and therefore tends to focus on concrete information relevant for people working at nonprofits. Although pure research for its own sake has value, the NTEN research really delivers for people who want practical information on the topics that affect the nonprofit sector every day.

Another tool for small to medium-size nonprofits comes from the nonprofit organization NPower. Through their work with many nonprofits, NPower has developed a plan for budgeting for technology. The plan encourages a three- to four-year planning horizon, which helps provide a true road map for technology investment. The resulting technology plan addresses required funding levels as well as the timelines and sequences of projects and operational investments. The plan also examines multiyear impacts and their funding implications, which provides staff with the information and perspective needed to create a solid road map. The inclusion of staff from all levels gives people the chance to gain important planning and budgeting experience. At the same time this multiyear, mission-aligned thinking allows everyone to better understand the big picture.

## Knowing What You Control

It's also comforting to know that for good or bad, much of the technology budget in any given year is significantly out of your control. To make an impact on the portion of IT budgeting that you do have some control over, you need to have initiated the right types of planning and analysis well before budget season, and, as mentioned earlier, you must make wise decisions based on a multiyear view. This process should lead to a solid technology plan with estimated schedules and investment levels that will come into play in the later stages of the budgeting process.

At this point it is good to first develop a good grasp of which expenses are in your control, which are only relatively in your control, and what part of the budget is truly up for evaluation. By "eating the elephant one bite at a time" you will find the task to be much less daunting. Although those in the public finance world tend to divide expenses into mandatory and discretionary, there is value in a more egocentric "What can I control?" approach. No matter how you decide to organize the effort, applying principles with this perspective will ease you into a manageable understanding of your expenses.

## Expenses Beyond Your Control

Most budgets have a significant number of fixed commitments already in place. For example, multiyear contracts and subscription agreements with difficult and expensive exit clauses will consume a portion of your budget. You should identify items of note for strategic planning purposes to evaluate opportunities for longer-term flexibility and improved ROI; then take these expenses and subtract them from your budget management total, and from your worry!

## Expenses Only Partly in Your Control

There are some expenses that would entail serious organizational implications if they, and their corresponding activities, were eliminated. These may include projects already under way (particularly those for which outside support was received), personnel, and regular hardware and software maintenance and upgrading. If there are one or two bold moves you want to take or some minor percentage adjustments you are interested in evaluating, identify those and the relative potential financial implications. For the remainder (likely the vast majority) of these expenses, put them with the "out of my control" ones and again, remove them from your worry! Now take a moment to pause and evaluate your handiwork. You will see that you have eliminated the vast majority of your near-term budget from being a concern. Congratulations!

## Expenses Possibly in Your Control

Up to this point the budgeting process has been very top-down. For the expenses that *are* possibly in your control, we turn to the bottom-up collaborative budgeting process that is so loved in the nonprofit world.

*Bottom-Up Budgeting.* With the top-down view firmly in hand, it's time to face the biggest challenge—people. More specifically, your staff. You may be reluctant to solicit your staff's IT budget wish list, anticipating requests that border on the extracurricular or recreational, but there are methods you can employ to reduce that likelihood.

Now is the time to reap the rewards of all that preplanning. Your team's solid technology plan will help the remaining budgeting work fall into place with relative ease. With a strong top-down view of the existing budget, and a planning-driven (bottom-up) idea of what the team would like to undertake, the group should be in a strong position to hash out the final details.

From a top-down perspective, you have a general frame of reference for the overall IT budget and know what portion of that budget is up for discussion. At this point you are ready to bring your top-down information together with your team's bottom-up plan and see if you can find the place on the technology plan where costs line up with the available funds.

When communicating the top-down budget information, it is important to provide some context. You may want to explain how this budget lines up with the benchmarking you have done and the implications of other organizational initiatives and realities on the budget. Another key piece of data is how firm the initial budget number is, so the team has an idea of their ability to influence it through their efforts. Generally, top-down guidance in the nonprofit world is as well-received as a piece of anti-pork-barrel legislation in Congress. That being said, if you keep reinforcing the fact that the whole organization needs to share its limited resources and maintain a genuine communication style, you will undoubtedly have the team enthused about tackling the budgeting task at hand with the resources available.

One of the first tasks is to tighten up the financial estimates of the items and projects provided during the planning process that made it into the budget. This is an opportune time to identify any "low-hanging fruit" donations or deep discount opportunities that may shift the equation. It is important for the team to review the technology plan and be sure to identify the true total cost of ownership for the expenses (which include expenses for the following year[s]) that the organization is signing up for when they take on this project. The team needs to be particularly aware of these implications of in-kind donations. Although companies can be willing providers of short-term commitments of assets and time, it is often difficult for them to make long-term commitments. If there are long-term costs associated with an in-kind donation, your organization needs to be ready to absorb them. Remember to be cognizant of the "expenses out of your control" and "expenses only relatively in your control" that this year's expenditure is creating.

## For Those Who Didn't Plan

At this point, many of you are thinking, "Thanks for the information, but if I already had a technology plan, do you think I'd be spending my free time reading about IT budgeting?" For those of you caught in the eleventh hour who need to have a working budget to go forward, rest assured, there is hope!

First of all, as noted in the top-down section, much of current-year and next-year budget is fairly well determined for you. We'll then take a logical step to planning out your key activities to quickly attain a working IT budget.

## Budgeting Without a Plan: A Quick and Dirty Approach

- Locate and review the technology items from the last twelve months' profit and loss statement (P&L).

- Perform a physical walkthrough of your facility and a mental walkthrough of all major functions—noting existing technology and potential information or other IT needs.

- Review the organization's calendar, noting the technology requirements associated with the organization's key events and activities.

- Review the list of technology needs and expenses based on estimates and information in your P&L. Be sure to understand the long-term cost obligations.

- Work with your team to reduce spending to fit within the available budget. Look for and eliminate any duplicate budgeting of the same expense. Focus on fully implementing the highest-ROI projects rather than underfunding as many initiatives as possible.

## Break Out the Detailed P&L

Before you get started budgeting, you should grab the detailed profit and loss report for the prior and current years. This will let you know what items have cost in the past and the general technology expenditures that occurred over the course of the year. Although it may be dull reading, a perusal through the list will prepare you well for the adventures ahead.

## Survey the Scene

The next step is to try to identify the general operational expenditures that need to be in your IT budget. If practical for your mission, actually walk around your main facility and make notes:

> I see PCs on some desks . . . phones . . . the field folks have laptops . . . what's up on Brad's laptop? It looks like he has our client assessment system up . . . he was complaining about how that it doesn't capture some of the data needed for the grant reporting . . . Here's a printout of our recent online donors, though . . . Let's see what's over here . . . oh yeah, Michael the IT guy, I forget about him all the time . . . he's got a bunch of wires and stuff in the computer closet . . . maybe I better just come back and ask him . . . or maybe I'll just send him an email.

After the physical walk-through, take a mental walk-through of all the audiences your organization touches—donors, suppliers, internal people, partners, regulatory authorities, the board, the end people served, and so on—and think about how their interactions depend on technology.

From this exercise you should have an initial list of line items that need to be maintained, replenished, and updated on an operational basis. Although this "budgeting by wandering around" may give you too much information in some areas, Michael will be glad to know he wasn't overlooked at budget time.

## Mark Your Calendars

Now that you have a baseline view of the basic areas requiring expenditures on an ongoing basis, take a couple of trips through the calendar to help you identify other areas where IT support will be required. Walk through your organization's calendar from the perspective of each of

## What to Look for When Surveying Your Organization

- Observe the physical technology devices (hardware) you see around the organization. For each one, find out about any support/services or related data access charges and the like. Note any potential for the item to need replacement this year.

- Ask employees and observe what software applications they use to perform their jobs, perform research, report on their activities, and so on. Understand any maintenance costs, subscription fees, and so on, and also—if they know—where those items currently fall in the budget. Also note any free services they use, and any potential need or benefit to upgrading to a fee-based version.

- Note any custom spreadsheets or other data-capturing and -organizing tools employees have developed to manage and store their information. Note similarities among employees and departments capturing similar data in disparate ways.

- Discuss big-picture information—technology performance or other challenges people have within the organization.

your major areas (programs, development, marketing, board, finance, and so on), identifying key activities, events, milestones, and the like, then determine any unique IT support requirements there. After this you can walk through the calendar from a solely IT perspective. This order is important because it helps reinforce the fact that in the end IT is a support function and should serve to enable the other functions' ability to achieve their potential to do good. Of course, as you review your IT calendar, the first item on your list of IT-initiated projects should be the development of a Technology Plan and follow-up monitoring process.

### Pull It All Together

At this point, take your list of desires and goals and line up projected costs with each item. Your trusty P&L will be a good source of potential cost data. Exhibit 6.1 shows an example of how you can format a simple technology budget.

## Exhibit 6.1. Sample Technology Budget Format.

| Category | Total Amount | New | Existing | Comments |
|---|---|---|---|---|
| *Personnel and Related* | | | | |
| Salaries and Other Payroll | | | | |
| Benefits / Overhead | | | | |
| Training and Development | | | | |
| Other | | | | |
| *Contract Labor* | | | | |
| Consulting | | | | |
| Service Contracts and Tech Support | | | | |
| Other | | | | |
| *Software* | | | | |
| Licenses and Maintenance | | | | |
| Subscriptions | | | | |
| Custom Application | | | | |
| Other | | | | |
| *Hardware* | | | | |
| Personal Computers and Related Servers | | | | |
| Networking Equipment | | | | |
| Mobile / Field Devices | | | | |
| Peripherals | | | | |
| Other | | | | |
| *Data and Telecommunications* | | | | |
| Internet and Data Access | | | | |
| Hosting, Data Center, and Backup | | | | |
| Cellular / PDA Access and Usage | | | | |
| Other | | | | |
| *Miscellaneous Supply* | | | | |
| Paper, toner, and other consumables | | | | |
| Data tapes, local storage, cables, and so on | | | | |
| Other | | | | |
| **Total** | | | | |

| In-Kind Donations | Value | Long-Term Costs | | Comments |
|---|---|---|---|---|
| Software | | | | *Note the value of the in-kind dona-tion, but do not include in your budget total. Also record long-term costs associated with any in-kind donations.* |
| Services | | | | |
| Hardware | | | | |
| Other | | | | |

By employing these guidelines, you will have created a complete and realistic financial image of your technology goals. Now prepare for that image to be, at the very least, refined into a smaller but clearer picture of the budget you can actually implement.

## Whittle It Down

Of course, as with most aspects of your organization, as you go through the budgeting process your resource budget for technology is likely to fall short of the anticipated costs of your desired tech plans. As with budgeting in the areas you are more familiar with, you may need to begin the process of whittling down your budget to match up with your available funds. Before breaking out your pocketknife, a few guidelines may help you more surgically trim and shape the budget to the appropriate size.

The easiest reductions are ones that don't take place at all, of course. One potential source of funding may be right in your organization's overall budget. It's common for IT costs to be double budgeted by small to medium organizations, especially those without an established history and processes for budget creation. Because IT is a support function, technology-related expenses often find their way into the budgets of the teams that IT is there to support. Be sure that you have uprooted any duplications.

To develop perspective for trimming costs, go back to your original vantage point about overall goals, objectives, and where each part of the organization should be on the technology curve. Identify points of convergence, where a project may help in more than one area of your organization, and talk to each team about the relative importance and ROI associated with every technology investment. If you have to cut back on a project for budgetary reasons, then be sure to trim the scope, timing, and outcomes as well. There may be some projects that can be broken out into phases, which can reduce risk, ensure quality, and spread spending over a longer period of time.

In the nonprofit environment, there may be a strong pull to choose to underfund many different projects, rather than appropriately resource the most important ones. As an executive, part of your role is to help the team make difficult investment decisions, and to not use the funding of lower priority projects as a team satisfaction tool. Keeping the big picture in mind will likely separate some of the higher-priority investments from the lower-return ones, reducing the pain of choosing to postpone or eliminate valuable items. From that point, before giving up the ghost on some technology projects, identify those projects for which there may be potential for receiving additional outside support based on the investment's merits. This provides a platform for additional resources to fuel your team's efforts. Later in the chapter we will review how to pursue corporate funding for these technology programs.

tips from the field

When putting together your final budget, don't forget the following:

- When budgeting staff costs, include the full, loaded costs of the people—employer-side taxes, benefits, training, and the like—along with their salaries.

- Budget some contingency funds, especially when you are including new projects, to reduce risk and heartburn later in the fiscal year.

- Document your assumptions, so as the year progresses, and the world doesn't run the way you planned it to, you'll understand the assumptions on which your work was undertaken, and you'll be able to explain them to others.

- Document and budget any ancillary costs for supporting in-kind technology donations.

- Plan on the front end which programs, areas, and other categories each expense will be charged to, making it easier to execute the financial processes and ensure clarity on which group's "bucket" will be absorbing which costs.

## Financial Classification of Technology Investments

Now that your budget has been approved and the vendors are eagerly gathering, it's time to ensure that these expenses don't improperly tip your metrics to a point of apparent inefficiency.

As noted in Chapter Four, nonprofits are often measured under the yardstick of efficiency, as defined by the percentage of money spent on programs versus on support and fundraising functions. Higher overhead and fundraising costs can have a negative impact on public perception. At the same time, cost savings that can be realized by strategic technology implementations require investment in hardware, software, and consulting. Accurately reflecting the timing of the value as well as the true nature of the expense helps organizations appropriately communicate with the public regarding their investments. This section outlines some methods to ensure that your investments are reflected in the appropriate light rather than being categorized as a short-term overhead expense.

## Differentiating Capital Expenditures

Often as organizations make significant technology or other purchases, they merely note and report that expense in the same way they do salaries, paper clips, and refreshments for the annual volunteer appreciation day. Differentiating capital purchases from true expenses can help nonprofits achieve an appropriate treatment of their expenditures.

Capital expenditures are investments in assets that have a multiyear lifespan. The expense incurred in a given year is offset by the value of the asset, both of which are reported on a balance sheet. The asset value is reduced (depreciated) over the lifespan of the asset. Fundamentally, because the organization made a purchase so they can receive value from it over several years, the cost associated should be spread over the time period in which the value is received. This allows for strategic investments that won't be mistaken for wanton spending by a potential donor or others in the public. Purchasing a new building, buying a new file server, or paying a large sum to make a donated piece of property usable are all examples of capital expenditures.

## Definition

A capital expenditure is an investment in an asset that has a multiyear life span.

How do we distinguish capital expenditures from ordinary expenses? In general, purchases made to support day-to-day operations are considered expenses. Recurring costs—such as salaries, Internet usage fees, and rent—are expenses. Staff training and other investments in ongoing resources are also treated as operating expenses. An item can be identified as a capital expenditure if it meets the definition of a one-time purchase: a cost associated with making a long-term asset usable, or an initial purchase related to a new initiative. For technology implementations, new software (not license renewals or upgrades), hardware, and consulting services that are directly related to the new project all can be capitalized. There is a minimum cost that a capital expense must meet or exceed, and there are some variances in how that minimum is determined, but to put it simply, a $29 software purchase is unlikely to qualify, but a $1,000 computer probably will. Your head of finance will know how your organization makes these determinations.

## Place Only Appropriate Items in Overhead

The second type of classification to be cognizant of is that you should not arbitrarily dump all technology costs into the administration (overhead) bucket. It is widely accepted that IT assets are just as critical to program personnel to achieve their goals as many of the other tools of their trade. Often an IT investment may have common benefit among several programs or other categories, and of course costs should be appropriately shared across the functions benefiting from them. Choosing this more appropriate classification of certain technology programs (or other categories), rather than defaulting them to overhead without consideration, will provide a more accurate and improved set of metrics, supporting your organization's reputation for delivering on its mission.

## Strategies for Funding Technology

Technology requests can outstrip your IT budget alarmingly quickly, and can make you feel like it is time to hunker down, hoard resources, and take on a scarcity mentality. But there's no need to defer strategic

IT projects until a major windfall arrives; you can make the decision to push ahead and go get the money you need now!

Proposals for technology projects can be some of the most compelling that an organization will create. Like any proposal, these involve putting the right request in front of the right people.

## Understanding Your Audience

Many nonprofits shy away from making funding for a technology project a top priority, no matter how compelling the investment is. They believe that if they even ask for funds for such endeavors, these projects will be viewed as overhead and their organization will appear too internally focused. It's true that some donors may not appreciate technology investments. Happily, other donors will realize the role technology has played in raising the business world's level of efficiency and understand that the same should be true for the nonprofit sector. Many of them are actually lamenting the fact that their philanthropic causes won't or can't invest in obtaining the same level of performance through technology.

Gaining the buy-in of potential technology funders starts with understanding these audiences and their unique perspective. Building relationships with the program officers and other staff at foundations and other funding sources will help you understand their perspective so that you can align your proposal with their values. If you delve into the backgrounds of the board members of foundations, you will often find a member or two with strong connections to corporate operations, business consultancies, or direct technology business experience. Drawing the parallels between corporate initiatives or aspects of board members' professional careers and the projects you are seeking to fund will increase advocacy for the project and may even bring you other sources of support for the project.

Again, technology proposals aren't for everyone—so as you identify those people of vision, be sure to understand what is appealing to their "inner geeks" and be sure to incorporate those perspectives in your proposal.

## Creating Compelling Technology Proposals

One of the most common mistakes made in technology proposals is focusing too heavily on features and functions rather than impact and results. Compelling technology proposals will start with the basic improvement or expansion of the good work that the investment will enable and then expand to the abilities unlocked by technology and the improved activities that technology will support. Of course, employing numbers related to impact, where possible, will often further your case in a tangible way. Quantifying anticipated results in terms of direct impact will provide clarity for both the technology minded and those still impressed with their fax machine.

## Teaming Up

As you strive to improve your organization's capacity through technology, there is a great chance that your project could have value for organizations other than your own. In fact, if that's not the case, it begs a few other questions. Part of what can make a proposal unique and even more powerful is to expand the ROI by expanding the deployment of the project across multiple agencies. Working together to develop improved capacities in a common area also demonstrates a practical commitment to partnership that will be heralded by funders and the community at large. Also, consider other types of new partnership efforts—starting with your technology service providers on the project. This is a particularly good strategy if you are leveraging one of those technology products or service organizations out there that is also a nonprofit organization. These groups have expertise in raising technology funds, as their mission is to unlock your technology potential.

## Using Your Technology Road Map

Be prepared to discuss the technical aspects of the program for the techies in the audience—or, if your presentation is in written form, provide a brief amount of technical information as an appendix or in a shadow box. Even in these sections, you can help the audience stay focused by opening and concluding with how this technology furthers the mission of your organization and is in alignment with or provides flexibility for your organization's long-term plans. For less technical people, focusing on results rather than tools can help them follow each component of the proposal. Included in this information, and high-lighted at the summary level, should be the value of your in-kind do-nations (if you indeed have technology donations associated with the proposal). A persuasive aspect of technology projects is that your team will frequently be able to acquire at least some of the project costs on a donated basis. With the high cost of these components, highlighting the in-kind investment can help make your case for the remaining funding even more compelling.

In a live presentation of your case, if you are not a technical executive, confidently delivering two or three sentences about the technical com-ponents of the project can carry a lot of weight with an audience. Then having a charming, perhaps humorous, deferral at the ready when the next level of inquiries comes in should satisfactorily settle the matter.

## Funding Technology Is a Team-Building Exercise

The fact that the project has a strong technical component is actually an opportunity in your organization to bond your team in new ways. In particular, these projects can help connect your development folks to the front lines of battle for the organization. Often as organizations mature, the development department does a great job of grasping the mission and service delivery values and then articulating these to fund-ing audiences. This excellence reduces the need to often put the other teams in front of potential funders. Technology-based projects are a chance to shake up the culture of isolating your support team members from the role of having to go out and passionately communicate about the value of your work. These types of projects can enable your IT folks to add some new value to the overall team efforts. It will also help the IT staff appreciate the work of their teammates on the rainmaking side of the house. Finally, having the IT folks engaged in the funding process will help the development team prospect for new sources of support, as we cover in the next section.

Now that you have developed a simple, creative pitch, focused on how the project furthers your mission, and memorized some of your techie buzzwords, and the staff is at the ready, it's time to get out there and bring in the funds to pay for that new technology.

## Prospecting: Locating Technology Initiative Funders

It's really no wonder development professionals change jobs on a fairly frequent basis. They learn an organization and become part of it and its amazing work. They are given the privilege of sharing the organization's great vision with prominent people in the community. But after years of delivering similar messages to the same people, they just get bored, which is pretty much the kiss of death for anyone out there working as the face of an organization.

Fortunately, new technology programs can inject some energy into your development staff, helping them engage with their current funding network in new ways as well as engage with new funding communities about the mission of your organization. Technology thus becomes a tool for increased efficiency at the same time that it serves as a human relations motivator.

Engaging in a new technology program shows off a new side or reinforces an image of your organization that you work hard to ensure is relevant and ever more effective in a rapidly changing world. Organizations that take on these ventures in a quality way are demonstrating a commitment to growth and an evergreen approach to achieving their mission. Your long-time supporters will be galvanized by your efforts, and ideally some will want to be directly involved with the project.

This support from your current circle certainly is important, but these technology projects provide a real opportunity for your group to venture out on safari into new and uncharted lands to try and capture the elusive "new money." It may help to start out in the "charted but previously barren" lands. From there you can move on to those few groups that actually post for funding technology initiatives. Organizations that post a funding for "capacity building" grants should also be pursued, because clearly most technology programs fall within this arena. Within those groups, it may prove more fruitful to specifically target those who have a board member from a technology or consulting background.

You should also share your story with groups that have a heavily "donor-advised" component, such as many community foundations. These groups place a value on making their donors aware of unique projects taking place. For those donors who made some of their wealth in the technology arena, your project may be particularly compelling. You may find that even initial small investments from this sector may turn into new long-term relationships, as these funders see your organization as a progressive, vibrant organization that is trying to leverage the same tools they did in the business world.

As you begin exploring completely new sources, you will need to take some guides with you. These sherpas into the unknown may be a little foreign to you and there may be some language barriers, but at least they know the terrain. Your own IT staff may even be able to help find undiscovered sources of funding treasure. Keep in mind that many technology firms are younger in their development and growth cycles, which could mean that their processes for philanthropy are much less rigid or defined.

Work with your IT staff to identify the technology organizations in your geographical area. At the same time, don't be afraid to cast a wider net for technology firms that have products or services that may be of interest to you. The organization may have at least some local presence (such as a sales office) in your area that could partner with your organization.

Be prepared to approach your engagement with these firms in untraditional ways (see the in-depth Corporate Engagement section for more details on these concepts). Also, when a technology organization has services or technologies you are interested in, consider complementing your financial ask with a request for pro bono (or deeply discounted— "low bono") services as part of the partnership request. These companies often want to have a relationship that goes beyond checkbook philanthropy. By leveraging their products and their people, you can create a holistic relationship that could bring you more cash, more technology, and more techies running around volunteering at your facility.

Overall, while you are making your technology pitch, keep in mind the overall mission of your organization and how this program will enhance that mission through the power of technology. Identify new sources to approach with your message, and be willing to engage with these sources in unconventional ways. Stay focused on communicating on how this proposal relates to your organization's higher goals. Your laser focus on achieving those goals outlined in the program that will make a specific, measurable impact on those you serve are the key to securing funding for your project.

## Leveraging Technology to Engage the Corporate Sector

Trying to gain corporate support can become an all-consuming task for an executive director, transforming a nonprofit leader from a great hero for social justice to someone closer to Captain Ahab in search of the white whale. Larger nonprofit organizations dedicate staff to nurturing corporate relations. The flip side of this is that many larger corporations have personnel assigned to corporate responsibility, or community liaison, or other such titles.

### Elevating to Partnership

Many nonprofits have negative perceptions of corporations that interfere with the ability to form true partnerships. Those within the private sector often have a comparative perception that nonprofits "don't understand how the real world works." Consequently, the giving landscape, even for major organizations, often depends almost entirely on the relational skills of the development staff and the old adage that "people give to people." Developing a rich, multilayered relationship with your corporate partners, based on aligned goals and processes, will create a relationship based on mutual benefit and return. This will both raise the level of investment from your corporate partners and provide stability in the relationship that doesn't hinge on single, personal relationships.

### Achieving Alignment

Small to medium business-to-business (B-to-B) companies often thrive on their ability to serve larger corporations' niche needs. These organizations focus on a particular need of a corporation and become its problem solver of choice. Corporations, in a complementary way, serve as a central brand and assembler of smaller, independent resources to accomplish their goals. This puts corporate personnel increasingly in the mode of looking for supporting organizations that align with their goals and processes and can bring them value in their areas of interest.

Your initial advocate in a corporate environment may not be from the philanthropy department. If you can build the interest of internal advocates who work with the corporation's main operations or finance, marketing, HR, or other department, this may help you refine your message. Then, having these advocates bring your case to the philanthropy department almost always will give your proposal a leg up (or more) above other requests coming in.

As a leader of an organization that wants to engage the corporate sector, you need to align your organization with corporate processes and goals. Although some in the nonprofit sector may bristle at this notion, there *are* common areas of interest and opportunities for alignment. When you approach a corporation, not with a begging bowl in hand but rather with plans to enhance their corporate performance, you are perceived as a partner and are invited to the table. Fortunately, non-profit executives tend to be strong facilitators of consensus both internally and with their client communities; they can use these skills in a significant way to successfully engage with the corporate sector.

## Conclusion

For most nonprofit executives, the budgeting process can feel like doing your taxes—and budgeting for IT can feel like doing your taxes in Russian. Having an awareness of the tools and sources of information available can bring some familiarity to the task. Understanding how to tap the potential of your staff to collaborate with you in the process will help you meet the challenge and deliver results. Throughout the process, you will find that IT budgeting can actually bring clarity and stability to your organization.

With a solid plan in place, you are now armed with an entire new arsenal of community engagement opportunities—opening the doors to new funding and increasing levels of intimacy with your supporters as you use technology as a lever to realize even more of your organization's potential.

## Note

1. http://www.nten.org/research.

# The Tools

> Any sufficiently advanced technology is indistinguishable from magic.
>
> —Arthur C. Clarke

On good days, technology feels like magic; when things go wrong, it feels like a curse. If you're not a technologist, how or why technology works or fails can seem like a mystery. That's part of why managing technology is so difficult for nonprofit leaders. How do you manage something you don't even understand?

But technology is just like any other aspect of your organization. You don't have to be an accountant to successfully manage your organization's finances. You don't have to be a human resources manager to successfully manage your staff. Likewise, you don't have to be an expert in technology to manage it well. What you need is some basic understanding of how key systems work and then strategies for making good decisions.

We give you both in this part of the book. We open with a primer for all the basic computing systems in your organization, then take you through the world of online communications, fundraising, and evaluation. Finally, we close the book with chapter on the future of nonprofit technology, giving you a small glimpse into the trends that will matter most for your organization.

# CHAPTER 7

# The Foundation: Introduction to IT and Systems

*Kevin Lo*
*Willow Cook*

To establish a solid technology foundation in your nonprofit, you need to understand the basics of information technology and systems. Knowing a few IT fundamentals can help you get the most out of your existing IT infrastructure, communicate effectively with tech consultants and other IT professionals, and make better technology decisions for your organization.

This chapter gives you broad, high-level criteria to help you determine whether your core systems—such as desktop computers, networks, and servers—are performing at an acceptable level. We explain some of the nuts and bolts of back-office infrastructure, websites, and databases, giving you a foundation for understanding basic information technologies and practices. Finally, we offer resources that you can refer to for simple, timely advice on purchasing, implementing, maintaining, and troubleshooting technology.

## Your IT System Basics

What you consider a basic IT necessity will depend, in large part, on your organization's needs. For a small nonprofit, a computer, an Internet connection, and a great blog may suffice; larger organizations may include multiple servers, hosting providers, enterprise software, and data centers on their list of operational necessities.

Yet whether you're a large or a small nonprofit, knowing how some basic technology tools and systems work can provide a good foundation for making IT decisions. In the section that follows, you'll find an overview of some core IT tools, how they work, and how they might fit into your organization.

## The Daily Hardware: Desktop and Notebook Computers

A computer is, in many ways, the foundation of your IT system. Before you can consider what software to use, how to create your online presence, or almost anything else technology-related at your organization, you will need at least one computer per employee.

As a nonprofit, you may find that computer options abound. A wide variety of new desktop and notebook computers for every budget are widely available online and through retailers, and your nonprofit status may afford you special discounts on certain machines. You may also be considering donated or refurbished models, out of either budgetary or environmental concerns.

Before purchasing any machine, though, take some time to evaluate whether it will operate the way you want it to. Does it have the power to run the software programs you rely on? Is it compatible with your current system? Factors to consider when choosing a computer include number of processors, processor power, the graphics card, memory, and hard-disk storage.

### Number of Processors

Each computer has one or more central processing units (CPUs), or core processors. Nowadays, it is common for computers to come equipped with "dual-core" processors, meaning two CPUs; generally, these perform better than single-core processors. High-end servers can come with up to four processors, but whether you truly can harness that computing power will depend on the compatibility of the programs that run on it.

## Processing Power

Listed in units of megahertz (MHz) or gigahertz (GHz), processing power refers to the speed at which a computer can perform. The higher the frequency, the faster the machine. For general desktop work, Internet research, and word processing, any machine faster than 1 GHz is sufficient. For multimedia applications, however, the faster the processor, the better the program will perform.

## Graphics Card

Also known as a *graphics processing unit* (GPU), a graphics card is the part of the computer that outputs instructions or calculations to the computer screen. Graphics cards can be discrete (installed separately) or on-board (built in). For most day-to-day tasks, on-board graphics suffice, but for multimedia tools (such as graphics and video applications), a computer with discrete graphics will offer better performance and scalability.

## Memory

Measured in megabytes (MB) and gigabytes (GB), a computer's memory reflects its capacity to perform functions. As with processing power, the more memory, the better; in fact, increasing your computer's memory is one of the most cost-effective ways to improve its functionality. Memory also determines a computer's ability to run multiple programs simultaneously, allowing the user to multitask. It is often measured in multiples of 128 MB (1,024 MB = 1 GB); 256 MB is the minimum memory required for general office tasks, such as online research and word processing.

## Hard-Disk Storage

Also measured in MB and GB, hard-disk storage refers to the amount of data your computer can store and the number of applications you can install on it. Your storage needs will depend on your organization's data scheme, as well as on how many programs a particular machine needs to run. As cost per megabyte has fallen dramatically, and as data can be stored in more devices (and even remotely and online), a hard drive with more than 40 GB of hard-disk space will suffice for a work-station that doesn't need to generate large amounts of data. Computers that scan photos or run video files, however, will require as much space as possible. External storage—such as external hard drives—can easily be added to expand storage capacity as well.

## Used or Refurbished?

Another option to consider when choosing what type of computer system will work best is whether a used or refurbished computer will do the job. There is a general perception (which is perhaps not entirely inaccurate) that nonprofits will gladly accept any donated item, especially used computers. As enticing as a free computer may sound, try not to take just anything that comes your way. If it turns out the computer doesn't function properly or can't do the work you need it for, you may end up shelling out a lot of money to repair or upgrade it. And if you decide to get rid of it altogether, be advised that some computer recycling centers will charge you a fee to dispose of equipment.

Always have an IT staff member or other knowledgeable person test a computer thoroughly before you accept it. Consider how it will fit into your system and how you will use it. A basic, slightly outdated computer in good working condition might be just right for a part-time intern who spends most of his or her time doing Internet research. However, a low-end machine with a broken drive will be more trouble than it's worth. (See also "The True Costs of Long-Term and Cost-Effective IT Solutions" later in this chapter.)

A more viable alternative to accepting a donated computer is to buy a refurbished computer from an authorized reseller. Refurbished computers are typically a year old, but have been inspected and updated by a professional. Not only is this solution usually more affordable than buying a new computer, it is also a more eco-friendly option. As with a

## Desktops Versus Notebooks

If you are trying to decide between a desktop and a notebook (also called a laptop) computer, here are some factors to consider.

*Price.* Keep in mind that notebooks tend to be more expensive (about 30 to 50 percent more) than desktops for the same specifications. However, notebooks' affordability continues to increase with their growing popularity, and as of this writing, there are several pared-down options with basic functionality on the market for less than $500.

*How often are you required to travel?* If you work solely from the office, or if you plan to share files from your computer, a notebook probably isn't worth the extra expense. But if you travel frequently or spend a lot of time in the field, a notebook may be a more practical option.

*Will you be sharing the computer with other staff members with different work schedules?* Depending on your situation, this scenario presents arguments both for and against purchasing a notebook. Although a shared stationary computer is easier to keep track of (and less likely to be lost), a shared laptop can be more convenient if someone on your team needs to work from home or attend a conference.

*What are your anticipated upgrade and repair needs over the next three to five years?* Upgrading or repairing a desktop is a lot easier than upgrading or repairing a notebook computer. It is easier to add or replace devices on a desktop, and the components tend to be less expensive. Although the growing ubiquity of external Universal Serial Bus (USB) devices has made it easier to replace notebook peripherals, desktops remain more affordable to repair and update.

donated computer, always make sure that the refurbished machine you purchase meets your needs and minimum hardware requirements.

Budget permitting, it is advisable to purchase similar models of the same computer all at once, rather than acquiring them over time on an ad-hoc basis. Buying machines with similar or, ideally, identical specifications will make managing and administering them much easier. This can also simplify the setup process: If you need to set up the same configuration on each computer, cloning software can help you do so automatically, meaning you won't need to repeat the process for every new computer.

## Desktop Software

Desktop software refers to the applications you install on your computers to give them everyday functionality. Software programs allow you to collect and analyze data, write reports and documents, and communicate with your stakeholders. Although nonprofits use many programs, this section will focus on operating systems, productivity software, and databases, three of the most common types of desktop software used by nonprofits.

### Operating Systems

This is the software that runs your computer. Without an operating system (OS), your computer cannot use its processing power, memory, or hard-disk space. An operating system consists of programs—or drivers—that allow a user to carry out actions such as accessing a network, adjusting the computer's sound, or connecting to a printer.

### Mac or PC?

The question of whether to go with a Mac or a PC often comes down to personal preference. Macs use the same processing units as PCs, making them equally powerful. Macs tend to be more expensive, but some IT analysts would argue that the total cost of ownership for a PC is greater when you factor in extra software and maintenance (Macs come with more built-in multimedia software, for example, and offer fewer security risks). However, certain software applications—like donor-management systems—may not offer a Mac-compatible version. When trying to decide between a Mac and a PC, consider your current setup and requirements. Make sure any software programs you need to run are platform-compatible, and think carefully before establishing a multi-platform office, which will require more planning, training, and support.

Most computers come with an operating system—typically a version of Microsoft Windows or Mac OS X—preinstalled, meaning you rarely need to purchase a separate OS. However, occasionally, you may receive a donated computer that does not come with an operating system, or you may wish to restore, upgrade, or change your current one. In this case, you would need to install a new operating system using a separate disk. (Note that many new computers include the OS software for an easy restore.)

All operating systems arrive with some core system-administration utilities and functionality, such as user-management tools, display properties, and network settings. Users should be trained in the basic functions of the operating system they are working with to help them get the most out of their computers' capabilities.

Just as it can be helpful to purchase new hardware in bulk, using the same (or similar) versions of an operating system across your network will ensure greater compatibility and ease of use. But when you consider upgrading to a new version of your current operating system, you should always check its compatibility with your software. This can help prevent headaches down the road if it turns out that other programs you are relying on incompatible with the new system.

## Productivity Software

This is the set of tools you use to accomplish day-to-day office tasks, the most widely used example being Microsoft Office. Other well-known productivity suites include the free OpenOffice, as well as NeoOffice and iWork for Macs. Online applications—including Google Apps—can perform similar functions, offering free and paid subscription levels that meet different types of need.

When selecting productivity software, take into account your current resources and how you plan to use the software. If your training budget is minimal, for example, the popular Microsoft Office—which comes with a strong user base, training materials, and support—may be the best option. New hires are apt to be familiar with Office, and should you require more complex programming on the platform, it shouldn't be difficult to find a consultant.

Yet if online collaboration is a priority and you don't have the resources to invest in a dedicated, in-house collaboration suite like Microsoft Office SharePoint Server, online office applications can be a viable option. Online office application suites like Google Apps, Zimbra, and Microsoft Office Live tout their built-in collaboration capabilities as alternatives to their installed counterparts. Keep in mind, however, that online office suites may lack some of the features and interfaces you are accustomed to finding elsewhere, and if you are working offline, experience network difficulties, or are working on a slow connection, you won't have access to your documents, making local backup copies a must.

## Databases

For many nonprofits, choosing the right database is just as high a priority as selecting an operating system or a productivity suite. Whether you're considering your first database or seeking to replace your current one, this can be one of the biggest tech decisions you will make. Your database is likely to be a key component of your operations; it can help you extend your geographical reach, broaden your membership base, analyze constituent trends, and increase donation rates. For this reason, it is important to evaluate each aspect of the system with care.

A database, in essence, serves as a repository for different pieces of accumulated data that it helps you sort into understandable and potentially actionable information. A good database can not only store and retrieve data, but also help you uncover relationships and trends you might not otherwise notice. Because it will likely be used by a variety of staff members—and not just specialists—try to examine its ease of use more from the perspective of a user than from that of an IT implementer or a database administrator. Trying to make sense out of what may be years of data collected from a variety of sources is not an easy process; the software should make that task easier, not more difficult. Information should be easily retrievable, in a format that is easy to understand. Most database packages geared specifically toward a nonprofit audience will come with built-in reporting functionality, but you should always check to ensure that these reports are easy for users to generate. Also check to see whether the database is easily customizable;

many allow for some flexibility when it comes to how you organize and enter your data.

Database software should be tried and tested, free from any showstopping bugs. The more well-established and well-known database vendors tend to offer packages with fewer serious problems, but keep in mind that they may also be slower to innovate because of a large user base or a legacy code. Any database you choose should make it easy to retrieve your data as well as to back it up to an external location for an easy restore.

Your database package—be it off-the-shelf, customized, packaged, or online—should make its data available to users when they need it. Ideally, it should also allow you to set different privilege levels for the types of information it stores. Even if you don't need these types of permissions features now, it may be worthwhile to consider them should you need them down the road. When evaluating an online solution, you should consider both data portability issues as well as security-compliance laws, especially if sensitive data will be stored off-site.

Databases come in a wide range of prices, with donated and discounted options available to many nonprofits. Buy the best-quality package you can afford, taking into account hidden costs and training needs. If you are trying to decide between a boxed or online version of the same product, take a close look at each of their demo versions to see which option works best for your style and needs. Online versions can offer more flexibility (you can access it anywhere) and are more likely to be platform-independent than their boxed counterparts, but may offer reduced functionality and security features. In addition, an online edition may simply be a web based interface for the same product, hosted on the vendor's servers, meaning it may not be as user-friendly as some of the free web applications you are accustomed to but with some of the same downsides (you won't be able to access it if you don't have Internet access, for example).

When considering any database package, be sure to look beyond the initial purchase price to the financial demands of maintaining that database over the long run. Although many database vendors offer a variety of support packages, some of these options can end up being costly, especially if you should require more support or more customization than you had anticipated. When examining any database package, be sure to ask these questions:

- Are support calls affordable, or will they end up costing more than the software itself?

- Do you have someone in-house who can help when you need assistance, or will you need to rely on an expensive consultant?

- What about other ongoing maintenance and subscription costs?

- How often will you need to upgrade, and how expensive will that be?

Keep in mind that switching to a new database and migrating your data is time-consuming, costly, and complicated; for this reason, choosing well in the first place can be invaluable.

# Networks

Computer networks are a fundamental component of any organization's technology infrastructure. A network allows you to connect devices and people, helping you to share information and work more efficiently. The type of network you set up at your nonprofit will depend on a variety of factors, including your security and bandwidth needs, the sophistication of your setup, and your projected growth. In this section you'll find descriptions of three of the most common types of networks: local area networks, wide area networks, and virtual private networks.

## Local Area Network

A local area network (LAN) allows the computers at your office to communicate with each other, share resources such as files or peripherals like printers, and connect to outside networks such as the Internet. Given the importance of both internal and external information-sharing to almost every organization, maintaining a strong LAN is critical.

A LAN comprises more than one computer, with network interface cards (NICs) connected with one another via a networking device such as a router, switch, or hub. These connections can be made either with networking cables or wirelessly using common standards and protocols.

## Wired Networks

In a wired network, cables transfer data between different network devices. There are network appliances that perform a variety of different office functions; here are a few of the most common:

- *Hub:* The most basic type of network device, a hub allows you to increase the number of users who can access a network.

- *Switch:* Unlike a hub, a switch offers some traffic-control features to allow you to regulate the movement of traffic in and out of your network. A managed switch offers even more functionality than a regular switch, and it usually costs more.

- *Router:* This offers the most features for networking and connecting different devices. A router can direct traffic in your network, determining who can access the network, at what times, and by what methods. The more sophisticated the router, the more expensive, and the harder it may be for nontechies to manage.

The network cables you use to connect these devices will depend on the devices themselves. The most common types of cables are category (CAT) 3, CAT 5, CAT 5e, and CAT 6. The higher the category number, the greater amount of traffic it can handle. A CAT 3 cable can handle only 10 megabits per second (Mbit/s), whereas CAT 5 can carry up to 100 Mbit/s and Cat 6 can handle up to 1 gigabits per second (Gbit/s) of traffic. CAT 5e can handle both Mbit/s and Gbit/s of traffic. Some devices won't recognize the connection if the cabling isn't supported, so always read the device specifications before making a purchase. If you are still running CAT 3 cables on 10-Mbit/s devices, for example, your network probably isn't running at the speed that your data demands.

## Wireless Networks

Wireless networks operate on the same general principle as wired networks, except that instead of using physical cables, you connect over the air using wireless routers and signals. Because they are easier to tap into, wireless networks require slightly more sophisticated configuring to ensure that they are accessible only to authorized users. Settings you should be aware of when setting up a wireless network include the service set identifier (SSID), wireless standard, encryption protocol, and media access control (MAC) filtering.

The SSID is the name of your wireless network, which you can search for using your wireless device. Although you usually have the option to hide this identifier from those outside of your organization, some devices will not allow you to connect to the network with an SSID. Experiment with different settings to see what works best for your users and their devices.

The wireless standard, analogous to the CAT 3/5/6 designations used in cabling, refers to the speed and method by which devices connect. Common wireless standards are 802.11a, 802.11b, 802.11g, and 802.11n. Although many devices offer multiple standards, it is preferable to use one standard across the entire organization, setting your routers or access points to transmit at "b only" or "g only," for example. Uniform standards will help ensure the best network performance possible; you can experiment with different settings to learn which is the most compatible with the most devices.

Unlike an Internet café or a library hotspot, where networks are often accessible to all, office networks should be encrypted to prevent others from using your bandwidth or accessing your resources. Two widely used encryption protocols are wireless encryption protocol (WEP) and Wi-Fi protected access (WPA). WPA, the newer of the two, provides more protection and is preferable to WEP, which tends to be used with older devices. When setting your protocol, choose a hard-to-guess password; using predictable passwords (like the name of your organization) can open your network to unauthorized users.

In addition to encryption protocols, MAC filtering is another measure you can take to secure your wireless network. MAC filtering allows you to whitelist the network cards permitted to access your network, offering you further control. This authentication does not work with all devices, so be sure to double-check that your device can access the network if MAC filtering is turned on. In addition, bear in mind that hackers have found ways to "spoof" (pretend to have a certain signature) to circumvent this protection, meaning MAC filtering should not be your only method of authenticating wireless users.

## Wide Area Network

LANs connect computers and devices within a limited area; a wide area network (WAN) is a computer network that spans great distances. (In fact, the Internet itself is a type of WAN.) WANs can be used to connect different LANs to a larger network, allowing nonprofits with offices in several locations to share files and applications, a central authentication system, and even a backup system over the same network.

Some WANs are private, or built using leased lines; others are managed by Internet service providers (ISPs) to connect LANs over the Internet. Although private and leased WANs tend to be secure and offer guaranteed service levels, they can also be resource-intensive compared to off-the-shelf LANs. WANs must be set up by dedicated network professionals—an expensive process requiring coordination with the participating ISP.

Whether a nonprofit should consider a WAN depends greatly on the level of data sharing it requires and on its organizational structure. Your need for a WAN will depend more on the level of centralized administration you need than on your geographical reach. Even if you have multiple offices spread across the country, if those offices operate independently, the costs of setting up and maintaining a WAN will outweigh the benefits. Moreover, newer technologies like virtual private networks have superseded WANs in many ways, making WANs the preferable networking option only in specific situations.

## Virtual Private Network

A virtual private network (VPN) is a tool used by one network to encrypt private data before sending it across another—often public—network, such as the Internet, making it "virtually" private. A VPN allows you to create a secure "tunnel" within a public network to securely communicate with your own network.

There are two types of virtual private networks: *remote-access* and *site-to-site* (also called *router-to-router*). A remote-access VPN allows users to access an internal network by logging on to a VPN server from an external one; a site-to-site VPN provides an uninterrupted, secure connection between multiple locations. The type of VPN you need will depend on how you work. If you have multiple offices that frequently share information and resources, a site-to-site VPN is a good option; however, if your offices work independently and staff work off-site only occasionally, a remote-access VPN may suffice.

A VPN is reliable, widely used technology whose implementation costs are low compared to the security and convenience it can provide. A VPN can be valuable to your nonprofit in a variety of ways; for example, it may allow you to do the following things:

- *Offer greater flexibility to remote workers.* The primary reason to implement a VPN is to allow workers who are not on the premises to securely access files and resources. If your organization frequently engages in field work or off-site research, you'll appreciate that a VPN allows remote workers to safely share data with the home office.

- *Enforce more stringent security controls.* Because workers need to securely log into a VPN to access files and other data, a VPN provides an additional security barrier for your organization, reducing the need to share sensitive information through less secure means.

- *Make your IT systems more scalable.* Whether in remote access or site-to-site implementations, VPN greatly expands your options for scaling your organization. The cost to securely add new users to the network is marginal, and you can accommodate remote or telecommuting workers without adding extra office space.

Yet a VPN's capabilities are limited. For example, a VPN will not do the following:

- *Instantly secure your network.* Although a VPN can provide added security, it's not a panacea to your security woes, and it cannot stop phishing, malware, and other hazards. Indeed, because VPN-enabled networks can be accessed remotely, an incident such as the loss or theft of a notebook computer could increase your security risks.

- *Lessen your administrative burden.* A VPN, like any complex technology, requires oversight to ensure maximum performance. A VPN must be monitored occasionally by a network administrator, with system patches applied as soon as possible.

Ultimately, decisions about networking should reflect the size and needs of the organization. Once you've devised a plan for networking your nonprofit, the next step is to get your nonprofit connected to the Internet.

## Internet Access

Once your computers are set up, your software applications installed, and your networks connected, you will likely want to connect to the Internet. Although some organizations (especially those with public computing labs) may elect to keep a few computers offline, this tends to be the exception rather than the rule. An Internet connection is necessary for many aspects of nonprofit work—from sending email to conducting online research to updating your website—making fast, reliable Internet service not a luxury but a basic requirement.

There are many ways to connect to the Internet, each with its own advantages. The services available to you may depend on your budget or location; here are some popular options.

### ISDN

Integrated Services Digital Network (ISDN) was one of the first higher-speed ISPs; it has been superseded by DSL in popularity and ease of use. Yet in some rural areas, it is still the fastest level of service you can find, and remains a vast improvement over dial-up services.

### DSL

Digital subscriber line (DSL) allows you to access the Internet at high speeds using your phone line. DSL is generally more affordable than cable Internet service, and it can often be bundled with your existing phone line and cell phone service for a discount.

## Cable

Some cable companies also provide Internet service, often at higher speeds than DSL for the same price. Although this option used to be available only to home users as a cable TV tie-in, some cable companies are expanding into small- and medium-sized business markets, and this option may be worth exploring.

## Dedicated Leased Lines

This type of service is the standard for many businesses, offering guaranteed service levels—at a cost. Dedicated leased lines are considerably costlier than DSL or cable, but if your needs are beyond just research and email, you may require this level of service, especially if your organization plans to grow quickly and must have a reliable, consistent connection between multiple offices.

## Fiber-Optic Networks

Fiber-optic networks are almost three times faster than cable and six times faster than DSL, but tend to be much more expensive and less available than either of these options. Although optical carriers are often employed by large enterprises and data centers, they are less commonly used by home or small-business users, although this may change as they expand their reach. Nonprofits that need to transfer large amounts of data (such as large video files) may wish to consider this option if it is available in their area.

## Cellular Networks

Increasingly, mobile phone networks transmit not only for voice, but for data as well. Many handheld devices can send and receive email, as well as browse web pages, albeit on a small screen. As connection speeds and quality have improved, these networks have become an increasingly viable high-speed option for both mobile and office-based workers. Using a special wireless card that plugs into your notebook computer, you can use the Internet anywhere there is a cell phone signal. If other options are unavailable, this could very well be the fastest network you can access in your area.

Now that you've connected your organization to the Internet, it's time to connect your organization to the world with a great website.

## Your Organization's Website

A good website can be a critical tool for promoting your cause, branding your organization, and connecting with others. Your site may feature your mission, your programs, and your staff; highlight news and upcoming events; and showcase your accomplishments. It can be a means to establish your legitimacy as an organization and provide a platform for reaching out to constituents, funders, and partners.

Because of this, for many new organizations, building a website is just as high a priority as setting up core IT systems or even the office itself. Before you begin planning the layout or content of your website, however, you will need a domain name and a hosting provider.

### Domain Name

A domain name is the address or Uniform Resource Locator (URL) visitors use to arrive at your website; www.yourorg.org is an example of a domain name. To lay claim to a domain name, you must purchase it from a domain registrar. Typically, this works through an agreement by which you pay the registrar a periodic fee for the rights to use that URL. In other words, the domain registrar is leasing you the rights to the domain, not selling it to you. For this reason, it is important that this agreement be signed and maintained by someone within the organization, not a volunteer, consultant, or web designer. Using an internal contact will reduce the likelihood that any notices or important information will be lost, which could result in your domain being resold to another party. A final tip: When registering your .org, register the .com and .net equivalents to prevent them from being used by another party. You don't want potential supporters ending up at someone else's site just because they got the suffix wrong!

### Hosting Provider

Once you have a domain name, you need a place to host your website. Although large organizations may opt to host their own sites, smaller organizations may choose to use a third-party web hosting provider, which will store and back up your site data for you. Web hosting services range from free, ad-supported services with few features to shared and managed services that give users considerable control over their data. Some providers also offer additional services, including email, site metrics, and other site-management tools. When selecting a hosting provider, look for a reputable service with a high uptime and helpful support features. There are many host-ranking sites out there, such as www.hostindex.com or www.topwebhosting.com, that rank the different providers based on user feedback. Migrating to a new host can be time-consuming and laborious, so do your research before signing a contract.

## Data Security

Security is a vast, complex, and quickly evolving issue that relates to nearly every facet of an organization, from the physical security of your office to the electronic security of your clients' data. For this reason, security can be one of the most daunting aspects of your IT system. New security threats—and tools to protect your organization—are constantly emerging, making it difficult to keep up. Nevertheless, there are some basic security measures you can take to safeguard one of your organization's most valuable assets: its data.

Knowing where data lives, how it is backed up, and how it can be restored is an important first step in securing your network from both intentional (for example, a hacker) and accidental (say, a fire) threats. Once you have identified the location of your data, take measures to back up or protect it, if you haven't already done so. (This is especially true when it comes to your constituents' personal information, for which you may be legally subject to more stringent data-protection requirements.) This may involve a combination of encryption, backup, or other safeguarding measures. If your data is stored off-site, examine the security policy of the third-party provider to make sure you are not inviting additional risks.

Once you have identified where your data lives, the next step is to locate the places in your system that are most vulnerable to attack. This may be your network, but it could also be through your online connections. Network intrusions, viruses, spyware, and phishing are some of the most common threats to your data's security.

*Network intrusions* are attempts to gain unauthorized access to your network via the Internet, whether motivated by a desire to gain control of your resources, to plant malicious code, or to simply snoop around for personal information. Routers can provide rudimentary protection from this threat using network address translation (NAT), which works to hide your computers' identity from those outside of your network. More advanced protection, however, may require a firewall—either a dedicated hardware device that inspects all incoming and outgoing network traffic or software that performs a similar function. Although both Windows and Mac OS X come with built-in software firewalls that perform some basic network intrusion deterrence, if security is a particularly important concern for your organization, you may want to consider purchasing a dedicated firewall appliance.

Probably the most infamous of the security threats, *viruses* are programs that run on your computer without your permission and can self-propagate to infect others. As the different ways in which people interact online increase, these, in turn, create more ways in which viruses can spread. They may come in the form of email attachments, downloads, or even bundled with other software. A good antivirus program, which works by scanning files as they are opened and checking them against its virus definitions file, is an effective way to prevent infection. Your system administrator should verify that the virus definition file is updated periodically to ensure that it functions properly. Keeping your subscription to your antivirus program's database current, moreover, will ensure that any new updates released by the vendor are made to your system automatically.

Although *spyware* is a relatively late arrival to the field of online threats, it has become one of the main nuisances on the Internet. Spyware refers to programs that are installed on your computer without your knowledge or permission, which then track your online activities and compromise your privacy. (One common point of entry is through pop-up windows.) Although spyware cannot propagate itself like viruses can, it does tax your machine by eating up computing power, and it can report your online habits and personal information back to a server. Anti-spyware software, like the free Spybot-Search and Destroy, does a good job of removing spyware from a computer. However, being vigilant about the windows, program prompts, and links you click is an important preventative measure as well.

*Phishing* is a deliberate, nefarious attempt to steal your personal information by tricking you into entering credit card and other sensitive data to a seemingly legitimate site. This is often prompted by an email that appears to be from a legitimate source (such as your bank or credit card company) asking you to log in to confirm your information. This ill-gotten data is then used to steal your identity or commit online fraud. If you receive an unsolicited email from a financial institution asking for your password, be suspicious. Many banks and credit card companies now offer more advanced authentication methods on their site to prevent this kind of spoofing, and browsers like Internet Explorer and Mozilla Firefox are helping by automatically identifying and flagging suspicious sites.

Finally, keep in mind that one of the most cost-effective security deterrents you can invest in is user training and education. There is no greater security point of failure than the uninformed user, so spend some time warning your employees about what to look out for and how to respond if they suspect a threat.

## Back-Office Equipment

Back-office equipment consists of the devices you use to perform your day-to-day office tasks; it includes printers, fax machines, and file servers. Although some of these may not play a critical role in your organization, they will surely add to your stress and frustration if they do not operate smoothly.

### Printers

Depending on your organization's size, your office should have one or two good laser printers for shared printing, as well as an inkjet printer for occasional color printing (larger printing jobs should be outsourced to a copy shop or a printing press). Look for printers that offer features that will allow the printer to be shared over a network, including the ability to manage large print queues. (Keep in mind that if you are using a print server, it must be turned on to accommodate print sharing.) Although inkjet printers are less expensive than laser printers, inkjet paper and ink cost much more, and inkjet printers typically don't last as long as laser printers. No matter what printing solution you choose, use it responsibly. In many cases, an electronic document is just as effective and far more eco-friendly.

## Fax Machines

Email messaging has eclipsed fax machines' popularity for outreach and campaigning, but most organizations still require a fax machine (or service) to send and receive documents, especially if a physical copy is necessary (for example, documents requiring a signature). To avoid needlessly generating waste, make a good effort to seek out paperless solutions, emailing or sending files electronically when possible, or consider using an e-fax service, which allows you to receive faxed documents as electronic files. If your fax volume is low and you do not require a dedicated fax machine, multifunction fax-copier-printers can be a good option.

## File Servers

Although all operating systems allow users on the same network to share files, if you need to share data among ten or more users, you may want to invest in a file server or at least a dedicated file-and-print server combination. File servers can also help streamline your backup process by allowing it to be managed by a single system administrator, minimizing the burden on individual users who may forget to back up their data manually. There are a variety of devices on which you can store your backup data, including tapes, CDs, and even DVDs; your choice will largely depend on the size of your organization or your storage needs.

Organizations looking for an all-in-one file, print, and backup solution may also want to consider a network attached storage (NAS) device, a small machine that can be connected to your network to share files, manage printing functions, and schedule backups. NAS devices usually come with a browser interface that allows you to set up options such as user privileges and power settings, and they are easy to use and accessible from any networked device. NAS devices cost less than a stand-alone server and draw a lot less power. If file sharing, printing, and backups are the only back-office functions you seek in a server, this could be a fine option for your nonprofit.

# Critical Success Factors for a Healthy IT Infrastructure

Determining ways to measure performance and success is important in all areas of nonprofit work, and IT systems are no exception. Yet many nonprofit staffers find themselves unsure of where to begin when faced with the vast array of machines and volume of data their organization uses on a day-to-day basis. To many nonprofits, just getting a computer to work or being able to get their data reliably may already constitute a success.

To build long-term success and to encourage decision makers to view IT as part of an organization's overall operations, there are four comprehensive goals to work toward. These are high-level goals that can be easily understood by a nontechnical decision maker, no matter what an organization's staffing, level, or budget size.

## Smart IT Planning and Management

Increasingly, information technology is not just a utility you must have to run your office, but a core component of your operations. Technology can turn data into information and can be used to deliver services effectively. Be it donor tracking, community outreach, or financial management, you need to be able to plan for technology changes in order to better achieve your mission.

Having enough information to make decisions and to communicate your needs to different staff is a big step toward successful planning and management. If you are a budget decision maker, by using resources like the ones we list at the end of this chapter or participating in community events, you can learn what your peers are doing to better their work.

If you haven't already incorporated your IT spending into your funding or programming conversations, it's never too late to start. In addition, just taking the time to listen to your line staff about their day-to-day functions will give you ideas on not only the best decisions to make, but also the best questions to pose when making those decisions.

## The True Costs of Long-Term and Cost-Effective IT Solutions

Like many nonprofits, your funding model likely determines not only how much money you can allocate to IT each year, but also the types of IT investments you can make. Although the cost of hardware, software, and other IT resources has fallen considerably in the past few years, it remains a significant—even overwhelming—expense for many nonprofits.

It is no surprise, then, that many organizations find themselves irresistibly drawn to the promise of anything labeled "free" or "low cost." In some instances, this can be a viable option; in others, a cheap short-term solution can be a terrible long-term investment. For this reason, it is critical that you carefully evaluate the lifetime costs—including training, maintaining, and integrating—of any equipment or service you are considering.

Say, for example, someone wishes to donate a used computer that appears to be in good working condition to your small organization. Unbeknownst to you, however, some of the programs you use don't run on the computer's current operating system and the computer's disk drive is unreliable. All in all, when you add up the expenses of upgrading, parts, and labor—not to mention staff hours devoted to the project—you were better off declining the offer, or even purchasing brand-new equipment.

Choosing cost-effective software can be even more complicated, especially given the often overwhelming variety of options out there. In addition to the free, donated, and discounted, many nonprofits are beginning to consider *software as a service* (SaaS) applications, which are deployed and accessed via the Internet. Although in some cases, these options truly are more affordable, in others, the training, support, and maintenance costs can quickly outweigh any immediate savings.

Understanding different options and cost scenarios vis-à-vis your tech plan and budget will give you confidence to make the best decision. Making an IT decision based on up-front costs alone can end up costing you a lot more in the long run. This applies to IT service providers, donated hardware, or free or low-cost software. As IT becomes a core asset of your operations, you need to know how to decide whether you really should take that used equipment, sign that service contract, or purchase that subscription license.

## Reduce Catastrophic IT Failures and Spend Less Time Putting Out Fires

If you manage an organization with its own IT department or have a reliable consultant who manages your IT infrastructure, you are probably well on your way to achieving this goal. However, if your organization lacks dedicated IT staff, the "accidental techie"—program staff that are more technically inclined but whose main task is not IT—may devote an inordinate amount of time to dealing with serious IT problems, taking time away from program work. Catastrophic failures are defined as those that immobilize normal day-to-day activity, often affecting more than one staff member or department.

Reducing incidences of catastrophic IT failures will thus allow you to spend more time helping your clients and less time trying to fix the IT needed to run your organization.

If you experience critical IT failures, it may be due to outdated equipment, insecure computing, or a lack of basic knowledge.

### Outdated Equipment

If your equipment is more than seven years old, the components have likely reached their end of life. Corporations often replace their IT equipment every three years, but if they are properly maintained and haven't had extraordinary mileage (like those that were used for basic office tasks), an extra three to four years of life is not uncommon. For example, you are more likely to get more life out of a computer whose main function was light data entry at your local bank during business hours than from one whose main function was to perform complex calculations or data analysis for long periods of time. Be sure to budget for upgrades and replacements on a regular basis.

### Insecure Computing

If you have a network, especially a wireless one, or use the public Internet to work without a secured connection, you are more susceptible to online threats. A malware nuisance, a virus outbreak, or even an outright deliberate attack could immobilize your office. Recovery from such down time would also be unpredictable, as it could involve investigative work or restoring a backup. Likewise, if you don't have virus protection, or you use poor passwords that can be easily guessed, you are also more likely to suffer down time. Being secure and taking basic precautions will prevent or limit extraordinary down time.

### Lack of Basic Knowledge

More often than not, prevention is better than treatment. By keeping abreast of technology trends and how they may affect your work, for instance, you can know what tools are out there to prevent you from falling victim to basic problems. Being informed about online threats and security issues, however basic, will allow you to gauge effectively what measures are needed to counter these threats. Last, implementing best practices across the organization to keep your IT infrastructure secure will reduce the incidence of catastrophic IT failure.

## Reliable Systems Decrease Time and Expense

Staff hours are often wasted troubleshooting unreliable systems. Although this is less severe than the impact of catastrophic down time, your organization can spend a significant portion of IT budgets (if you have one) on supporting poorly maintained systems or systems that don't accurately match the workflow and processes of your organization. Even if you are moving toward web-based or online applications, you still need a sound IT network and infrastructure to access those systems; the burden of maintaining those types of software is shifted to the online provider, but this increases the need to maintain the reliability of your core systems.

Many of us, IT experts included, spend some time of our day trouble-shooting minor issues. Ten minutes here, half an hour there—sooner or later we are talking about real time being lost. To decrease the time lost to troubleshooting, there are several steps you can take to keep office technology trouble-free:

- *Have a maintenance plan:* Like a car that needs scheduled maintenance, computers (and to a lesser degree networking devices and peripherals) need to be regularly maintained to run optimally. Virus-scanning and spyware programs must be updated periodically to protect against the latest threats. Devoting a set time to check for these problems will decrease the time needed overall and reduce the chance of catastrophic IT failure.

- *Build good computing habits:* Good habits and best practices will reduce the need to troubleshoot. Are your users visiting potentially unsafe sites or clicking pop-ups that lead to spyware being installed? Are users unable to discern what is legitimate email and what is spam or phishing email? Although computers do sometimes behave unpredictably (as any computer technician will tell you), they aren't supposed to deteriorate over time. If your IT infrastructure gives you problems, you should consider investigating why that may be, or have an experienced professional look into it.

- *Keep a troubleshooting log:* When problems arise, you should try to keep track of your IT issues, however informal the method may be. That way, you can begin to see a pattern and establish a basis for where the pain points are. If you are line staff and need proof that your network experiences outages more than 50 percent of the time, a simple spreadsheet that logs the date, time, nature of the problem, and its resolution is a good way to show that productivity is affected and desperately needs to be addressed.

By promoting healthy computing practices in your organization and handling IT issues in an organized, efficient manner, you'll be able to spend more time carrying out your organization's goals and less time troubleshooting.

## Where to Find Technology Help

Technology assistance and advice abounds on the Internet, for die-hard techies and tech novices alike. If you need help getting the most out of your current tools, making a decision, troubleshooting, or just learning more about technology in general, the following resources can help.

## Technology Definitions

Sometimes, half the battle is simply knowing what a technology term means. Tech Encyclopedia (http://www.techweb.com/encyclopedia), WhatIs.com (http://whatis.techtarget.com), and even Wikipedia (http://wikipedia.org) are all good places to start. Or use Google's search engine; the operator "define:" tells Google to look up definitions of a word or phrase.

## Technology Reviews, Tips, and Trends

CNET (http://www.cnet.com), ZDNet (http://www.zdnet.com), PC-World (www.pcworld.com), and Macworld (http://www.macworld.com) offer product reviews and comparisons, tips, and news about the latest technology offerings, and can be a good place to keep up with general technology trends.

## Nonprofit-Specific Technology Advice

Idealware (http://www.idealware.org), NTEN (http://www.nten.org), NPower (http://www.npower.org), ICT Hub (http://www.icthub.org.uk), and TechSoup.org (http://www.techsoup.org) offer technology comparisons, reviews, webinars, and how-to's geared specifically toward nonprofits; nonprofit technology blogger Beth Kanter's wiki (http://bethkanter.wikispaces.com) is a treasure trove of information for nonprofits seeking to learn more about social media. Have a specific question? TechSoup.org's forums (http://www.techsoup.org/community) offer free technology advice from an international community of experts.

## Technology Help for Libraries and Community Tech Centers

WebJunction (http://www.webjunction.org) offers tech-planning tools and a community forum for libraries; TechSoup.org's MaintainIT project (http://maintainitproject.org) shares public computing tips and techniques in its articles and tech-planning "Cookbooks."

## Product Help and Support

If you're having trouble installing, using, or troubleshooting a particular product, sometimes it's best to go straight to the source. But before you call tech support, keep in mind that many product vendors offer official help sections, complete with help documents, online forums, product updates, and more—free of charge.

## How-To Videos

Sometimes the best way to learn about a complicated technology is to watch a video about it. Common Craft (http://www.commoncraft.com) offers a well-edited selection of how-to videos; WonderHowTo.com (http://www.wonderhowto.com), a directory of how-to videos culled from various sources around the Web, has a great selection of technology how-to's on everything from networking to programming.

## Conclusion

Carrying out the mission of your organization with the resources available to you should be the primary factor in every technology decision you make. By understanding the basics of building and maintaining your IT infrastructure, you can choose hardware, software, and networking solutions appropriate to your needs, your budget, and the size of your organization. Educating staff users about preventing security threats and preparing your office for major catastrophes will save your organization time and money. Bookmark and share the array of resources, assistance, and donations available to the nonprofit community for future reference. Understanding the fundamentals of IT will help ensure that your organization's technology infrastructure and budget don't get overstretched, allowing your organization to better focus on its important work and mission.

# CHAPTER 8

# Where Are Your Stakeholders, and What Are They Doing Online?

*Michael Cervino*

Where should you focus your efforts to find out where your stakeholders are and what they are doing online with and for your organization? What data is meaningful? What is trend, and what is simply trendy? These are the questions that drive the research and analysis that inform the program design of the highest-performing online organizations. The answers that come back validate, over and over, that the Internet is a constituent-driven channel unlike any other. Keeping pace with constituents' evolving interests and behaviors online enables an organization to make strategic choices about programs and tactics to engage those constituents. If you want to improve your ability to target your outreach, serve your constituents, and engage in the online dialogue about your organization, it pays to know the networks in which your constituents participate, the websites they visit, the discussion lists on which they lurk, and how they spend their time online. There is a wealth of data in some areas of constituent engagement and a paucity in others. Yet just as the technology advances, so too do the access to data analysis and the tools for making that analysis. This chapter presents suggestions to help you develop a better understanding of online user behavior.

## Let Your Objectives Be Your Guide

An organization's Internet program exists for specific reasons. Whether it's a public website, Facebook page, intranet, or extranet, an investment in user-facing technology is made to create value through the online interaction of an individual with an organization. The organization must make that desired value explicit through clear objectives. As every graduate business course stresses, *simple, measurable, achievable, realistic,* and *timebound* (SMART) objectives enable the teams working on the program to design strategies and tactics aligned with the value the organization wishes to create. In the absence of clear objectives, the online work will inevitably break down into scattershot one-off tactics that may do more to erode value than to create it.

This is evident now in many organizations' haphazard commitment to social networks, social media, and the virtual world medium. Too many nonprofit organizations whose email marketing programs have been strategically driven for years by specific, measurable goals now drink the "new medium" Kool-Aid and put up Facebook pages, build Second Life islands, and slap up YouTube videos because they "need to be there."

## Be Clear About What You Want

In our recent work with an organization on their Facebook strategy, we asked the question: "What is the value you hope to derive from this initiative?" The initial response—"We need younger audiences"—was an aspiration, a goal. It was not a clear objective.

To craft a more clear objective, we led the organization through a series of discussions on user behavior in social networks to ground their expectations in what might actually be realistic and achievable. These discussions covered how people are using social networks to connect to business associates, classmates, family, and friends. We explored how different social networks can attract different profiles of people for different purposes (for example, LinkedIn as a professional networking community, Facebook as a personal networking community, Care2 and Change.org for social causes.) We researched who in the networks had self-identified already as a supporter by creating a page, posting a message, or linking to someone within the organization.

We examined the power of individuals in the network to champion a cause and spread that cause's message to others in their network through messaging, applications, extensions, widgets, and other tools available through the social networks. By stirring about in the active stew of these networks, the organization came to understand the essential ingredients they needed to reach new constituents by engaging those they already knew in those networks.

They also explored where the limitations are for nonprofits in these social networks—what institutions can and cannot accomplish in these communities. Through an evaluation of high-performing organizations in the social network space, they learned what investment in staff and resources to expect to make and how these initiatives do and don't integrate into other online and traditional channels.

Grounded in a new understanding of how people are evolving in their use of social networks and what opportunities this presented for their organization, the team articulated a new SMART-er objective: "Create a network of 100,000 within 12 months whose engagement on behalf of the organization can cover the cost of staff resourced to the initiative within 2 years."

The most powerful piece of this objective was the stipulation of "engagement on behalf of the organization." This has provided the team a liberating focal point for their efforts. They have "permission" to research, test, and deploy techniques to directly convert those networked individuals or harness their enthusiasm to be advocates and volunteer fundraisers to achieve their objective.

## Establish Your Baselines

The second focus area is the twin star of the first: establish a baseline against which you can measure progress. This baseline can be derived from users engaging directly with your web presence (for example, 1 percent of average monthly traffic joins the email list or 0.05 percent of users use Forward This Page to a Friend) or on behalf of your organization (5 percent of our "a-thon" participants advertise our event on their social network presence, or five hundred individuals blog about our organization each month).

The baselines should be directly aligned with the objectives. Likewise, the objective's measurability should tie to the baselines created.

You may be asking, "Which comes first? Do I gather my baselines, then set my objectives? Or do I set my objectives, then go gather baselines?" Start with your objectives; they are derived from the business value you want to create and are the guide for what you want to measure. Consider this: if you cannot create a baseline for an objective against which you can measure progress, then you do not have a SMART objective. In the earlier example, the current social network may be zero individuals today, but future growth can be measured against this number.

Not all metrics are meaningful when it comes to measuring objectives. A truly meaningful metric will measure programmatic change rather than a specific tactical activity within this larger picture. For example, you could count the number of clicks on the home page icon for "Join our social network." You can create a baseline and measure growth or decline in clicks on this icon. You could go on to determine whether your stakeholders click the icon more from the home page or subpages and whether they prefer blue or red icons. Does this mean your objective should be to "increase the number of clicks to X for our social networking icons"? For measuring the success of the icon, certainly, but as a strategic objective guiding program decisions, the answer is "No." A more meaningful programmatic metric would be the percentage of new engagements from the website versus those joining from within the network. If all growth in your social network is coming from the website, is the organization truly tapping a new market or simply redirecting its current audience?

Understanding who your stakeholders are and what they are doing online requires two types of baselines—one for overall objectives and another for specific tactics. Once you have these, you then need to be disciplined in monitoring progress (more on this later) and be sure not to confuse the two.

Some organizations have a rich history of monitoring and analysis; others are starting from scratch. No matter where you are in that continuum, here are a few suggestions for building or expanding your baselines:

- *Mine the data:* Invest in analysis tools that can deliver the analysis on the metrics you need. Analysis tools, and an increasing array of analysis services, can measure website, email, social network, and social media engagement.

- *Survey constituents:* Asking for their input is invaluable in validating assumptions about your constituents, and the mere act of engaging them for their input communicates their value to the organization.

- *Compare to peers:* Find five of your peer organizations who will share their metrics. Be prepared to share your overall findings with each organization as a "thank you" for participating. Weigh the value of these metrics carefully, relative to the maturity and investments in their programs versus yours. Take into consideration how their positioning, issues, and user experience may be driving their numbers. Most important, learn where they are finding new constituents online and at what return on investment.

- *Study nonprofit benchmarks and metrics:* Associations like NTEN, vendors, consultants, and various publications are producing more benchmark data than ever.

- *Review other industry metrics:* More broadly, overall metrics on Internet behavior like those on the Pew Internet & American Life Project are useful.

With the foundational elements of objectives and baselines in place, let's examine the suggestions for tactical areas to explore in your research and analysis into online behavior.

## Track What Is Relevant

Regardless of the online medium, you can distill the pressing questions about online activity down to three:

1. How are constituents finding out about us or connecting through to us?
2. What are they doing when they interact with us?
3. When are they leaving and why?

Because *online activity* and *interaction* can be defined so broadly on the Internet, let's look at just a few enduring principles as well as some examples that may not endure, given the ever-changing nature of the technology.

### Discovering How They Found You

How do you discover how your constituents are finding out about you? A good starting point is to assess whether there is a data trail somewhere that you can follow back to the origination point of the interaction. If there is, dig into it. If there is not or if the costs of trying would outweigh the incremental value, determine whether you can build that data trail going forward and analyze from there. Each medium has different paths to tracing back to the origin of a constituent interaction.

#### Site Logs and Traffic Analysis Tools

There are numerous tools available that allow you to analyze your website traffic. This analysis will tell you what sites, domains, and pages your users are coming from, where they are going, how long they stay, and what content seems the most important to them The following are important categories of information to look for in your site logs:

- *Referring sites:* Knowing where your users are coming from can help define where to spend online advertising dollars, create comarketing partnership, or conduct partner outreach. They also provide insight into your user profile—if they are using these sites, what other similar sites might be out there?

- *Keywords:* Users will search for you by typing words or phrases into search engines. Link these up with the pages they go to from those search results, and optimize that experience. Target ads by analyzing other keywords like the ones they use.

- *Linked sites:* Who's linking to you? What do these sites say about the profile of your constituents online? Use Google, and type in the URL of the link (omitting http://).

- *Entry pages:* What pages are people entering on, and where do they go from there? Although most enter at the home page, many come in directly through search or other means to sub-pages. Do you understand why these are highly used entry pages, and are you making the most of those interactions?

## eCRM Data

Organizations with email lists, advocacy tools, online donations, and other data-rich applications are continually pushing for more meaningful insights from this data. Here are some things to look for:

- *Frequent referrers:* Who joined as a result of someone forwarding a message to them or referring them, and who made that referral?

- *New join source:* Source code your onsite and offsite promotional links, links in emails, and other engagement driving links. Find out for sure what inspired new subscribers, donors, activists, and the like to join your cause.

## Social Networks

In social networks, the principle is generally that your trusted network is the influencer to others. As of this writing, there is little transparency on the social networks as to who recommended whom to you. But there are a few things that are useful to examine:

- *Influencers:* Who is linked to you, how big are their networks, and how active are their comments and actions on your behalf?

- *Evangelists:* Who has created pages, posted a badge, added a link, installed an application, or taken some other personal action on behalf of your organization?

- *Growth calendar:* How do spikes in your social network growth align with your in-network and out-of-network marketing efforts?

- *Promotional click-through:* Where you can, track click-throughs to promotions you control that drive people to link to your network profile. This can be off network and, increasingly, within the network using advertising.

## Social Video

This refers to YouTube and similar sites. Much like actions driven from social networks, most social-video-inspired activities are difficult to trace. Highly watched or recommended videos in the network garner views and can simply "take off." However, you don't know *who* is signed up for your channel, just *how many*. Here are some tips:

- *Track your promotions:* At a minimum, you can filter out the views you know are driven from your email or other marketing to get a "net" on who found you through other means.

- *Follow comments:* Some networks allow you to reply to comments, which can help unearth what drew people.

- *Contact "friends":* For platforms that enable it, contact the friends or subscribers who have signed up for your video feed.

## Blogosphere

In addition to the web logs for your blogs, monitor the following:

- *Commenters:* Both on your blog and on their blogs, use Technorati or other blog search engines to determine who regularly comments on your blog, as their blog helps both drive traffic and define the profile of those interested visitors.

- *Promotions:* Track your own onsite and off-site promotions to your blog.

- *Content analysis:* Which posts draw the comments and traffic? Is there a theme, style, or chord you strike that resonates with your audiences?

### Social Links

There is an emerging class of social media tools—like Digg, Stumble-Upon, and Del.icio.us—where people are sharing favorite links. These networks' mentioning or "voting" of a link, up or down, can drive both users of those networks and outside them, due to their impact on search engine rankings, into your sphere. Some pointers:

- *Track as referrers:* Isolate these networks in your web logs to monitor traffic from them.

- *Creating a profile:* Most of these networks foster connections among their users. By creating a profile and investing time in creating a presence as a valid member, you can find those who are helping to rate you up.

## Following What They Explore and Say

Using the approaches just outlined, organizations can deepen their understanding of their stakeholders' needs and interests by following past the point of entry on through the click paths and engagement actions they take. Consider the question from this angle: "What are my constituents interacting with today that would inform the content, offers, or services I should release tomorrow?" Online marketing is shifting from a demographics-based targeting medium to user profile–driven marketing. A twenty-five-year-old male and a fifty-five-year-old female may both enjoy the same YouTube video on social justice and follow the same blogger on human rights. Their interest profile and interaction profile (video/blog) create a persona you can market to through your outreach and content.

Following the trends for these interest profiles over time reveals what they find popular and therefore what could be most useful to integrate into your program. The rush to be on YouTube is a logical trend in this context. According to a Pew Internet & American Life January 2008 report, 15 percent of American adults watched video online last year, a growth rate of 45 percent over the prior year. Creating content for this audience is smart—it is going where the audience is. But in that context, understanding what your user profile prefers is critical to shape what video is created, how it is tagged and promoted, what bloggers are pitched to review it, and what the call to action in the video pulls viewers through to take the step of joining your cause.

Here are four of the most useful approaches for getting meaningful insights about these types of engagements and constituent profiles out of traffic and activity data. These skew more heavily toward website and eCRM analysis, where the analytics are more available, than toward social media and networks, where data is less available.

### Content Themes

Most organizations focus on the popular pages of the day. You can take things further and monitor the trend lines of popularity over time. Look at popular pages, but also work toward grouping your content together by themes and looking for those that may consistently draw more interaction.

### Features Use

Analyze which features are popular and which are not. If a feature is rarely used and is taking up valuable real estate or marketing effort, reconsider whether it is truly useful for meeting your objective. Many commercial enterprises are using feedback comments and rankings on features to continually align what is offered with their audience's interests. For example, if you create a Facebook game application to expand your network and raise awareness of your mission, does it push through requests for comments and suggestions to improve the game?

### Discussion Topics

Whether on discussion lists, websites, the blogosphere, social media, or social networks, monitor the discussions about your organization and your issues. A time-saving way to keep on top of this is to use content search and aggregation tools like Yahoo! Pipes. These tools allow you to enter keywords, like your organization's name, to receive updates when your organization is mentioned in web pages, discussion lists, and blogs. Staying on top of who is talking about the organization is invaluable in identifying potential sources for online advertising or media outreach. Entering into the discussion or responding to a post can create a positive impression of your organization and a new contact for your network.

### "Submit" Trends

A crucial part of understanding your user behavior is tracking and trending their online actions—donations, advocacy alerts, registrations, product purchases, downloads, media views, and other interactions that leave a data trail when they click Submit that can be monitored. It can be informative to look at today versus yesterday, this week versus the same week last year, or even this effort compared to that last similar effort. What is most revealing for these types of actions is indexing an average. Many clients find trailing charts to be most informative— whereby you create a rolling three-month or twelve-month average or aggregate and monitor whether that trend is going up or down. For example, donation submits today may spike up because of an email ask, but last year there was no email ask on this same day—it was a week earlier. Comparing day to day or week to week isn't useful, but looking at a cumulative of the last ninety days compared with a ninety-day cumulative in the same window the prior year can help normalize the bumps and provide insight about your growth or decline in donations, sign-ups, or other priority engagements. By plotting each day's trailing ninety-day total, you create a trend line that reveals whether you are headed up or down.

## Figuring Out Why They Leave

Many organizations monitor the exit pages (the pages from which users leave your site) from their site. They also pay attention to email opt-out rates. They monitor time on site, how long visitors watched a video or interacted with a Flash piece or stayed on a blog post. Far fewer organizations pay attention to click paths—which pages are clicked on, in what order, and how many users follow that path versus other paths. Only recently are organizations paying attention to process abandonment—the number of people who only start a process compared with those who finish the process. These are crucial metrics for determining if what is happening now is better or worse than what happened previously. But they don't always explain why online users are choosing to leave. Here are three areas to focus on to get beyond the "what" to the "why":

- *Ask the constituent:* Solicit the reason from the individual at the point of their taking that action. For example, if someone is unsubscribing, ask them why on that form. If someone is bailing out of a process, intercede to ask their input on why they are doing so.

- *Analyze click path patterns:* If you can analyze click paths, determine whether there is something present on the page that may be consistently triggering bailouts. There may not be some deep psychological driver for why your constituents are dropping out of a process. Something as simple as placing a "Cancel" button right next to the "Continue" button can create click error and increase bailout rates.

- *Multivariate testing:* This refers to testing multiple variables on a page or form or in an email at the same time. The technique is invaluable in helping to isolate which creative, layout, or process factors work better than others at driving the desired outcome. The simplest form is A/B testing—one creative against another, or a three-step process versus a two-step process. As the costs of the technology have come down, more sophisticated testing of many variables at once is now an option for nonprofits.

You can generate these insights about your online audiences and their relevant activities both on your organization's site and on your behalf on other sites or in other networks. Getting it done requires aligning your research efforts to your objectives, leveraging good analytic tools, and, most important, creating the space and time to work on it.

## Use Relevant Engagement Metrics

Organizations regularly ask, "What's relevant to look at for my online constituents?" and "What should I spend my time pulling together?" Increasingly, the list of key metrics has had to evolve as new interactions and media enter the market and established ones evolve. Here are three guiding principles that are highly useful in determining what metrics to gather:

- *Track volume:* How many people have donated, provided feedback, contributed comments, posted media, or taken other priority actions I can track?

- *Normalize using rates:* What percentage of my constituents has engaged in a particular action? What percentage has done one thing, two things, three things, and so on?

- *Follow trends with rates of change:* Are volume and participation rates changing significantly over time?

Tracking the total count of new members is difficult to interpret "at a glance" due to the dramatic rise and fall of counts on a daily basis (see Figure 8.1). Perceiving the underlying trend is challenging. Tracking the rolling thirty-day average of new members smoothes out the peaks and valleys of the daily raw counts to reveal the underlying trend of gradual upward growth (see Figure 8.2). The rolling average is a sum of the end date plus the prior twenty-nine days divided by thirty.

Monitoring the engagements like those measured with these metrics will reveal where your program has problems and potential. For example, inactive rates have a natural tendency to rise after organizations have a spike in sign-ups due to hot news or a compelling issue action. During these high-profile periods, the net is cast more widely and brings to the organization constituents who are one or two rings outside the bull's-eye of the true loyalist profile. Monitoring the inactive rate over a short newcomer window of thirty or sixty days reveals this dip. Rather than continue "communications as usual," the organization can test different content and calls to action in their new constituent welcome series to find ways to maximize engagement.

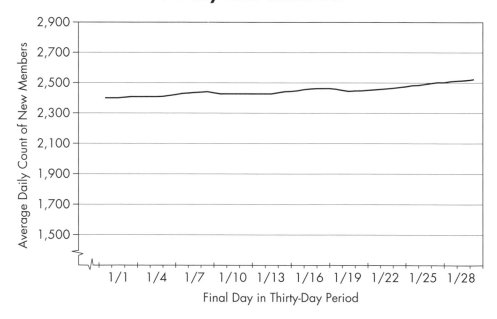

**Figure 8.1. Daily Count of New Members.**

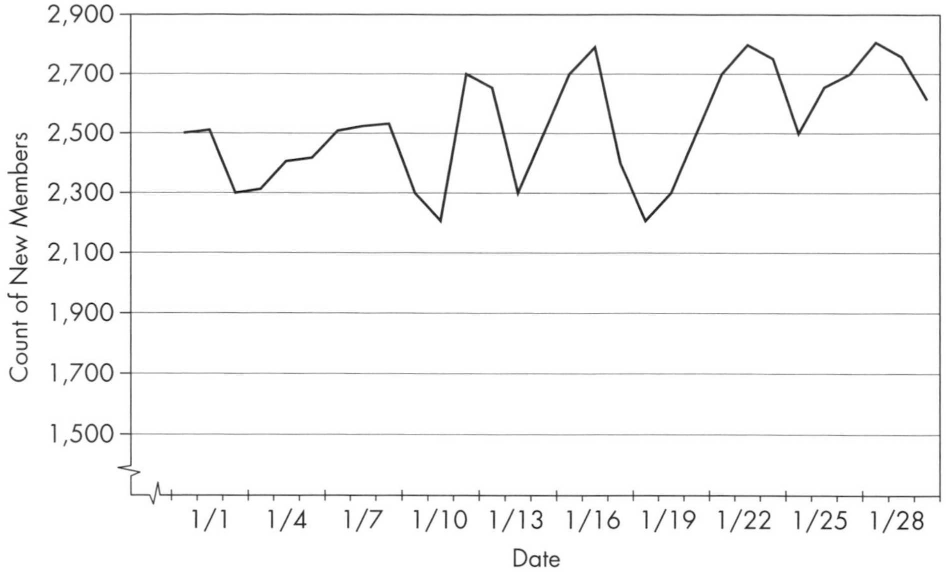

**Figure 8.2. Rolling Thirty-Day Average of Daily New Members.**

## Metrics for Monitoring Trends

*Engagement rate of your list by action type:* Measure of the percentage of contacts who take each type of action you offer (donate, advocacy, and so on).

*Multi-action versus single action takers:* The percentage of contacts who take only one type of action compared with those who take multiple types of action.

*One-time action takers versus repeat action takers:* The percentage who have done only one thing once versus those who repeatedly engage.

*New contact conversion rate:* The percentage of new contacts who have converted into action takers within their initial period of engagement (typically sixty to ninety days).

*Retention rate:* The percentage of contacts who acted in the prior period who have taken action in this period. For donations, this may be annually. For advocacy, this should be a shorter time horizon for an active program.

*Comment/update rate:* The percentage of contacts who have updated their contact information or submitted a comment. Although seemingly neutral, these interactions indicate a high level of interest in connecting with your organization.

## Survey Your Constituents

Surveying your users can reveal their reasons for finding you and for the behaviors they exhibit on your site. Survey efforts are particularly useful for getting a handle on who your stakeholders are and what they are doing online, and gaining some insight into what they expect or would like to do with or for your organization.

Obtaining useful constituent input does not require an annual constituent survey. Online survey tools and feedback forms are inexpensive to deploy, albeit requiring some expertise to define the survey's purpose and craft appropriate unbiased questions. If you have discussion lists, posting questions for input can elicit valuable insight. In redesign projects, techniques like online card sorting and usability testing get constituent input on critical design questions. A number of organizations have created advisory groups of volunteers who sign up to answer questions or provide input on the direction for a program. These groups can be invaluable for providing insight into which websites, blogs, lists, and networks they belong to and why. This more intimate dialogue with a representative group can reveal where to explore placing ads or conducting media outreach. A sophisticated online program will build constituent input into their program design in a variety of ways.

Short of gathering actual behavioral data, there are few methods better than surveys for getting input from your users on what they do online and what they would do with you. Surveys can consist of as few as two or three questions that get to the vital information you need to inform a decision, or require fifteen to twenty minutes of time for more comprehensive input. Where your list or traffic is high enough, determine the sample size you need for statistical validity (see Google's "survey sample size calculator" for a variety of free choices). Using smaller audience sizes permits more frequent surveying by asking different representative groups each time.

Usually, the demographic questions are the easy ones to define. "What is your ZIP code?" "Are you between the ages of twenty-five and thirty-five?" From there, we get into the science and art of survey work. Start with the more fundamental question: "What do we need to learn through this survey?" List those goals and then determine which questions, validly posed, will provide the data you require.

## Conduct a Cross-Channel Analysis

The "holy grail" for analysis is the deeper understanding of the relationship across marketing channels. Is there some offline connection driving online behavior and vice versa? This leads to classic cross-channel marketing questions, such as, "Did the direct mail piece drive the online gift? Did our TV, print, or radio story drive online interactions?"

## Case Study: Heifer International

Heifer International wanted to learn whether bloggers and socially networked people who were on the Heifer email list would be interested in helping in a campaign to raise money in these spaces. Before launching full scale into the blog-raising campaign, Heifer sent an email out to a sampling of the list with ten questions, some of which were demographic, and then these four:

1. Do you have a MySpace, Facebook, blog, or other social media site? (Yes/No)

2. Which do you have? (Checklist of the major players)

3. What is the URL? (Open Text)

4. Could Heifer contact you about your social media site? (Yes/No)

Heifer gained two crucial pieces of information through these questions. First, they found they had a critical mass sufficient to test the program—more than 30 percent of respondents indicated they were willing to be contacted. Second, Heifer had a concrete list of several hundred individuals with their URLs and their interest in helping on the campaign.

The organization successfully engaged more than 150 of those individuals in a pilot blog-raising campaign—in which individuals used their blogs and social spaces to solicit donations for Heifer from readers and friends. By the end of the campaign, the number of participating blograisers reached nearly four hundred.

Heifer used surveys once again at the completion of the program to find out what the participants did and did not like about their experience. They also asked participants what motivated them to undertake the effort and what they learned from it. All of this input was then used to improve the next generation of the program.

Fortunately, the marketplace has shifted tremendously since 2006. Organizations are demanding greater visibility into this mystery and, in response, the systems, vendors, and consultants are actively working toward meeting this need for ongoing, systematic cross-channel analysis. Until the "seamless integration" is realized and the reports and tools to leverage the data become available to a broader range of the market, many organizations will continue to struggle with data pulled from different channels and systems and how to get the analysis done. There is no quick fix for this challenge, but there are ways to take advantage of the opportunity.

*Hire professionals.* If your organization can afford to do so, hire the staff, a reputable vendor, or a consultant who can take your data sets and produce meaningful cross-channel analysis. Make sure your effort includes both the conducting of the analysis and a focus on how to improve data collection practices to increase the knowledge gained from future efforts.

*Track where you can.* Where you control the advertising on TV, radio, or print, use marketing URLs or provide codes for your promotions, or both. Although many people will still go through your main page, alternative URLs tied to particular ads or channels can yield some insights. For example, many child sponsorship organizations use wholly different URLs for different TV ad spots to track creative and monitor traffic during ad buy periods.

*Cross-channel communications calendar spike monitoring.* Match significant events from your cross-channel communications calendar to your web traffic and engagements. These enable you to see whether there are spikes timed to the days or hour of an offline event.

*Matchback analysis.* For direct-mail fundraising, in particular, matching back online donors to the list of those who were part of a prospect, renewal, or special appeal campaign provides an indicator of who your "channel-switchers" are and how big a portion of your donations and donors this represents.

*eCRM to donor database data exchange.* With more and more organizations passing summary data about online engagement from their eCRM tools into their donor database of record, and vice versa, the potential to draw on this data for meaningful cross-channel analysis improves. Although integrated data may not definitively indicate what really influenced the individual to act, the analysis can provide greater visibility into who is in relationship with the organization across channels and allow a more strategic design to messaging. Nonprofits are using the specific values in marketing—such as the highest previous contribution (HPC) to personalize ask amounts—but also the mere presence of a value (for example, learning that a person is a volunteer and an advocate to include in a cultivation email). Here are a few of the more meaningful aggregated data points that organizations are exploring for the value they provide in shaping their programs and tactics:

- HPC, most recent gift, and frequency of giving (the classic RFM data points)

- Cumulative giving (last twelve months and lifetime)

- Years as a constituent (separate figures for being an activist, donor, volunteer, and so on)

- Number of online actions taken in the last twelve months (typically includes separate figures for advocacy, surveys, and other major actions)

- Email responsiveness (rating based on regularity of opening email and clicking through)

- Connection to the organization through a social network

- Referred friends

Leveraging these data points requires creating the reports that integrate these elements into your view of your constituents.

*Limited-purpose analysis.* Comprehensive analysis or data exchange is not necessarily required to analyze specific cross-channel tests or more limited scope analysis. If you define up front what data you will need to accomplish the analysis, you can ensure that it will be there on the back end when the testing needs be done. For example, you can test whether an email sent before or after a phone call or mail piece has an impact so long as both online and offline reporting systems are cleanly tracking the participants, segmenting the efforts, and coding the responses. It is not terribly difficult to determine the donor value of people whose first gift came from online ads versus email asks, so long as you have sourced the origin of that first gift online and can pull those individuals and all their subsequent giving history together for number crunching.

*Ask your constituents.* Where hard data may not be accessible or the analysis effort is too onerous, consider asking your constituents what you seek to know directly. Pull-down lists on submission forms can be highly useful in a directional way. The responses to questions like "How did you first hear about us?" "What brought you to our site today?" and "What motivated you to take this action today?" are revealing, especially when tracked over time to see changes in trends. However, be cautious not to overread into the responses—take into account both the inherent limitations to the structuring of these and the user interpretation of the question when they self-report.

The tools and techniques for ongoing, systematic cross-channel analysis are still emerging. Fortunately, organizations can be clever and resourceful in finding alternative ways like these to shed some light on their program.

## Listen to What They Are Saying About You

The Internet is a wonderful thing. People will talk about *anything* on discussion lists, blogs, in social networks, and on websites—including your organization. You can't control this dialogue, but you can embrace it as a reality and seek to learn from it, if not outright participate in the discussion.

It is impossible to monitor everything said about your organization or your issues, but here are four suggestions for how to tap into the conversation that is going on about your organization on the Internet:

- *Automated content search:* As mentioned earlier, create a Yahoo! Pipe or use another content feed service to automatically tell you what new things are being posted on blogs, published on websites, in social media, and the like that match keywords you enter into these tools.

- *Blog search:* Search tools like Technorati's Watchlist let you create a search and save it, making it simple to get a daily or weekly check into what's being said in the blogosphere.

- *Discussion list mining:* Several companies have developed software and services for mining discussion lists for conversations about your organization and compiling those into summary reports of new issues and trends. Simpler tools like BoardTracker will deliver alerts to you when discussion lists mention your key terms.

- *RSS feeds:* Google, Digg, Reddit, and many other search and social tagging sites offer RSS feeds based on your search terms. These are far more efficient than typing your terms into every property each day. As you become familiar with the specific websites, blogs, and networks that your constituents frequent, or that mention you often, you can subscribe to the RSS feeds from those properties to monitor the conversations about your organization and more generally what is being covered. This context can be helpful in understanding your constituents' interests.

Here is a practical example of how monitoring the dialogue about your organization can help you capitalize on those conversations.

## Case Study: ACLU

In January 2008, the ACLU's director of website communications, Eric Schoenborn, was planning the web outreach for a campaign to commemorate the sixth anniversary of the arrival of prisoners at Guantanamo Bay. Bloggers had been critical voices speaking to issues of torture and indefinite detention, and as the anniversary neared the ACLU wanted to provide incentive for bloggers to continue this discussion.

The ACLU knew these blogs attracted the profile of constituents they wanted as members and activists. With the anniversary and accompanying campaign sure to increase chatter on a core issue for the ACLU, they saw a chance to "recruit while the iron is hot." Their objective: introduce the readers of these other blogs to the ACLU's blog and get them to become regular consumers directly from the ACLU. The ACLU executed a threefold strategy to attract the readers of the third-party blogs to the ACLU.

With the help of Henry Copeland at blogads.com, the ACLU placed a series of innovative blog ad buys with the targeted blogs. The ad investments themselves piqued the interest of the blog owners. Many bloggers rely on their advertising to keep blogging, so they pay attention to who is advertising and on what. Some will use their blog posts to give a "shout out" to their advertiser's issues.

The second key activity was conducting blogger outreach directly through email, by commenting on bloggers' posts and using other techniques to increase blogger awareness of the ACLU blog and its content. The result: the top bloggers began commenting on the ACLU's posts and mentioning their blog in their posts.

The third tactic was the use of an innovative new technique created by blogads .com—dynamically inserting the title of a blog post from a third-party blog relevant to the ACLU's issue. By inserting the blog post title from third-party bloggers, the ACLU gave visibility to those bloggers talking about the ACLU while at the same time promoting the ACLU's own blog as the focus of the ad.

The result: bloggers increased their mentions of the ACLU's posts in an effort to get their blog post titles into the ACLU ads. Readers saw both the ads with constantly updating headlines and more and more blog posts about the ACLU's issue around the blogosphere. Within a week, the ACLU tripled unique visitors to their blog, and overall site traffic increased 20 percent. By monitoring the marketplace for who was talking about them and their issues, the ACLU was able to grab the attention of consumers of other blogs and bring their attention to their own blog.

## Perform Trend and Benchmarking Studies

Staying abreast of broader nonprofit sector and Internet industry trends and benchmarks provides a tremendously important context for comparing, interpreting, and predicting your constituents' online behavior. Nonprofit data-driven studies on trends and benchmarks are too few. Despite this, the effort to stay abreast is invaluable for the information discovered. Here are examples of some reliable and time-tested sources for good studies.

## Sources for Benchmarking Studies

**NTEN:** Usually the first to know about reputable studies, and the organization is working to increase the frequency and visibility of research.

**Other Associations:** Consistent publishers and promoters of relevant research, include organizations like American Marketing Association, Direct Marketing Association, and ASAE, among others.

**RSS Searches:** By configuring a Google RSS search feed for nonprofit research and white papers, you can surface consultants' white papers, vendors' reports, and other contributors' data analysis that you may not otherwise hear about. Do the same on Technorati to monitor the blogs of nonprofit thought leaders.

**Pew Internet & American Life Project:** Found at www.pewinternet.org, this project of the Pew Charitable Trust regularly publishes reports on online behavior and technology adoption. From social tagging to rich media use, uses of email to types of actions taken online, Pew Internet & American Life covers it.

**Applicable Commercial Sites:** There is a proliferation of sites one could follow for online trends in user behavior. Some of the more useful sites are Sherpa-Marketing, MarketingProfs, Nielsen BuzzMetrics, and Media Post.

These are just a start. Usually the best sources for trends can be found by asking those around you who are knowledgeable: what lists do they belong to, what feeds do they follow, which sites do they regularly visit to stay abreast of the trends?

## Monitor Your Progress

This chapter began with objectives and baselines; so too shall it end. Monitoring your progress against your baselines must be an ongoing discipline. This does not have to be a daily discipline for everything, but rather a regularity appropriate to the objectives you are tracking. Given the breadth of what's possible, here is a general guide for how frequently to monitor various metrics:

### DAILY:

- Abnormal spikes in comments and negative events (such as unsubscribe requests)
- Results as they come in from multivariate tests, promotional messaging (emails, ads, and so on), and survey responses, to spot actionable results as they emerge
- Content feeds through RSS, Yahoo! Pipes, and the like
- Social network, blog, social tagging, and discussion list activity
- Web logs for significant shifts in key words, referrers, or traffic patterns

### WEEKLY:

- Trailing charts and rates for priority engagement actions
- Multivariate test results, survey results, campaign reports, email reports, and so on for efforts completed that week
- Cross-channel calendar matching
- Significant changes in new constituent behaviors

### MONTHLY:

- Macro growth changes, such as list size, network size, opt-out rates
- Constituent engagement metrics (such as retention rates and multi-action rates)

For most organizations, the frequency of monitoring will be determined primarily by the nature of the metric and the time and expense required to support that frequency. No matter what your resources, it is far better to monitor your progress on your objectives against a few key metrics less frequently than to do no monitoring at all.

## Revisit Your Strategies and Objectives

A high-performing online program monitors constituent inputs and analyzes trends daily, weekly, and monthly. Staff do not wait for the "annual strategic planning process" to make the changes in the program when the data reveals something must be done today. For example, when retention of new constituents is an objective, identifying a decline in the rate of new constituents who are converting to action takers requires aggressive testing of techniques to reverse that trend. Your organization may need to rethink a year-long program designed to expand your social network for fundraising if, six months into the program, the revenue results are dismal and the prospects for a turn-around bleak. You will need to reexamine the program with the larger picture in mind: "Does the network itself and its nonmonetary benefits add value to our organization, engage our constituents, and support other objectives such that we should continue?"

The process of regularly reviewing progress and evaluating the strategies and tactics of your program has an inherent shortcoming. There is a natural tendency, in this examination, to skew resources and attention for the future toward the highest-performing portions of the program or toward repeating what worked the last time. The failure of a single test or a pilot program may scuttle an initiative. But failures along the way are not necessarily a reason to abandon a chosen path. If you have done your homework and your constituent research demonstrates a viable market, then learn from the failures, adjust your tactics, and try again.

Businesses—including nonprofits—are continually changing the ways they market themselves, conduct business, share knowledge, and create social change as ever-increasing bandwidth, storage, and the pace of technology innovation enable better ways to build their lists. In response, consumers try, and eventually adopt and use, those tools, sites, networks, or widgets that fulfill their needs best. Charting your way through this evolving landscape requires a clear sense of direction and constant evaluation of the steps you are taking and who is following your path. It can be easy to lose your way in the Wild Wild Web, but if you do the work, the knowledge you gain about where your constituents are online and what they are doing with your organization will lead the way.

# CHAPTER 9

# Effective Online Communications

*John Kenyon*

Imagine your online communications are kept attractive, accurate, coordinated, and up-to-date in only hours a month. Fresh, engaging content flows like water, bringing a steady stream of new and returning visitors. Your every fundraising, educational, or advocacy campaign's online components spark throngs to action. You are safe in the knowledge that you have a plan flexible enough to keep you nimble yet solid enough to keep you prepared and help you weather unexpected challenges.

All this is achievable for nonprofits with the right planning—along with knowledge, skills, and the will to improve.

The Internet has effectively erased time and geography for nonprofit organizations. Online, your nonprofit is open twenty-four hours a day, seven days a week, with no geographic boundaries. People from around the world can learn about issues, take action, and increase their involvement with any size organization, regardless of location. To remain competitive and relevant in this context, the burden is on you to communicate effectively online via your website (or sites) and electronic communications.

In this chapter we explore the essentials of successful nonprofit communications, including planning, engagement, effective websites, email, tracking activity, and learning from results. I am confident that by learning about these important concepts and seeing examples of them in action, you will be able to get closer to the communications utopia just described.

## Preparing for Online Communications

To be successful with online communications, it is essential to create plans, to know how to turn those plans into action, to understand the importance of listening, and to accurately assess your organization's capacity.

### Planning to Succeed

Just like in-person and print mediums, websites and email are merely channels for communications. Organizations get the most out of these channels when they make them part of a larger communications plan. To be successful, communications efforts must fit into the larger context of an organization's strategic, fundraising, advocacy, technology, and other related plans. If your organization does not have clear goals and plans in these areas, this is where you need to start. Your communications plan relies heavily on your goals and strategies for achieving your mission, maintaining a healthy organization, raising money or awareness, educating, or any other core activities. Without these plans to strategically align communications, you are, as the saying goes, "planning to fail."

Developing mission-aligned communication goals is the first step for organizations who want to improve their online communications. Articulate a vision for communications along with overarching organizational communication goals, then develop more specific goals—internal and external, strategic and operational, online and offline. Articulating these goals makes the process of creating and managing online communications much simpler and lets staff understand how to focus organizational resources. The goals serve as guideposts when deciding what elements, tools, and content to include in online messaging activities. They also help prevent organizations from wasting resources on communications that don't support their goals.

Here's an example of how goals and an organization's mission can align:

- *Vision:* In support of our mission to promote civil rights, [Organization Name] communicates creatively and responsively with our constituents. Along with communicating stories about our past, present and future, we listen to and learn from all of our communities.

- *Goals:* We will connect our various communities by providing a variety of safe forums for discourse and tools that support effective communications.

  *Goal 1:* To actively coordinate all online and offline communications.

  *Goal 2:* To use the strengths of the online medium to support all organizational goals, including fundraising, volunteering, and education.

  *Goal 3:* To collaborate with each department to assess how the elements of the communication plan relate specifically to the work of the department.

  Mission → Vision → Goals → Plans (Strategies, Tactics)

Without plans, you are making your job much more difficult when it comes to designing your website and online communications, choosing what content to collect and use, what functionality you want, and especially selecting appropriate tools such as bulk email management tools.

## Turning Goals into Action

Plans are essential, but how do you turn them into action? How do you "operationalize" those goals? Based on the goals, specific operational strategies need to be articulated. For example, if an organizational goal is to share success stories, there may be internal and external strategies for collecting and distributing those stories as well as when and where to communicate them. An organization might adopt a strategy whereby every month one program person is responsible for a five-hundred-word story about a success. That story is then circulated internally to give staff a chance to provide feedback or to add content. Once feedback and any additional content are incorporated, the story is published in a specific section or sections of the website and may even be used in an enewsletter or email campaign. The impact of that content is then tracked and evaluated based on user behavior and the information gleaned is used to improve future communications. Plan operationalized!

## The Importance of Listening

The primary elements of effective online communications are a website and email (including text messaging), but there are others. If staff members post comments to other websites or blogs, that is another form of online communications that reflects on the organization. If others write articles or post comments about your organization, that also becomes part of what is being communicated online. Obviously, you can't control what others write, but you can certainly respond. You can only respond, however, if you are listening. As we will see in this chapter, half of being successful communicating online is listening. This includes paying attention to which pages on your website people visit most or least, which links in your emails people click on—or don't—and what others are saying or are not saying about you online.

## Organizational Capacity: Are You Ready?

Although this chapter is not an operational "how-to" guide to websites and email, we will touch on some important related operational practices to be aware of beyond planning and listening.

*Managing content.* No matter the size of your website or volume of email, you must manage the content they contain. Both text and image content must be selected, collected, produced, formatted, and edited. Organizations that have some sort of offline publishing process (print newsletter, annual report, and so on) already have the capabilities of collecting and publishing content. Organizations that currently have no such process will need to develop that capacity.

*Managing data.* Data management is the other essential practice necessary to the success of online communication efforts. This includes data on who wants to receive which kind(s) of communications, the areas of your mission that stakeholders are interested in, and metrics indicating the content that holds the most (and least) interest for stakeholders. Without good data management practices and tools, truly effective online communication isn't possible. I regularly advise people, "If you don't love your current database, start divorce proceedings, start dating other databases, and find one that is a good match to your needs."

*Human resources.* This is perhaps the most important readiness factor. It is nearly impossible to succeed without a person designated to manage everything that online communication efforts entail. It can be challenging for that person to succeed without the knowledge and skills necessary. This means that your organization must provide the training, mentoring, and consulting support necessary for success.

*Time.* Internet communications are so immediate that organizations often fail to plan enough time to properly conceive of and implement website and email strategies. Email may be instantaneous, but good campaigns are not. You need to give your staff the time to learn about good practices and tools, craft plans, investigate options and strategies, and track the effectiveness of their efforts.

*Money.* Online communications don't have to be expensive to be effective, but they will cost money. You need to plan to pay for the resources you don't already have, including staff, email and content management tools, website development, hosting, and expert advice.

## The Meaning of Engagement

Online engagement encompasses all of an organization's online activities and communications focused on engaging stakeholders. The foundational elements of these activities are the website or sites and email or text communications, but they can also include content posted on other websites, like video and photos (YouTube, Flickr), profiles (MySpace, Facebook), articles, listserv or blog posts, and any other "official" organizational content posted online.

A website and email are essential elements in moving people up the "ladder of engagement." Traditionally, organizations try to attract prospects, engage them so they become supporters, get them to commit through an action, and then retain them (see James Greenfield's *Nonprofit Handbook* for a description of the traditional "ladder of engagement"). The same is true online, but you are using different tools.

To attract prospects, organizations must drive traffic to their websites and attract new email subscribers. The best site in the world won't attract visitors without strategies to drive traffic, which we will discuss a little later. Once traffic is being driven, email addresses need to be collected, as email is the only way to stay in touch with prospects who visit a website. Prospects are then engaged through regular email contact and by providing web content that interests them. Once engaged, actual supporters are identified when they take an online action, whether it be making a donation, registering for an event, or signing a petition. To keep those supporters committed calls for more personalized email and web communications that speak directly to each stakeholder's interests and allowing each stakeholder to speak directly to your organization in some form.

## Effective Websites

One of my favorite clients, the Sisters of Notre Dame de Namur, California Province, were contacted out of the blue by a funder who offered them $40,000 based solely on information about a naming opportunity found on their website. This was a funder that they had never heard of and would not have thought to contact, but by having an effective website they were able to attract and receive that funding. Without an effective website, this would have been a lost opportunity—and they would not even have known that they lost it. This example may sound like a long shot, but consider the number of new potential donors who are coming to your site every day. When they arrive, your online presence carries the full responsibility of securing their support. If no additional funds are needed by your organization, this may not be a concern, but most organizations cannot afford to miss funding opportunities.

An effective website can engage new and existing stakeholders, strengthen the personal relationships that are at the heart of fundraising, increase organizational credibility, and bring in financial and other resources.

An ineffective website can turn off new and existing stakeholders and weaken both the personal relationships you've built and your credibility— it can even harm your chances of receiving much-needed resources.

## The Four Cornerstones of Effective Websites

There are four main characteristics of an effective website: credibility, cultivation, clickability, and content.

### Credibility

Your website has the job of showing that the organization is credible— it is the public face of the organization. Many supporters don't get to meet staff members or satisfied clients in person; it is up to your website to communicate their stories. Information about operations, staff, events, constituents, partnerships, and finances all contribute to a perception of a credible organization. Information about past events and initiatives also contributes to credibility, so have summaries of them with appropriate related images.

As reported in the *Chronicle of Philanthropy*, only about 20 percent of people feel that nonprofits do a good job with the money they are given. So how do you combat this overwhelmingly negative perception? One important tactic is to be as open as possible about your finances, especially online. Include financial data from your annual report, charts and graphs showing where money comes from and where it goes, and specifics about what you accomplish, as shown in the Mercy Corps examples of Exhibits 9.1 and 9.2.

### Cultivation

When thinking about the language and tone of a website, I always suggest that organizations ask themselves "Does our website have its arms open?" Does your website use inviting language that cultivates relationships and engagement, such as "Join Our Work," "Become Part of the Solution," "Work with Us to . . ."? Or does your website simply make

## Exhibit 9.1. Mercy Corps Home Page Content.

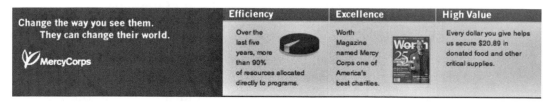

## Exhibit 9.2. Mercy Corps Website.

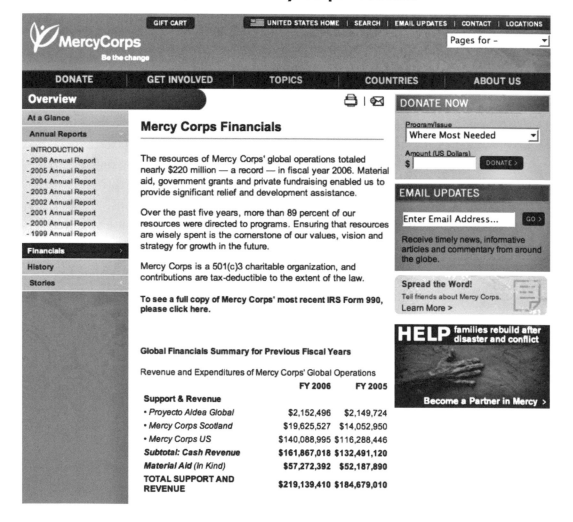

statements—"This is what we do, these are our programs, and you should help"? This tone is not very engaging or supportive of establishing and maintaining a relationship.

You want to increase people's interest in being involved with your cause(s) and their depth of understanding about what you do and how you do it. Visitors come to your site to learn and then to act—are you encouraging action and making it easy for them to donate or take other actions? Using positive language is also emerging as a best practice. People are interested in issues but are more often motivated by solutions. How can you highlight your successes and the progress you are making?

Exhibit 9.3 shows the use of positive and inviting language on a website's home page. Language used includes "solutions," "we are succeeding," and "we can solve . . ."

### Exhibit 9.3. The We Campaign Home Page.

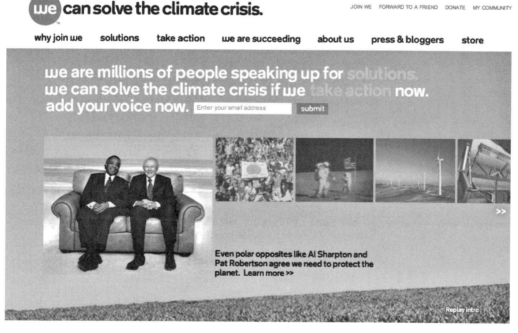

## Clickability

Providing different types of information and interactive elements that a visitor can click on make a website more engaging, appealing, and interesting. Clicking is a kinesthetic experience that mimics a conversation. Can your website carry your half of the conversation? A conversation might go something like this:

"Hi, what does your organization do?"

"We support children at risk through programs for children, parents, and grandparents."

"I am interested in your programs for parents."

*Click* to the Parents program overview page: "We have programs for adoptive parents, parents of teenagers, and general parenting skills."

"I am interested in your parenting skills program."

*Click* to the parenting skills program page: "We have evening and weekend programs in various local areas."

"Several of these would work for me; first I'd like to know about the Saturday program in my town."

*Click* to the page with Saturday programs, times, location information, and signup form.

Beyond carrying on a conversation, clickability also provides the website visitor with a variety of options for interacting with the organization. This calls for clear navigation to make the options easy to find. These interactive options can include surveys, quizzes, maps, community discussion areas, video, audio, games, and many others. The goal is to have options that match the varied interests of your visitors—and that are easy to find.

In the example in Exhibit 9.4, there are many clickable items that link to information about the issues of focus, current work in those areas, successes, positions on issues, ways to help, a photo contest, and even a podcast.

## Exhibit 9.4. The Nature Conservancy Home Page.

The mission of The Nature Conservancy is **to preserve** the plants, animals and natural communities that represent **the diversity of life on Earth** by protecting the lands and waters they need to survive.

SAVING THE LAST GREAT PLACES ON EARTH

Search [GO]

How We Work | Where We Work | News Room | About Us | Great Places Network

**great places** NETWORK

JOIN NOW >> | FREE

**how you can help**
donate online
renew membership
estate planning
gift ideas
volunteer
activities
merchandise
magazine
conservation science
e-newsletter

*Nature Conservancy* magazine

Read highlights from the **Spring 2007 issue** and find out how you can subscribe.

**Future.**

**Photo Contest Winners Coming Soon!** See the winners of our 2006 digital photo competition here on Thursday, Feb. 22. And check out the entries on the Conservancy's Flickr™ group!

**Air Potatoes?**

It's a vine, it's a tuber...it's a dangerous invasive plant. Learn more about the air potato and how we're fighting its spread.

**2007 Farm Bill**

The 2007 Farm Bill could be a crucial tool for conservation in the United States. Hear what we'd like to see in the Farm Bill.

**Turned a River**

Nevada's Truckee River was nearly dead. Read how the Conservancy led the fight to turn the river and bring it back to life.

**Nature Stories**

Angel's Landing in Zion National Park seems just like a place angels would alight. Climb up with us in this new podcast.

## Content

Content is the most important of these four elements, and it requires regular input. Creating a great website is practically pointless if the content is not updated on a regular basis. Nothing destroys an organization's credibility and stakeholders' feelings of confidence like a website whose main item announces an event that happened three months ago or whose content never changes. Since the website is a reflection of the organization, if the content is "asleep," visitors will likely get the impression that the organization itself is not awake.

As discussed earlier, an effective website provides multiple levels of information on an organization's activities. From a broad description of the organization's focus, to information on specific program areas, down to the detail of exactly how those programs work, who runs them, and who participates in them, it is best to have a depth of information so that visitors can find both broad and specific information. Consider making available a variety of information, including statistics, data, downloadable documents, and biographical information. Using a content management system (CMS) can help make updating content easier to manage.

The content must be not only fresh but also well organized. Websites need clear, consistent navigation elements to make finding various information as easy and intuitive as possible. Usability testing and

## Technology Heads-Up: Content Management Systems

Content Management Systems are software packages that assist in the management of website content. Rather than using HTML code to program a website, code line by code line, most content management systems use an interface similar to that found in most popular word processing programs; this opens up content management to those not familiar with HTML.

Another benefit of these systems is that they allow distributed publishing. Rather than all website updates being funneled through one person, responsibility for managing content can be shared by many people in the organization. With the proper setup, these systems allow specific sections and pages to be updated by the appropriate person: development staff can update the development-related pages, program staff the program-related pages, and so on. Most systems also provide additional functionality such as blogs, wikis, and other community tools. This distributed publishing requires that an editorial function be created to make sure the right tone, language, and even facts are used. This editor is often also the "approver" who approves and posts the content contributed by the various authors after it is reviewed.

providing a place for feedback on the site are good ways to gather data on ways to improve the site's organization.

The site shown in Exhibit 9.5, for example, has clear navigation and a variety of rich content that is regularly updated from podcasts and videos to slideshows, downloadable reports, and event registration.

### Exhibit 9.5. The Doctors Without Borders Home Page.

## Seven Considerations for Highly Effective Websites

Beyond the four foundational considerations, there are seven other important considerations that affect a website's ability to communicate, its interactivity, and its "stickiness"—that ability to keep visitors at the site.

## Audience

Unless you are Honda or Google, your audience is not everyone. Identify your top three or four audiences and what they want and need from the site. For example, if a primary audience is younger people, is your use of language appropriate to that audience? Can they get your website updates sent to their phone via text message? Does the organization have a presence on sites with heavy youth traffic like MySpace, pointing to further content on the website?

## Outside-In Language

Look at your site's language from the *outside in*, not from the *inside out*. Use language and terms that anyone can understand. Using acronyms like IOC, UVT, and COS in navigation or content distances visitors from an organization, so find terms that mean something to people on the outside. Along these lines, the layout and language used must be appropriate for the audiences. If you deal with complex issues, find ways of clearly explaining what you do first before going into the complexities.

## Content Styling

Content comes from a variety of sources, but it does not work to simply insert content designed and formatted for print publications. People rarely *read* websites; they *scan* them. So to be successful, your content must be as scannable as possible. Make content more online-appropriate by using highlighted keywords, bulleted lists, and lots of links. Keep to one concept per paragraph as well.

## Fresh Content

If your website content isn't fresh, your organization looks stale. Make sure you have a strategy for routinely getting new content up on your site. In addition to setting up a schedule for staff to create content, you can recycle or rotate existing content, or republish content from various news sites (check their attribution policies).

## Accessibility

People whose sight, hearing, or physical movement is impaired often use special tools to navigate the Internet. Blind or visually impaired visitors may use a content reader that speaks the content of your site to them. If a site is not accessibly designed, you may be making this a much more difficult task for those visitors. Ensure that your site is built within accessibility standards so you eliminate this roadblock to people's ability to use your site. An excellent collection of information on accessibility can be found at http://www.w3.org.

## Encourage Action

As noted earlier, people come to your website to learn and then to act. To get people to take an action online, they must be asked or persuaded, and it must be easy for them to take the action. A site that doesn't indicate a need for donations anywhere but on the donation page is not "making the ask." The same is true whether you are trying to promote volunteering, advocacy, or any other activity. Ask visitors to take the actions desired and give them compelling reasons to act. Provide tools that make these actions easy, like online donation tools, event registration tools, and email sign-up tools.

## Policies

Have your policies posted on your site in clear language. Especially important is your privacy policy. This tells people who provide you with personal information exactly what you will do with that information, such as email or physical addresses, phone numbers, and especially credit card information. Other policies to have clearly stated, often referred to as "terms of use," cover the kinds of content you allow visitors to post in comments to articles, blogs, or other content, as well as who owns submitted content. (See http://www.etrust.org/ for more ideas and information.)

## How the Eco-Grinch Stole Christmas

In December 2007, Earthjustice launched an online year-end giving campaign based on their work to move energy beyond coal. During the campaign planning, staff came up with the idea of sending a lump of coal to the people who are the top environmental polluters—the "Eco-Grinches" of the year. Initially, they thought they might send a virtual lump of coal to the polluters or to get constituents to send e-cards of coal to those polluters. Unfortunately, most of the decision makers use online forms to allow people to contact them, rather than public email addresses, so this was not feasible. Earthjustice came up with the idea to set up an online poll and ask people to vote for the biggest grinches. They sent an email to their supporters and explained that they would send the "winner" a virtual lump of coal and let them know they were the Eco-Grinch of the year.

The results were remarkable. More than twelve thousand people responded—shattering records from all of Earthjustice's previous online polls. The traffic was almost four hundred times the volume of responses that they had had on any similar initiative. This greatly exceeded expectations and resulted in a huge audience engagement. Interestingly, Earthjustice didn't do a press release or any PR work for this campaign, so there wasn't any media coverage, but there was still a great response. They also received over 150 letters and many emails talking about other people who should be on the list or why someone voted for a certain person. The campaign not only drove a lot of traffic to Earthjustice's site, but the visitors often spent more time on the site having some fun, and even donating. The campaign also aligned nicely with their year-end fundraising campaign about coal. Although previously Earthjustice had seen advocacy, awareness, and fundraising campaigns as disparate, this campaign showed the connection among those areas.

## How to Drive Traffic to Your Website

You can't expect to drive thousands of people to your site overnight, but you can increase your traffic significantly by focusing on a few small basics:

• Have a distinct and succinct web address (URL).

• Promote your URL everywhere—in print, in person, and at events.

• Participate in online communities where you can recommend content on your site.

• Link to partners and appropriate outside content.

• Link back to your site in emails and enewsletters.

## Effective Email Communications

In his "Gilbert Email Manifesto," Michael Gilbert states that email communication is more important than a website to an organization. (Although this is generally accurate, it may not be true if you are just beginning to build an email list or are an organization, like a university admissions office, whose website and application form are more important than email, because you don't have the email addresses of those prospective students!) Another truism is that websites alone don't raise money—emails do. These ideas underscore how essential email is when thinking about online communications. Without effective email communications, organizations are seriously hindered in engaging their stakeholders.

Email and enewsletters can tap the power of the community, as people can pass on messages to people in their networks which is a much stronger tie than just happening upon a website. Not only do people usually respond quickly—80 percent within forty-eight to seventy-two hours[1]—but they also pass on email more often than they make an online donation. In addition, email has a higher response rate than direct mail[2] and usually costs about two-thirds less than direct mail.[3] The quality of these messages is vital, as people will only respond to and pass on emails with compelling messages.

## Effective Enewsletters

Enewsletters come with their own techniques for effectiveness. Effective newsletters have one to several short blurbs and related images, both designed to entice the reader to click through to the full story on your website. The aims are to inform, motivate action, and drive traffic to the website. Here are a few elements common to effective newsletters:

*An easy-to-read table of contents.* This lets readers know quickly what is in the newsletter and allows them to find the content that sparks their interest.

*Consistent look and feel.* You want readers to recognize your brand at a glance.

*Tease the content.* Craft an enticing "teaser" to get readers to click on a link to get the full story on your site.

*Write for readers to scan.* People don't usually read word for word online as they do in print, so use keywords, bulleted or numbered lists, and other techniques to make the content easy to scan and digest.

*Be regular.* Establish a regular schedule for your enewsletter and stick to it! Don't promise a weekly or monthly enewsletter if you have never created one.

## Four Cornerstones to Effective Email Campaigns

Email is most effective as a communications tool for organizations when it is personal, targeted, integrated with other communications strategies, and trackable.

### Personal

Personalizing content can go a long way to help the reader feel important to the organization. "Dear Juan, Thank you for your $1,000 gift on May 2nd" is much more personal than "Dear donor, Thank you for your recent gift." Collect and maintain as much information as you can about your stakeholders so that you can use this personal information to appeal to them directly. This will have the short-term effect of increasing response to your messages and the long-term effect of keeping that individual subscribed to your lists.

You can also make email more personal with your tone. If you are writing to a younger audience, write emails that are more casual and use language that appeals to that demographic (without pandering, of course). If you are writing to a group of lawyers or academics, you might use a more serious tone.

## Targeted

To accurately target your email communications, it is important that you have the ability to segment your list. Beyond just address or donor level, this requires having fields in your database to indicate which programs or efforts a person is most interested in, along with other relevant information that you identify as useful.

The ASPCA famously showed the importance of segmentation when they sent *almost* identical emails to cat owners and dog owners. For cat owners, they included cats in the email subject line and had a picture of a cat; for dog owners, dogs were mentioned in the subject line and the email had a picture of a dog. For those they didn't know about, they sent an email mentioning dogs and cats with pictures of both in the email. From the targeted recipients they saw responses increase— 230 percent from donors and 86 percent from non-donors. Knowing your constituents' interests and passions as related to your organization can make a significant impact on your communications success.

## Integrated

Communicating via email is part of relationship cultivation. If your friend Kim calls you only when she needs money and never tells you what she did with the last $100 you gave her, or how much she appreciates it, unless you are a saint you likely aren't motivated to continue the relationship. The same is true for your stakeholders. Provide a mix of email content, including update-only emails with no donation requests, straight fundraising or advocacy campaigns, and enewsletters with "soft" asks—for example, "To help us do more work like this, click here." Offer up a variety of content via email just as you do on a website, and make sure that the look, feel and tone of these communications all mimic your website and your other communications. This integration is key to building the brand of your issues and your organization.

Although it may seem that the whole world has gone digital, now is not the time to give up on direct mail and other communications strategies. When radio first came out, in the early twentieth century, it was said that newspapers would disappear because everyone could get their news for free via the radio, but almost a century later newspapers are still around. Keep doing what works for your organization; just be sure to integrate email into your campaigns thoughtfully.

### Trackable

In the days before email an organization would send out their mailings and over six to eight weeks or more responses would come in. The organizations could never know what subject in the letter a reader was particularly interested in or wanted more information about, what content triggered their donation, or even whether the letter was opened or put right into the trash. Email can tell you all of that and more.

Most email systems can tell you a lot about what your stakeholders are doing with your email. You need to track how many people are opening your messages, clicking on links, or forwarding the message. Track these metrics to learn what excites your stakeholders, and what doesn't, so you can adjust your communications appropriately.

## Six Considerations for Effective Email

Beyond the four foundational considerations, here are six other important considerations that can increase the effectiveness of your email communications:

- *Respect your subscriber.* You must have "Do Not Email" and/or "Do Not Send Enewsletter" fields in your database, and provide a way for anyone to unsubscribe in every email. If you have both email campaigns and enewsletters, have fields in your database that can indicate preferences for email and enews so people can opt to receive either one or both. Not respecting the request of a stakeholder is a quick and easy way to lose that person forever.

## Technology Heads-Up: Email Software

Bulk email systems are online software vendors that send bulk email for your organization. Their features vary, but generally they will do the following:

- Create a database of email addresses
- Allow you to conduct email campaigns (send bulk personalized email)
- Provide the functionality that allows you to put a "Subscribe to Our Newsletter" function on your website
- Allow recipients to unsubscribe and subscribe to email lists
- Let you send both text and HTML emails (some even have HTML templates)

Key elements to look for in email systems:

- A clear spam prevention policy
- Good Internet service provider (ISP) relationships
- Ability to set "To," "From," and "Reply "addresses
- Easy subscribe and unsubscribe
- Automatic removal of unsubscribes and bounces
- Subscription confirmation option
- Easy-to-understand user interface
- Ability to segment list
- Trackable URLs so you can analyze email recipient behavior
- HTML sniffer to detect whether to send the HTML or text version of a message to each email address

See the Idealware report "A Few Good Email Tools" for some email software options.[4]

- *Maintain an email privacy policy.* Have and post an email privacy policy on your website and linked prominently from your email signup page.

- *Build your lists the right way.* Never rent or buy email lists. For email lists to be useful and high quality, you must build them one interested person at a time. Always *ask for* and *document* permission to email. If you can, tell subscribers specifically what they will get and with what frequency (our weekly e-update, our monthly newsletter, and so on).

- *Make the "envelope" of your email compelling.* Your subject line should be descriptive, catchy, and urgent, without being alarmist. The "From" name in the email should be a real name and email address rather than a generic organization mailbox address. Avoid punctuation and sensational language as that can trigger spam alerts.

- *Select HTML over text.* The benefits of HTML email far outweigh the effort of producing it. HTML emails look better, instantly identify the email with your brand, more closely match the graphic look of your website, and are more likely to be clicked on.

- *Test out different email programs.* Different email systems will interpret the format of your email differently, so sign up for free accounts from a variety of clients (Yahoo, Google, MSN, and the like), and send your emails to those addresses first to see what your readers will see. Send out emails to a small group of staff or board members before sending to the general public to catch any errors the author may have missed.

## Evaluation, Metrics, and Benchmarks

So now you have nice site with good content, and you're routinely driving traffic to it. All the pieces are now in place, which means it's time to find out which parts of your plan are working and which need adjusting. Once content is being managed well and systems are in place for driving traffic to the website, how do you know how which parts of your plan are working and which need adjusting? By using evaluation, metrics, and benchmarks.

Evaluating activity and tracking online metrics is a new process and skill for most organizations. It is essential to your success in online communications that you incorporate this activity into your process and build skills in this area. Metrics provide some of the most valuable partnership and marketing data you can find because they accurately benchmark what people really care about. By evaluating this activity and learning from it, you can improve your online communications based on data. By learning through tracking, you will reach the sectors you really want and serve up programs that keep people coming back. Without tracking, you are likely just repeating the same mistakes and ineffective strategies.

## What to Track

There are myriad pieces of data you can collect about what people are doing on your web site and with your emails. To use these statistics in the most efficient and effective way, begin with the business questions that are most important to your organization. These questions will guide you through which data to look at, limit the amount of time spent on the tasks, and let you focus on the most important data.

For example, if your mission is to educate consumers about the advantages of compact fluorescent light bulbs (CFLs), you might want to track how popular those pages are on your site and how many CFL fact sheets are downloaded from your site.

Key data pieces for website traffic usually include the following:

- *Unique visitors:* The number of unique visitors in a time period. An individual who visited the site three times in that time would count as one visitor.

- *Page views, most popular pages:* The number of times a given page was viewed in a time period.

- *Time spent on pages, longest visited pages:* The average amount of time spent on a particular page of a site by all visitors in a time period.

- *Document downloads:* The number of times a particular document was downloaded from the site in a time period. An individual who downloads the document three times in the time period adds three downloads to this figure.

- *Keywords used to find your site in search engines:* The search terms people are using in Google, Yahoo! and other search engines to find your site.

- *Traffic sources:* How visitors are finding your site; for example, search engines, links from other sites, directly typing in your website address.

Key data pieces for email include the following:

- *Open rate:* The number of messages opened divided by the number of people who received it.

- *Click-through rate:* The number of people who clicked on a link in an email divided by the number of people who received the message.

- *Response rate:* The number of people who took the action requested in an email (donate, sign a petition, and so on) divided by the number of people who received it.

### Exhibit 9.6. Dashboard—Google Analytics.

## Exhibit 9.7. Salesforce Email Reporting Example.

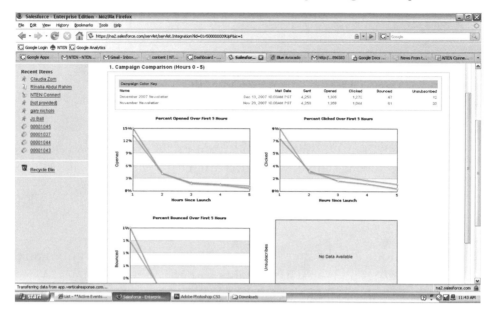

## Where to Find the Data

Website analytics in some form are available to most organizations from their website host (see Exhibits 9.6 and 9.7). There are different packages that present data in different ways from different sources, sometimes in pretty graphs and charts, sometimes as raw data. Contact your web host to find out what packages they offer. Some packages merely track activity such as which pages were displayed; other packages provide much more detailed information. Although they provide useful data, the more data-intensive services can also create an ocean of information that can be difficult to use effectively.

Most email services also allow you to track activity, though they all differ in exactly what they track. You will need to find a tool that can deliver the metrics most important to your organization.

## Collect, Analyze, Adjust

To really understand how effective your online presence is, you will need to continually follow—and repeat—an ongoing three-step process: collect, analyze, and adjust.

## Collect

Earlier in the chapter we outlined key information on what you need to collect to understand the effectiveness of your online presence. Once you know what metrics you want to track, start a simple spreadsheet and record your stats every week on the same day. Soon you'll have enough data to begin to see the trends and patterns you will use to tweak your strategy.

Likewise, you shouldn't act on your data every week. A good guideline is to review statistics monthly, then on a quarterly basis sit down with the data and see what you can learn from the trends.

## Analyze

Periodically, or after a big email campaign, you'll want to analyze your statistics and see what insights you can gain from them. At this stage, you want to evaluate the anomalies in your statistics. When you see big peaks or valleys, try to figure out what caused them. Here's an example:

Your organization has seen a drop in the number of online donations it receives each month. Using web site stats, you can begin to unravel the mystery. Looking at the statistics, we can see the following:

- The number of unique visitors to the site has remained steady—a drop in traffic can't be the culprit.

- The number of people that visit the donate page is also consistent with the last few months. So people aren't having a tough time finding it.

- People are spending *much less time* on the donate page in the last few months, so nothing there must be capturing their attention.

- The number of people who proceed from the donate page to the second step in the process has also dropped dramatically.

Clearly, the problem has something to do with the donation page. With the web team, you take a look at the page and realize that you changed the images and text on the page around the same time the decline started. Obviously, the changes are not working. You'll need to update the page and follow the stats for a while longer to see if you can reverse the trend.

## Adjust

Based on the data, consider what you might change or improve, try it out, and evaluate the impact. Even the largest organizations are constantly trying new techniques, designs, and language on their site in the attempt to maximize the effectiveness of their web sites and emails. Rigorously tracking and analyzing your metrics can give you the information you need to create compelling and meaningful experiences for your stakeholders.

## Interview: William Neuheisel

Neuheisel is the website and database administrator for DC Central Kitchen.

### Exhibit 9.8. The DC Central Kitchen Home Page.

JK: *Tell us a little about the staff at DC Central Kitchen.*

WN: Our staff of about seventy is mostly kitchen staff, with about thirty people in administration. Our development staff is six people, we have one technology staff person and outsource most of our IT work. Out of about seven thousand people in our database we have almost five thousand as part of our email list.

JK: *What do you think has been your most successful campaign?*

WN: The most successful one we did was last fall, focused on the beneficiaries of our services. We had been accepting online donations for about three years when we did this campaign.

We sent out our fall appeal through direct mail around Thanksgiving and we sent out matching emails to support the campaign.

We focused on our beneficiaries, having short stories about how people benefit from our programs. We make meals and ship them out, so we told the story of two partner organizations that we send meals to. They saved money by getting food from us and could then use that money for their other programs. On another email we included two stories of the graduates from our culinary job training program. Donated food is used in the training program to develop job skills—a twelve-week program that results in them being certified as food handlers. They then work in restaurants who we partner with to get food and donations.

We sent two emails before the direct mail piece—one half of our list got one story, one half the other. Then a week later we sent the opposite one—this bracketed the direct mail piece and helped us see the different reactions to the different pieces, the story about the graduates and the story about one of the agencies. The direct mail piece had the same three stories, so everyone got the same stories online and offline.

There were similar results for the emails, less than one percent difference in click-through and open rates. We used two different pictures—one an action shot, one a portrait shot of a face—the portrait one did a little better, we think because it was more personal and immediate.

We also integrated this campaign with our website. During this campaign we switched out our donate button to one of the pictures in the emails and had a little blurb with it which matched the emails. On the donate page we had the stories and the pictures with the donation form below that. In one week, we received around ten thousand dollars, almost the total we had done online in the entire past year.

JK: *What is your process for coordinating online communications?*

WN: Last year we started planning for communications in general. We sat down and planned out the year—newsletter, other regular communications, direct mail, all coordinated with our online communications. We created a comprehensive schedule. If we left the email scheduling to the last minute we could be sending out too many emails. In addition we have a daily staff meeting highlighting our activities. Development is good at being in touch with programs, as development generates most of the content from our office but coordinates closely with program staff to gather stories and highlight activities.

JK: *What words of wisdom would you share with others trying to master this?*

WN: That success hinges on having a lot of support and buy-in from management. Our leadership has always been enthusiastic about new technologies, so there were no arguments about having a blog or doing email or a MySpace page. They are open and embracing, willing to support it even if they don't understand it. They are interested in exploring online options.

For most things you have to just jump in and get started. You are learning as you go, even the best people in the industry don't have exact best practices like there are in direct mail. Just get started and figure out what works for you.

Our founder has been blogging and has even started a video blog. We are working on integrating video and people are responding—board members and donors compliment the communications. In fact, this week a corporate sponsor said that we are their favorite organization to hear from along with the Red Cross! Part of that success is because we have experimented and part is that we stay in regular communication with people—when there are months without communication people forget what they signed up for.

Overall, we have seen a 500 percent increase in online fundraising revenue over previous year. Four actions helped us achieve this:

First, making our online experience more donor-centric by letting our donors choose which programs they were most interested in hearing about, view giving histories online, manage their recurring gifts online, and print their own tax receipts.

Second, testing our approaches in an in-depth way to understand what was working (including polling for feedback right on the donation form) and using that information to improve our online communications.

Third, improving our content by making it more relevant, emotional, and concrete in terms of showing results.

And fourth, focusing on having consistent and coordinated communications through regular internal communication.

Interview used with permission from DC Central Kitchen, http://www.dccentralkitchen.org.

## Conclusion

Online success is about communicating effectively. In an increasingly competitive nonprofit landscape, organizations that communicate well will thrive. Those that don't will struggle or cease to exist.

An up-to-date, interactive website and regular email communication are the foundation of an effective online presence. Creating and implementing plans for content, campaigns, and engagement helps focus organizational resources. Setting benchmarks and tracking results allow you to continually improve your communications and reach your goals.

Now that you have read through these ideas and examples, I encourage you to reflect on what you can specifically apply to your organization. Think about how you can use these ideas and examples to further your mission, engage your stakeholders, and communicate essential information in interesting ways.

I wish you success in all of your online endeavors. Remember to keep your focus on the intended audience and the message you want to communicate, stay close to your data, and don't forget to have fun!

## Notes

1. Introduction to eMarketing, Convio Corporation.

2. The eMail Marketing Report, eMarketer 2001.

3. Jupiter Communications.

4. http://www.idealware.org.

# CHAPTER 10

# Donate Now: Online Fundraising

*Madeline Stanionis*

Online fundraising has become one of the most important—and exciting—aspects of the nonprofit technology world. With hundreds of thousands of people donating online for the first time in the past few years, online fundraising represents an opportunity that most groups can't afford to pass up. But it is challenging to determine the best approach, the right tools, and the appropriate structure to make it work. This chapter shows you how.

## How *Not* to Raise Money Online

Let's call our fictitious nonprofit organization "The Society for Doing Good in the World." The Society, a medium-sized nonprofit organization, was ready to amp up their online fundraising. Unfortunately, each department went about this in its own, fragmented way.

The communications department set up the email messaging software.

The development department set up the online donation processing software.

The political department set up the online advocacy software.

The IT department built a website.

And a member of the board set up a "widget" device—a small application that users can customize for their cause and place on their own website, blog, or social network to promote and facilitate donations—which allowed board members to raise money from friends and family.

So far, it seems like all this activity might pay off, right? Hardly. Here's how their uncoordinated approach ended up failing them just when the Society needed online fundraising to work.

You see, one day the sky fell in—a crisis occurred, and the Society was one of the primary organizations to respond.

The communications department used the email messaging software to send a press release to the media and an email solicitation to donors about the Society's response to the disaster—but it took two days of meetings about how to message their response.

The development department found that they couldn't edit their online donation page themselves to coordinate with the email solicitation and reflect how donations would be used to address the crisis. It took forty-eight hours to make the changes they desired.

The political department launched a campaign to build support for legislation that would prevent the crisis from happening again.

The IT department launched a blog about the crisis on their website.

The board member activated her widget, and one of her friends donated $1,000.

The results: No one gave as a result of the email solicitation. The media did not cover the Society's response to the disaster. Few people visited the blog. No one participated in the political campaign. Not surprisingly, the Society raised very little money online to support their work to address the crisis. And the board decided the widget was so (relatively) successful, they demanded that the Society build their entire strategy around these new-fangled widgets.

The Society made a lot of mistakes—they weren't technically or programmatically integrated, their tools were inadequate for their needs, they spent time and money on inappropriate strategies—and it looks like they were poised to make even more mistakes (building a strategy around a widget).

What would it have looked like if they had done it right?

## How to Raise Money Online

Let's take The Society for Doing Good in the World one more time—this time, with a much smarter approach.

First, they formed a multidisciplinary team and encouraged the members to spend time learning and understanding what's possible online. And they empowered them to make decisions quickly on behalf of the organization.

The team selected an affordable integrated software system—email, donation processing, advocacy—all in one.

The team put in place a mix of proven online strategies, like a solid email program, combined with some more creative ones, like an online auction.

When the crisis hit, the team went to work. Within an hour, they modified their website and donation pages to reflect their work on the crisis. Within two hours, they sent a short, specific, and honest email to their list, describing their immediate response plan and asking for contributions. They included a link to their website for more information and a press release.

The Society followed up the fundraising message with a call to take action on the legislation. And they continued to update their list over the following weeks and even promoted their blog. Within a few weeks, a number of celebrities had donated items to their online auction, and the Society went back to their list with the auction.

Oh, and the board member did again activate her widget and it did generate a $1,000 gift.

The results? Significant contributions in the first few days. Support for the legislation in the first few weeks. A deeper connection with the work of the organization for the people who went to the blog. And many people donated a second time through the online auction.

This time, the Society did a lot of things right. Their technology and programs were well integrated. They were ready to move quickly. They used tried-and-true methods and a few new ideas well. They were focused, strategic, and, more important, they raised money to support their work at a time when they really needed it.

Of course, there is no "right" way to raise money online, but the experience and knowledge gleaned from thousands of organizations during the past few years point to the hallmarks of a successful online program. Here's how you can be just as smart as the Society was the second time around (in seven easy steps!).

## Seven Steps to a Successful Online Fundraising Program

One reason why many nonprofit organizations struggle with online fundraising is because of the darn technology—so many tools and so much hype can be intimidating! It's easy to feel overwhelmed. But it doesn't need to be that way. The truth is, a good online program relies just as much on more old-fashioned tools like planning, coordinating, and communicating as it does on technology. Here are seven steps that break it down:

### Plan!

You may have noticed that the most impressive results in the online fundraising world occur after a natural disaster. You can't plan for that, can you? Well, no. But you can bet that the organizations that generate the most significant funds online after a hurricane or earthquake are those whose systems and people are capable of springing into action quickly and effectively. They may not have planned for a disaster—but they indeed had a plan. And that's where it all starts.

A solid online fundraising program starts with a plan. And that plan starts by putting together a small team whose members have a variety of skills, including technical, copy and content, and leadership. Most important, this is the group that should be empowered to make decisions on behalf of the organization.

You and your team would do well to consistently learn from other organizations as you develop and implement your own program Add your name to the variety of organizations who are raising money online, and you'll soon see trends and ideas that you can incorporate into your plan.

Your plan should address a few basic elements including your organization's website, an online donation processing vendor, donation pages, an email list of online supporters, and a way to email your supporters (messaging software).

Your plan should also include a selection of appeals and other communications like online renewals, issue based appeals, match appeals, year-end giving, e-newsletters, and acknowledgments. You may also look for a few new and interesting ideas that you've observed others use and are willing to try, like an online auction, a blog, or social network outreach.

Combine these basic elements into a simple calendar, and you get something that looks like Exhibit 10.1. You'll note that your plan and calendar will likely start with a more basic program than the one illustrated in the exhibit, but staying tuned into how others are using new and cool ideas as well as learning from your results will allow your plan to evolve over time.

# Exhibit 10.1. Sample Online Calendar.

## Sample Online Calendar
### 2007 Online Schedule

| KICKOFF | LAUNCH DATE | GOALS | | | | PROJECT | AUDIENCE | THEME / CREATIVE / CONTENTS | QUANTITY | RESPONSE RATE |
| | | Names | Action | $$$ | Good will | | | | | |
|---|---|---|---|---|---|---|---|---|---|---|
| **January 2007** | | | | | | | | (retainer) | | |
| 12/26/06 | 1/16/07 | | | X | | Supporter Drive Msg 1 | Full list, segmented | January is our Supporter Drive! | 95,000 | 0.45% |
| 1/2/06 | 1/23/06 | | | X | | Supporter Drive Msg 2 | Full list, segmented | Supporter Drive Follow-up | 95,000 | 0.70% |
| 1/3/06 | 1/31/06 | | | X | | Supporter Drive Msg 3 | Full list, segmented | Last chance! | 95,000 | 0.55% |
| | | | | | | | | MISCELLANEOUS WEB REVENUE | | |
| | | | | | | | | Monthly Total: | | |
| **February 2007** | | | | | | | | (retainer) | | |
| 1/15/07 | 2/5/07 | | | | X | Supporter Drive Msg 4 | Supporters | Thankyou to donors who helped us reach our Jan. Supporter Drive | | |
| 1/30/07 | 2/20/07 | X | X | X | | Testing strategy and implementation of 2 tests | Internal | Would include: - 2 A/B tests of different sub.s - Would repeat each test 3 times | | |
| | | | | | | | | MISCELLANEOUS WEB REVENUE | | |
| | | | | | | | | Monthly Total: | | |
| **March 2007** | | | | | | | | | | |
| 2/8/07 | 3/1/07 | | | X | | Monthly giving strategy memo & recommendations | Internal | Recommendations for FY 07 and beyond | | |
| 2/13/07 | 3/6/07 | | | X | | Monthly donor appeal | Full list, segmented | TBD | 98,000 | 0.07% |
| | | | | | | | | MISCELLANEOUS WEB REVENUE | | |
| | | | | | | | | Monthly Total: | | |
| **April 2007** | | | | | | | | (retainer) | | |

## Don't Plan!

Once you've put a plan together, be prepared to ignore it. Really!

You see, one of the most important lessons you can learn about online fundraising is that it is all about timing. The most successful organizations are able to take advantage of news and topical events quickly and persuasively. And by quickly, I don't mean "sometime this week." "Quickly" on the Internet means within a few hours.

Responding so quickly requires that you have a well-oiled machine in place. That's where your plan comes in: you'll need your technology to work fast, and your people should be able to pull together a strategy and execute it immediately. There are all kinds of timing opportunities, and most are a result of crises. Bad news, a natural disaster, an internal predicament—these are the moments you hope don't happen. But when they do, this is what the Internet does best. By all means, send a message out in all your online channels, including your website and email as well as your blog, social network, and other methods.

The Humane Society of the United States is an organization that knows how to respond quickly and effectively to news. One July evening in 2007, the news broke that a sports celebrity was accused of operating a violent and cruel dog-fighting ring. The Humane Society pulled together a campaign that launched first thing the next morning.

However, instead of responding with a fundraising ask, they launched an advocacy campaign (see Exhibit 10.2) calling on recipients to take action on the issue. After recipients took action, they landed on a donation page. This was a great strategy—if the Humane Society had only asked for money in their campaign, a relatively small fraction of their constituency would have ended up on the donation page. Because they asked for an action that landed folks on the donation page, far more people ended up seeing that donation page, significantly increasing their fundraising response.

A crisis isn't the only kind of timing-related online fundraising opportunity. The other kind of timing opportunity is around dates that you know are coming, like Mother's Day or year end. The biggest mistake

**Exhibit 10.2. Humane Society Advocacy Campaign.
The campaign launched first thing the morning after the
news hit. The Humane Society of the United States led
with an action request followed by a fundraising offer.**

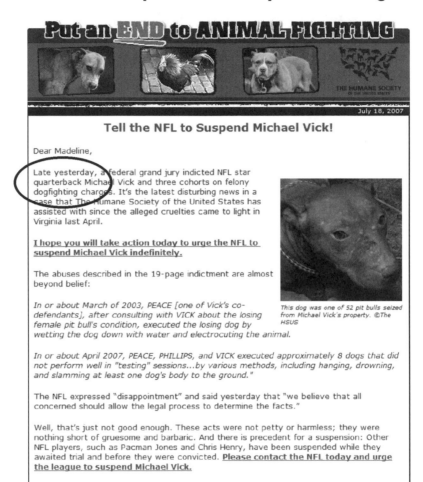

This dog was one of 52 pit bulls seized from Michael Vick's property. ©The HSUS

that fundraisers make around these holidays is forgetting that the Internet is best at provoking procrastinators to give. People tend to turn to the Internet most when they need to take care of something in a hurry. So although some will respond to a year-end appeal sent on December 15, far more wait until December 31. Take advantage of taxpayers looking for last-minute deductions with last-minute appeals on the days leading up to and on the final day of the year.

## Put Your Website to Work

For most organizations, unless there's a crisis, donors and prospective donors aren't your most frequent website visitors. Top visitors tend to be program participants, media, students, and activists. But donors may be among your most important audiences, so it's worth spending time looking at your website through the eyes of a donor. Does your site tell your story? Convince visitors that you are credible and trustworthy? Persuade them to become donors? Make it easy to be engaged? If you're not sure about your answers to these questions, read on!

### Design Matters (but Not Too Much)

Websites, email, blogs, and other online engagement devices each require an organization to think about "look and feel"—in other words, the images and layout of the items that your constituents experience. And unfortunately, nonprofits can spend *way* too much on making these items absolutely gorgeous. Gorgeous is not a bad thing, but warm, friendly, and credible is just as good (and usually a lot cheaper). When it comes to design to support your online fundraising efforts, it helps to use photographs that represent the impact of your work; think people, animals, scenic vistas—inspiration matters! You'll also need text that briefly explains your work and values in many places (not just the "About Us" page). Remember that you and your colleagues are not your donors. Choose the images, information, and items that you know are most appealing to donors, not only to "insiders."

And by all means, make it easy! Information on donating, learning more, finding a phone number, and getting involved should be easy to find and easy to use.

### Key Concept

Inspiring photos, brief text and making donating easy are all important elements of a well-designed online fundraising program.

Got it? Simple, warm, friendly, and professional is what you're aiming for in your web design.

### Functionality *Really* Matters

Functionality means that all of the things that allow people to engage with your organization work well. Signing up for your email list, making a donation, taking action, commenting on your blog, downloading your fundraising widget—all of these must be easy or people won't bother.

Exhibit 10.3 shows a home page that pays attention to design and functionality. The International Rescue Committee's site tells their constituents that they are bold and active; it makes it easy for people to get involved, and it contains just the right amount of images and information to inspire and inform.

### Make Your Donation Page Great

When your constituent lands on your donation page, your job is to provide the right mix of inspiration and ease to ensure that he or she completes the form and makes that gift. This is much harder than it seems! Typically, of every five people who visit a donation page, only one makes a gift.

## Key Concept

When designing the donation page, make it as clear and simple as possible to maximize donations.

The commercial world spends a great deal of time understanding what makes a shopper complete a form and make a purchase (the equivalent of our donation page), but the nonprofit world doesn't have nearly as much research available to help with our decision making. However, we have learned some useful information about how to close the deal on your donation page.

First, link directly to the donation form from your "Donate" links, rather than to an intermediary page. The fewer clicks people have to make, the more likely they will complete their donation. The introductory copy on the donation page should consist of a concise, compelling case for giving. You'll want to minimize this copy to ensure the donation

## Exhibit 10.3. International Rescue Committee Website.

form remains at least partially "above the fold"—that is, in the first screen view, without forcing the visitor to scroll down. Given the short amount of time online readers spend on any one page, a visible form above the fold sends the most immediate signal to give.

Customizing the page to reflect the reason your donor landed there will also help. Did she click on a link about a crisis? Then the page should briefly describe how her money will be used to alleviate the situation. Did your donor click a "Join Us" link? Then your page should illustrate the benefits of membership.

We've also learned to limit the options on the donation page. That means suppressing subnavigation if possible. It also means that the donation form should contain only those fields necessary for making a gift—don't ask for extra information on the form! If possible, preselect the dollar amount radio button that is slightly above your average online gift.

As simply as possible, you may also include a link to "Other Ways to Give" below the introductory copy on the donation form. This way you will still give your donors options and peace of mind, even as you streamline the path to the donation page. Options might include planned giving (bequests, estate gifts, charitable annuities, life insurance donations, and so on), sustainer gifts (Candidate of the Month, monthly, Victory Cabinet), or information on how to donate by mail or phone.

Finally, displaying a secure site badge on the donation form—ideally just above, below, or next to the fields collecting credit card information—is an important reassurance to donors concerned about online transactions.

This is a long list of tips—but put them all together, and you'll note that, as with site design, you should be aiming for simplicity and clarity for your donors.

## Create a Case for Giving

A well-organized, effective donation page increases the likelihood that prospects will follow through and become donors. But an effective page alone is not enough—getting donors to commit repeatedly requires a compelling case for giving. Making a case for giving usually means including success stories on your website, a brief financial report demonstrating your efficiency, and an annual report with accomplishments and plans.

The international relief organization CARE does an excellent job with their donation page—it's persuasive, easy, and includes elements from their case for giving right on the page (see Exhibit 10.4).

## Exhibit 10.4. CARE Website Donation Page.

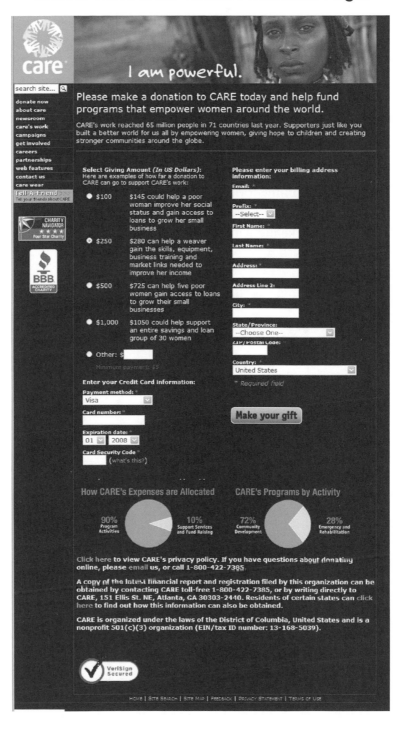

## Accept Help

Among the most amazing innovations that the Internet has brought to fundraising is the ease with which others can take up your cause and raise significant dollars. Never before has it been so simple for passionate supporters to create and run their own fundraising campaigns.

The adoption of this kind of fundraising, which many call *distributed fundraising*, parallels the rise of social media like blogs, social networks, and wikis. Distributed fundraising includes more traditional fundraising efforts, like walk-a-thons, which have become measurably easier with the use of online tools that make a participant's personal fundraising easy and even fun. Distributed fundraising also includes more unfamiliar methods, like the widgets we described in our opening scenario.

Some examples of widgets are shown in Exhibit 10.5.

### Exhibit 10.5. Widget Examples.

*Source:* Six Degrees

Distributed fundraising software and tools are becoming less expensive and easier to use every day. Thus it's tempting for an organization to invest significantly in distributed fundraising—what could be easier than putting the work into the hands of your supporters? However—and it's a big however—many organizations have found distributed fundraising to be difficult unless they in fact have a real-world event like a walk-a-thon that accompanies the online elements. Just like any other volunteer effort, most distributed fundraising campaigns are successful only when the organization running them also invests in staff who can organize, support, motivate, and manage the program.

## Think Campaigns, Not Appeals

Consider, for a moment, your donor's day. Think of all the places she is getting information and interacting with others. A chat with a coworker, the daily newspaper, email, a blog or two, the mail, a television show, radio, YouTube, a variety of websites, and maybe even a social network—all in a day's time. Your job is to figure out how you can get your important cause heard amid all this communication. It's wise to use a couple of media and repeat your message a few times—a letter, an email, or a radio ad alone just doesn't cut it anymore.

That's why successful online fundraising relies on campaigns. Campaigns require your organization to get organized and coordinate for a period of time across several communication channels, online and offline alike. Campaigns lend themselves particularly well to specific and time-sensitive projects or special opportunities, such as year-end fundraising or a time-limited matching gift, and they are most effective when current events already have your donor's attention.

### Tip from the Field

Cross-channel campaigns that include online and offline components can be more effective than stand-alone email appeals.

Elements of a good online fundraising campaign include repetition across channels; a story arc that is inspiring, clear, and authentic; and a realistic and inspiring goal. Avoid delivering other messages or one-off alerts while you're running a campaign, as distractions can confuse or overwhelm your donors. Finally, don't forget to tell people what happened and what's next.

Planned Parenthood ran a month-long membership drive in the spring of 2008 that included four email messages, promotion on their social network, enewsletter, and blog, and a homepage hijack in which they replaced their home page with a member drive donation page for the last few days of the drive. Messages came from several people, including staff and volunteers. The message in Exhibit 10.6 came from a Planned Parenthood employee who wrote a personal story about why he was a member.

## Be Creative!

One of the most magical aspects of the Internet is that a cause that was unknown yesterday can become a cause célèbre today. Why? Sometimes because news or urgency thrusts an organization into the limelight, but just as often because an organization uses creativity to garner attention and raise money.

Creativity is really just that special something that, especially when combined with smart timing and campaigns, can make your fundraising appeal more memorable and, of course, more successful. And because Internet fundraising is very low-cost compared to raising money through the mail or telephones, nonprofits can afford to try things that are more creative.

The challenge to be creative can be daunting to people who don't consider themselves artistic or unusual thinkers. The good news is that artistic and unusual are only two ways for your cause to stand out online. There are many others, including an authentic and genuine voice, using clever premiums, incorporating video and other new media, and taking advantage of the new interest in alternative holiday gifts.

*Be authentic.* Authenticity doesn't sound like creativity, but it's quite true that a genuine, personal appeal can capture attention simply because it is truthful and connects with people in an honest way. *The Nation* magazine enlisted favorite writer David Corn to author a fundraising email message for them—the result was a blunt, honest, and utterly successful fundraising effort (see Exhibit 10.7).

## Exhibit 10.6. Planned Parenthood Membership Drive.

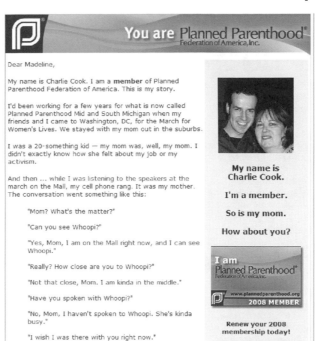

Dear Madeline,

My name is Charlie Cook. I am a **member** of Planned Parenthood Federation of America. This is my story.

I'd been working for a few years for what is now called Planned Parenthood Mid and South Michigan when my friends and I came to Washington, DC, for the March for Women's Lives. We stayed with my mom out in the suburbs.

I was a 20-something kid — my mom was, well, my mom. I didn't exactly know how she felt about my job or my activism.

And then ... while I was listening to the speakers at the march on the Mall, my cell phone rang. It was my mother. The conversation went something like this:

"Mom? What's the matter?"

"Can you see Whoopi?"

"Yes, Mom, I am on the Mall right now, and I can see Whoopi."

"Really? How close are you to Whoopi?"

"Not that close, Mom. I am kinda in the middle."

"Have you spoken with Whoopi?"

"No, Mom, I haven't spoken to Whoopi. She's kinda busy."

"I wish I was there with you right now."

"Well, why didn't you come?"

"You never asked."

**My name is
Charlie Cook.**

**I'm a member.**

**So is my mom.**

**How about you?**

I am
Planned Parenthood
Federation of America, Inc.

www.plannedparenthood.org
**2008 MEMBER**

Renew your 2008
membership today!

Renew Today!

My mom was watching the march on TV — while I was watching the Mall live and in person. We'd never even talked about it.

When I came home that evening, my mom and I had our first real discussion about why both of us are pro-choice. She spoke about the time before *Roe* when, at her high school, many of her friends had abortions that were illegal and unsafe — how she heard rumors of people using dangerous "home methods" — and how no one really talked about it, but everyone always knew.

This is when she said how proud she is of me for working for an organization whose goal is to ensure that no woman would ever have to go through that again.

It was late. We stopped talking. She tousled my hair (which I hate) and said, "Charlie. One thing: Next march, you invite me, ok?"

---

This is a special month for all of us at Planned Parenthood Federation of America. It's our member drive. I'm reaching out to everyone I know to give what they can to **become a 2008 member.** This is a big year for us. We have a LOT of work ahead of us. Reproductive health care is at the forefront of the political battleground — and Planned Parenthood and the people we serve are the bull's-eye target.

And, don't worry. This time, the first person I called was my mom.

Thanks for your help.

Sincerely,
Charlie Cook
Planned Parenthood Federation of America

P.S. Already made your membership gift for 2008? Please accept our apologies for this additional reminder, and thank you so much for your continued support!

You can also print a donation form to mail in here. Please mail your gift to:

Planned Parenthood Federation of America
434 West 33rd Street
New York, NY 10001

**Exhibit 10.7. The Nation Fundraising Letter.**

# The Nation.

Dear Member of the *Nation* Community,

I've never written a fundraising letter—not counting the few notes I sent my parents when I was in college. I'm a journalist. I write articles and books—about politics, national security, and the world around us. And I'm damn lucky; I get paid to do so by *The Nation*. But the magazine has been hit by a fiscal crisis—one caused by the sort of institutional Washington corruption I often cover—and I've been asked by our publishing team to ask you for help. **Please click here to pitch in.**

Last week, Teresa Stack, *The Nation*'s president, sent you a letter explaining this crisis. To recap:

*Postal regulators have accepted a scheme designed in part by lobbyists for the Time Warner media conglomerate. In short, mailing costs for mega-magazines like Time Warner's own* Time, People *and* Sports Illustrated *will go up only slightly or decrease. But smaller publications like* The Nation *will be hit by an enormous rate increase of **half a million dollars a year**.*

For *The Nation*, $500,000 a year is a lot of money. Believe me, I know. I've been working at the magazine for over 20 years. The pay ain't great. But there are few media outlets that allow their writers and reporters the freedom to go beyond the headlines and take on the powers that be—to ask inconvenient questions and pursue uncomfortable truths.

But starting July 15, 2007, *The Nation* will face this whopping postal rate hike. Not to be melodramatic, but **this rate increase is a threat to democratic discourse.** Why should magazines that can afford high-powered lobbyists receive preferential treatment? This rise in mailing costs will make it harder for the magazine to deliver the investigative reporting and independent-minded journalism upon which you depend. (Take my word; I see the editors and publishing people in our New York office freaking out about this postal rate hike and discussing possible cutbacks.)

*Offer a clever premium.* In 2004 and again in 2008, presidential candidate John Edwards offered donors his mother's pie recipe in exchange for their donation (see Exhibit 10.8). Is this something you can do only on the Internet? No, but it's also not the sort of thing you would spend printing and postage on.

*Use new media and new online destinations,* like video and blogs. Exhibit 10.9 shows Planned Parenthood's employee-written blog with staff-made videos of themselves at work during the fall of 2007. The blog

## Exhibit 10.8. John Edwards's Premium Offer.

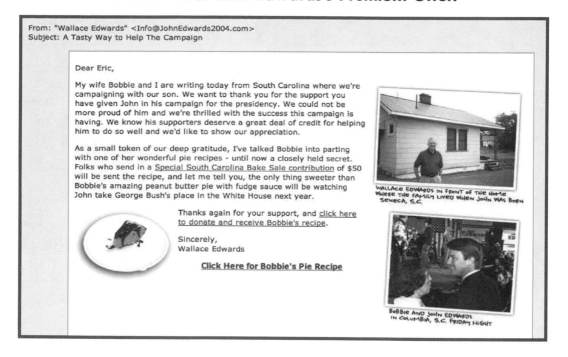

From: "Wallace Edwards" <Info@JohnEdwards2004.com>
Subject: A Tasty Way to Help The Campaign

Dear Eric,

My wife Bobbie and I are writing today from South Carolina where we're campaigning with our son. We want to thank you for the support you have given John in his campaign for the presidency. We could not be more proud of him and we're thrilled with the success this campaign is having. We know his supporters deserve a great deal of credit for helping him to do so well and we'd like to show our appreciation.

As a small token of our deep gratitude, I've talked Bobbie into parting with one of her wonderful pie recipes - until now a closely held secret. Folks who send in a Special South Carolina Bake Sale contribution of $50 will be sent the recipe, and let me tell you, the only thing sweeter than Bobbie's amazing peanut butter pie with fudge sauce will be watching John take George Bush's place in the White House next year.

Thanks again for your support, and click here to donate and receive Bobbie's recipe.

Sincerely,
Wallace Edwards

**Click Here for Bobbie's Pie Recipe**

WALLACE EDWARDS IN FRONT OF THE HOME WHERE THE FAMILY LIVED WHEN JOHN WAS BORN SENECA, S.C.

BOBBIE AND JOHN EDWARDS IN COLUMBIA, S.C. FRIDAY NIGHT

was created in response to protesters who descended on their clinics. Donors could "pledge-a-protester" and donate a token amount for each protester the employees encountered. It worked, both in raising money and in creating a more personal connection with blog visitors, many of whom commented on the videos and posts.

*Take advantage of alternative gifts for birthdays and holidays.* One of the ways people use the Internet most frequently is for shopping. Now, some organizations have figured out how to create emotionally satisfying shopping experiences for donors. "Oxfam Unwrapped" is one of the best examples of this approach. Created by the Oxfam international relief organization, the site, shown in Exhibit 10.10, allows donors to shop for a "gift"—typically an item that is delivered to a family in a third-world country rather than a traditional wrapped gift that is sent to the recipient. The donor can select the gift and then further select a card, which they can personalize and have sent by Oxfam to the recipient, notifying them of the item purchased in their name. Beautiful,

## Exhibit 10.9. Planned Parenthood Employee Blog.

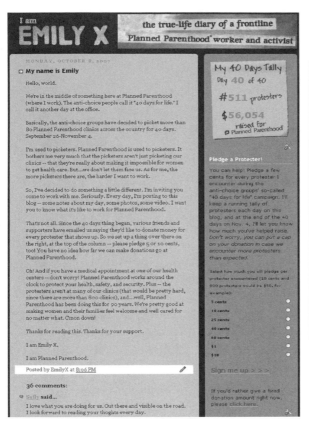

inspiring visuals combined with a smooth, easy process make Oxfam Unwrapped a smart and creative way to raise money online.

See? Lots of creative ways to get your online fundraising efforts noticed. But I would be remiss if I didn't remind you of one caveat: sometimes you shouldn't be creative. You see, it can be hard to get going creatively, but once you're on your way, it's just as easy to go too far. Make sure that your great ideas and new technology don't get in the way of your important campaign—the reason you're raising money in the first place. Ask your mom to test out your idea by trying to make a gift. If she can't figure it out, it might be too complicated.

## Exhibit 10.10. Oxfam America's Alternative Gift Selection.

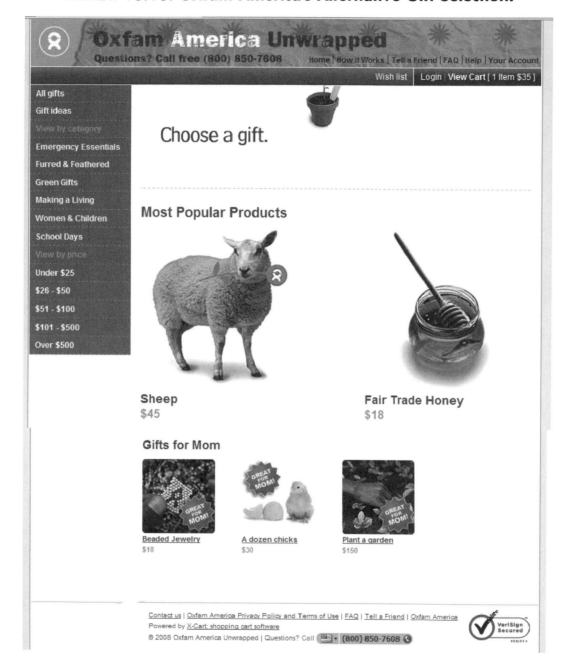

## Learn

Fundraising is, of course, about results—the number of people who gave, otherwise known as the *response rate*, and the amount of revenue you generate. Sometimes the most well-conceived, brilliant campaign tanks. And conversely, the appeal that didn't exactly appeal to you turns out to be the one that generates the most revenue. Why? Online fundraising—more than other fundraising methods like direct mail and telemarketing—provides you with ample opportunities to answer that question, learn from your results, and apply the lessons to future campaigns. The challenge is that the data can be quite overwhelming! Here are the metrics you should keep your eye on, and how you can test, tweak, and try strategies that can improve performance in each.

## Key Concept

Keep track of open rates, click-throughs, and conversion rates for all of your campaigns. These metrics will help you improve each successive campaign

*For email campaigns, the first metric you ought to pay attention to is the open rate.* This refers to the number of people who "opened" or read your message. It is important for the simple reason that people who don't open a message are not very likely to give. Unfortunately, the technology behind an open rate yields a metric that is not entirely accurate, but it is still a good gauge. Many factors can impact an open rate (including just how compelling your previous messaging has been), and it is worth testing them to achieve the best possible result. These factors include the following:

- *Time of day and day of week.* Some people read email at work; others read their messages during the leisure of the weekend. It is worthwhile to test the timing of your email campaigns to find out when your recipients are most likely to open your messages.

- *Subject line.* Testing subject lines often produces statistically significant results. Many organizations test a few subject lines on a small segment of their list and then roll out the winning subject line to the rest of the list. For example, a gay and lesbian rights organization tested the solicitation email subject line "Candidate of the Month: [Candidate Name]" against the more provocative "Going where no out candidate has gone before." The latter subject line won with a resounding 20 percent open rate versus 15 percent for the former.

- *"From" line.* Knowing and trusting the sender of a message certainly influences open rates as well. You may find that your organization's name is the best choice, or a more friendly personal name may work better for you.

*The second metric you should watch is the click-through rate.* This is the number of people who click on a hyperlink in your message. In an online fundraising message, the only possible link to click is usually a fundraising link. So the click-through rate in this case tells you how much interest your message generated. Variables that affect the click-through rate include premiums, link placement in the body of the message (near the top, in the P.S., or in an inset box, for example), the offer that explains what you are going to achieve with my donation. And of course a compelling, well-written, and clear email message can also make a difference!

*Conversion rate* is a particularly critical metric. When a donor clicks from your email message, advertisement, social network page, or wherever to your donation page, that person has told you that he or she is interested. Your job on this page is to close the deal. The number of folks who complete your donation form and make a gift is called the *conversion rate*. For example, if one hundred people land on your donation page and ten of them make a donation, you have a 10-percent conversion rate.

There are many factors that can increase or decrease your conversion rate, including limiting the information you ask for from donors, the giving levels presented on the page, the copy and use of images on the page, and the number of steps you ask donors to take in order to give. The amount of effort you exert in tweaking your donation page almost always pays off, even if it's for only the relatively small number of folks who visit the page. Those hundred or so visitors have demonstrated their interest by visiting the donation page. You can't afford to lose them just because you haven't paid attention to creating and testing the best possible donation page layout and user flow.

These metrics are only a few of the many you can measure in your campaigns, but they pack a punch! Watching and learning from them, then making tweaks and conducting tests with just these few metrics will almost certainly help you deliver more effective online fundraising campaigns.

## Key Concept

To provide oversight, many states require nonprofit organizations that are rais-ing money and the firms that serve them to register, whether they are fund-raising online, in the mail, or on the telephone. There are numerous services and law firms that can assist with this process. A good place to start is http://www.nasconet.org.

## Conclusion

So there you have it. Seven easy steps! With a good—and flexible—plan that takes advantage of your website and distributed fundraising, you are well on your way. Add in the use of cross-channel campaigns rather than stand-alone email appeals, throw in some creativity, and you're ready to take advantage of the opportunities presented by online fundraising. Of course, don't forget to go back and review your successes—and your fail-ures. Learning from your past efforts is the key to improving your future campaigns.

And here's one bonus tip: it is so hard to attract and sustain a strong group of online constituents amid all the YouTube videos, mommy blogs, pet tricks, nun jokes, work email, auction sites, and shoe stores, all competing for your donor's attention online, that you can't afford to be anything but remarkable! Let your passion and commitment for your cause show in your efforts. That's the secret ingredient you have that all the other online clutter lacks. Use it wisely!

# CHAPTER 11

# Where Will We Be Tomorrow?

*Edward Granger-Happ*

*"The art of prophecy is very difficult—especially with respect to the future."*
*—Mark Twain*

Mark Twain was right: predicting the future is difficult, especially for technology. When I was in graduate school, working in a data center that had a mini-computer the size of two large desks—with 16 K of memory—I never would have guessed that in just thirty years a digital wristwatch would have an MP3 player with 125,000 times more memory, for a tiny fraction of the price.

We all know about the huge gains in technology that have happened in our lifetime. And we know it's accelerating. If we are to make decisions about where to invest our donors' dollars, we need to make an attempt at prophecy. But for all the future-gazing and planning we may want to do, we also need the humility to recognize that some things are understood only when we go out and try something, recognizing that about half of what we need to know to be successful with technology, we learn by doing. And sometimes we may get it wrong.

As we attempt to peer into the future, to increase our chances of getting it right we need to listen to different points of view. There is a natural tension between the heads of IT at nonprofits—who worry about how to keep the "engine room" running and take advantage of the new technology before it is old technology—and the executive directors or CEOs who are concerned about how to serve a need and further a mission. IT is grounded in the operation of the organization; its key customers are employees. A CEO of a nonprofit looks outward, to the beneficiaries as primary customers. My goal as CIO is to push both to look more at each other's goals and imagination to ensure that the future will truly become more an era of technology for good.

This chapter gives an overview of key trends in the technology realm that nonprofit leaders must pay attention to. I also argue that the most strategic use of technology is to deliver wholly new programs, or existing programs in wholly new ways that would not be possible before the application of technology. Technology is one of the few buttons an organization can push to get the scale of capacity building to grow large enough to have the maximum global impact. Training and empowering helps, but without the better tools, we are just plowing the field with a more effective hand plow. And increasingly we will see donors demanding larger outcomes for their donation dollar.

## Key Trends

Looking from the past to the future horizon, we can see eight big-picture technology trends that will have the greatest impact on our organizations. Some of these are obvious; others are weaker signals for which we need to focus the lens on our telescope.

### Prices for Technology Are Falling

We can do much more with far lower investments than ever before. Figure 11.1 shows this in the starkness of a graph. Even against a logarithmic scale, the fall of prices is precipitous.

From 1953 to 2000, the price index for computers dropped 99.997 percent. That's an extraordinary change.[1]

**Figure 11.1. Price Indexes for Domestic Mainframes and PCs (1996 = 100).**

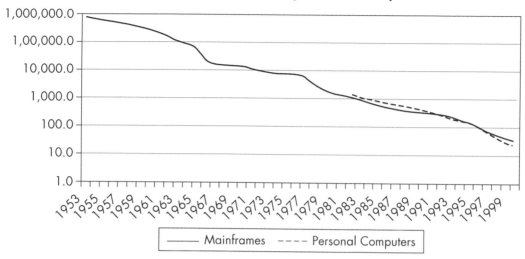

**Figure 11.2. Mobile Communication Costs for Disaster Relief.**

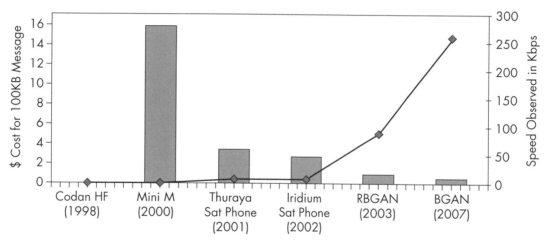

If we look at communications, we see the same thing. The members of NetHope, a consortium of the largest international nonprofit IT leaders, compared notes on the costs and bandwidth for mobile devices used in emergency relief.[2] In just seven years, costs dropped thirty-fold while speed increased four-hundred-fold. The chart in Figure 11.2 shows this. The bars in the chart show the dropping cost per 100 KB of information; the line represents the speed, which is indicative of bandwidth.

## The Continuing Explosion of Computing Power

The continuing explosion of the computing hardware triangle of bandwidth, disk storage, and CPU speed, with continued falling prices, will mean increasingly cheap global communications.

As all three of these factors accelerate, communications will also become faster while the technology that drives them will get cheaper and cheaper. As a result, we can expect to see applications distributed across the Internet, yet it will seem as if we are running programs on our desktops. As software distributes across the Internet cloud, the need for shared, central data in organizations will increase. Collaborating on projects—and most all types of work—across many locations and time zones will become possible and drive this centralization. Everyone will want to share and access the same data at the same time.

## We Can Collaborate More Easily

Cheaper and faster technology also means an increasing real-time involvement in each other's work and in donor participation in programs, time zones notwithstanding. This will drive greater levels of collaboration, but not always in ways we expect or want. For example, the fact that donors and providers will be able to virtually participate in program planning, delivery, and evaluation may not always be welcome, but it is inevitable.

Cheaper, faster information and communication technology (ICT) will also mean that *where* the work gets done will become less relevant and much more flexible. Working in real time in groups whose members are in different locations will become commonplace, as will employees working from anywhere. Rising energy costs will also motivate working outside the typical office.

These trends will also drive greater levels of collaboration within and among nonprofits. It will be increasingly possible to have real-time work groups between organizations as well as within organizations. This increased 24x7 connection will generate productivity gains but also rapidly produce information saturation and more stress. Managing work-nonwork balance will therefore become a major organizational issue and need in the near future.

## We Are All Connected

Global interpersonal communication will continue to grow geometrically as a result of the dropping costs and the worldwide frenzy to be connected by handheld devices such as cell phones. In five to ten years global video conferencing will be commonplace on every desktop and via handheld devices. Cell phones, PDAs, and laptop computers will continue to converge. Cell phones will increasingly become the computing device of choice in the next five years, with their power exceeding that of current laptops. Costs per conversation will continue to decline.

## Software as a Service

An IT category that has significant promise for nonprofits is software as a service (SaaS). SaaS applications are standard, bite-sized applications hosted by vendors and priced on a pay-as-you-go basis. Their cost structure is significantly less than that of other software solutions to date. They are especially attractive for commodity processes. But they mean accepting a standard, best-practice process and eliminating unnecessary custom applications.

Following the corporate trend, more run-the-business software will become prevalent in nonprofits. There will be nonprofit enterprise systems that will standardize and streamline all administrative processes. However, unlike the corporate enterprise systems, these will be smaller SaaS applications tied together. Enterprise systems will then extend to the processes of delivering programs themselves. They will be global, extending to wherever an Internet connection and a browser are available.

## A Changing Tech Employment Sector

The retirement of the seventy-nine million baby boomers over the next decade or two means that up to 50 percent of people working in technology will be leaving their jobs.[3] Their knowledge and experience will go with them. More important, there are fewer technology people to take their place. This will create a shortage that will drive up the price of technology professionals, and the competition for skilled IT people will become intense. The implications for nonprofits are first, a negative impact on staffing with a resulting "seller's" market and bidding wars among organizations.

Additionally, commoditization of technology means that more and more of the basic and intermediate building blocks for technology will move offshore and become, indeed, commodities. The IT technology professional will need to increasingly move up the food chain to system integration, business translation, and generalist skills. This means we need to hire for a different skill set than the support-oriented IT hires we make today.

We can expect to see an accelerating shift in our IT departments, from application development and network building to systems integration and management. Nonprofits are not in the software and network businesses; we need to stop acting like we are. We can expect to see our IT work move out of headquarters and to the regional and country offices where labor costs are low and skills are rising. This will require responses from nonprofit leaders. In addition to the shifts just noted, we will also need to use more standard, off-the-shelf software and tools that leverage existing staff time and skills more each year.

## More Scrutiny

Following the impact of Sarbanes-Oxley (SOX) on for-profits, we can expect an increasing regulatory framework for nonprofits.[4] This will cause increased expense and processes for security, operational audit trails, and verifiable processes. The effort required for compliance will detract from our charitable purpose and add demand for supporting technology. With the introduction of SOX, Statement on Auditing Standards 70 (SAS70) audits have become more common.[5] SAS70 was developed by the American Institute of Certified Public Accountants; it defines the standards that should be used in an audit. These comprehensive standards often include a review of technology concerns such as data collection and storage. Nonprofits must also be compliant with the Payment Card Industry Data Security Standards (PCI DSS) for donor credit card information or risk losing their ability to accept credit card donations.[6]

Evidence for the growth in compliance expense can be seen in total audit costs, which, for example, increased 38 percent at Save the Children between FY04 and the time of this writing; the IT portion has increased a staggering 50 percent, based on time required to complete an audit. This means that nonprofits will need more administrative and systems support to meet growing regulatory demands. Similarly, corporate and corporate-minded donors are increasingly demanding that we define expected, measurable outcomes as a condition for their donation. This will drive the need for more data collection and reporting, with the need to demonstrate impacts in real time via the Internet.

As a result, investment in higher-order systems will be required, such as executive information systems, balanced scorecard systems, and program tracking systems. We can expect that much more hard-nosed accountability will be required from nonprofits.

## Disruptive Innovations

Many industries in the for-profit world have experienced wrenching change due to the disruptive innovation that technology can bring.[7] Think about how the music industry—or, to cite an even more extreme example, the newspaper industry—has changed over the past decade. We can expect disruptive innovations to impact nonprofits in the coming years as well. Nonprofits have not experienced this in significant ways to date. However, the signs are on the horizon.

For example, the value chain for a typical nonprofit stretches from donor through fundraising and programs (nonprofit products) to beneficiary, driven by mission. Internet-based technologies are making it possible to directly connect donors to beneficiary projects, cutting out the typical role nonprofits play. This is not unlike the disruption caused by iTunes and MySpace in the music industry.

Three nonprofit "dot-coms" in particular provide cases to which nonprofits need to pay attention. GlobalGiving, DonorsChoose, and Kiva—all web-based organizations—provide a current challenge to the typical nonprofit value chain. The role that nonprofits will play will need to change from providing end-to-end donor-beneficiary experiences to unbundling programs, programs delivery, and quality assurance.

Social entrepreneurship is another emerging trend that could potentially be a disruptive innovation. Social entrepreneurs apply innovative business principles to social problems in order to address the root causes of those issues and enact large scale, long-term change. Grameen Bank, the pioneering microfinance institution in Bangladesh, is a notable example. By loaning small amounts of money to groups of people in need, Grameen Bank gives people the capital they need to lift themselves out of poverty. The system leverages the skills of the individuals and uses community dynamics to help ensure that beneficiaries act responsibly.

## So What? Strategic Implications

One of the questions I like to ask is "In which areas do we need to be great, the most innovative, and world class?" It is not possible (and not strategic) for an organization to try to be world class in every category. Save the Children's strategy team did a good job drawing out the top four areas where we aspire to be best in the world: Child Survival, Newborn Health, Early Childhood Development, and Emergencies. Technology is not on that list, and I'd argue that for a nonprofit it should not be. We can be "good enough," and that's "great" because it allows more focus and investment in the area where we aspire to be the world leader. In other words, "good enough" in many areas allow us to be great in the fewer, most mission-critical areas. That's the essence of what I call the *good enough* principle.

This means having humility. It also means being willing to look at your own operation and say, is there really something unique about the way we do email? No; everyone does email relatively the same way. Is there really something unique that we do for payroll? No; it's a generic application. Well, why then are we spending time trying to innovate and invest money in doing those types of applications? I venture to say that probably 80 percent of what we do in IT and other departments in nonprofits is commodity; it's the same as at other organizations, certainly the same as at other nonprofits. A little humility can go a long way in helping us invest our donor's dollars in services where we truly can have innovative impact. It's not going to be on email.

## Six Strategic Questions EDs and CEOs Should Ask

Given these trends and a focused strategic approach, here are the key questions nonprofit leaders should ask themselves to assess and prepare for the future of IT.

### How Can We Ensure Convergence Rather Than Divergence?

As organizations grow, adding more offices or chapters, we should ask ourselves, How can we ensure that our offices are all using a common set of applications and data? The thought of the staff in each office doing "their own thing" with technology results in a nightmare of complexity from which most organizations won't be able to recover. The costs of unifying an organization's disparate technologies after the fact are very high. So is the cost of living with a growing divergence of technology. CEOs need to ask: Are our technology choices narrowing? Are we standardizing on fewer platforms and fewer applications?

Customizing our choices for each location's needs may be a strong desire (and often the default), but customizing also means a cost that grows over time and is rarely justified. As organizations grow, there is an opportunity to standardize technology and share applications across all offices and members. Insisting on an IT principles or standards document, early on, is a starting point toward convergence rather than divergence. CEOs must choose to harmonize now or face the nightmare later. Redundant and diverging technology is ultimately a cost to donors and to beneficiaries. It also drives up the cost of interoperating in a unified world.

### How Do We Balance Innovation and Infrastructure?

Building basic infrastructure, like connecting field offices and increasing bandwidth, is the foundation on which all our technology dreams and plans rest. It is the prerequisite. Conversely, without the web-based applications that run on our field network, there is no return on our technology investment. The demand for infrastructure can easily consume our entire IT budgets. Our top opportunity is to enable innovative programs and make current programs more effective. We need to remember that we are in the programs business, not the software and hardware business. Therefore we need to manage our technology budgets as a portfolio, including infrastructure, workflow enhancement, and innovation projects. The majority of our investment may still go into the infrastructure bucket (in particular, growing the bandwidth and reliability of our Internet-based connections), but we must also invest in business process and workflow applications and reserve some investment for innovative programs that leverage technology directly for beneficiaries.

Ultimately we need to ensure that we spend our time innovating on true value-added processes and not on commodity processes, such as payroll, accounting, HR information systems, email, and even donor management. As noted earlier, it is likely that 80 percent of our processes fall in the commodity column and 20 percent in the value-added column. For commodities, we ought to adopt industry best practices and standards and eschew customization.

## What's the Technology Future?

The trends in technology are clear: we are moving away from custom applications, large enterprise solutions, and offline applications. These are past technologies. The future is small, standard, connected service-based applications. That may be hard to envision, but we need to remember where we were five years ago and think about where another five years will take us.

Remember this future-looking theme: *Don't bet against the network!* In the time it takes you to program around its pitfalls, it will get to where you need it to be. The last thing we should do is spend a fortune buying, building, and rolling out an offline system, only to find ourselves in a significantly better place for online systems when we are done. Our strategic bet is on playing "to where the puck is going to be"—to use hockey player Wayne Gretzky's measure of success.

There's a related question: *What new programs (that directly serve benefi-ciaries) have you helped engender that would not have been possible without the new use of technology?* This is the most strategic use of technology— that which directly moves the mission of your organization forward. For a nonprofit, it is hard to justify IT expenses that are focused only on the desktop or back office. IT success means new and revitalized programs that leverage technology.

## How Do We Meet Near-Term Business Needs While Building for the Long Term?

Large application projects easily take three or four years to complete. The result is that they then have very little impact on a five-year strat-egy, as they are delivered at the end of the period. Infrastructure build-ing, like large-scale field office wiring, also takes four or five years to complete, and it is often a prerequisite to web-delivered application projects. But business units and field offices have needs now. What do we do? We have three choices: build or buy software to throw away in a few years; put our near-term needs on hold, patch the old, and live with manual solutions; or buy small for the long term.

Two final points about business needs: First, we need to drill down on the pain point issues and ask what the particular difficulties are with our current systems. The root issue is often business processes and poli-cies, not systems. And solving the former does not necessarily require changing the latter. Second, mature and widely sold technology appli-cations usually represent the needs of a broad customer base; they are therefore an embodiment of best practices. In understanding our needs, we need the humility to understand others' solutions. They may suggest ways for us to change our processes. The application technology therefore needs a seat at the table at the outset, not as a later follower.

## How Do We Invest Enough but Not Too Much?

Many nonprofits underspend on IT. The U.S. NGO benchmark for IT spending is 2.5 percent of revenue.[8] Many large nonprofit organiza-tions spend 1 percent or less of revenue on IT. That may mean they are more frugal, but it also means their fellow agencies can run faster than they can, and they risk falling further behind. A serious question for CEOs: do you need to double your IT investment across your organization if you hope to be competitive with other organizations? Underinvesting often leads to a large backlog of technology projects—especially renewing aging infrastructure and applications—which makes it harder to do the newer, more competitive things we need to do (see the portfolio approach described earlier). We need to take an "evergreen" approach with our hardware and software, recognizing that most hardware has a five-year life, and almost no software lives beyond ten years. This needs to be a fundamental part of our annual budgeting and requires longer-term capital budgeting.

The flip side is the risk of spending too much by taking our lead from large for-profit organizations. Corporations who invested in large, enterprise-wide systems are now faced with the high cost of upgrades and increasing time to change applications—hardly a recipe for agility. Application choices can mean overspending. We therefore need faster, smaller alternatives. The time and cost prospects are driving the bite-sized approach. Yet even if the costs were not significantly less, the timing is not strategic; it does not enable or support the typical five-year strategy to deliver a project in four years.

## Where Will Disruptive Innovations for Nonprofits Come From?

As I've already noted, we are all aware of the significant disruptions that new technology has meant for the retail music and publishing businesses over the past twenty years. Nonprofits have been largely unscathed by these seismic changes. But that will change. CEOs need to be constantly looking to the horizon for the first weak signals of the disruption that technology changes can bring.

## How Have You Helped Your Organization Attract and Retain Knowledge Workers (and IT Professionals)

Think about the under-twenty-five crowd you are hiring as boomers retire. The baby boom generation retirement wave is pushing us all to a crisis point. There are only half as many "millennials" coming into organizations as there are boomers going out. They are going to need to be twice as productive. Are you providing the workplace technologies most familiar to them? While you are at it, are you providing the means to keep retirees engaged?

## What If We're Wrong?

What if we're wrong about the future of technology? What if we're wrong about the network? What if broadband is not going to be available in Africa in two years? Well, that's why we get paid as senior leaders. Strategy is about making bets. When we're making bets in nonprofit organizations, we're making bets with donors' dollars. We have to ask the question from the IT perspective: What's the most pragmatic use of that contribution? Where are we going to make our bets?

One final word before you make your bets: when there is rapid change and uncertainty, smart organizations vary like mad.[9] Run pilots, experiments, and test ideas. Throw away what doesn't work. Take to scale that which succeeds.

## Notes

1. *Deconstructing the Computer: Report of a Symposium*, National Academy of Sciences, 2005, p. 12. Raw data at Triplett (1989) and unpublished Bureau of Economic Analysis data, National Academy of Sciences, *Deconstructing the Computer: Report of a Symposium*, p. 107; http://www.nap.edu/catalog/11457.html.

2. See http://www.nethope.org for details about NetHope.

3. Dr. David Delong, CIO Year Ahead Conference. November 2005, noted that NASA has three times the number of people over sixty as they do of those under thirty. More than 50 percent of IT workers in the U.S. government are eligible to retire by 2013, and 40 percent of the Tennessee Valley Authority (TVA) staff is eligible to retire by 2010.

4. See http://www.icnl.org/knowledge/ijnl/vol7iss1/art_3.htm for an in-depth article on the impact of Sarbanes-Oxley.

5. See http://www.sas70.com/about.htm for more information about Statement on Auditing Standards 70.

6. See https://www.pcisecuritystandards.org for further information on the Payment Card Industry Data Security Standards.

7. The classic text on disruptive innovation is Clay Christensen's *Innovator's Dilemma* (Harvard Business School Press, June 1997). See also Christensen's "Disruptive Innovation for Social Change," *Harvard Business Review*, December 2006. "A disruptive technology or disruptive innovation is a technological innovation, product, or service that eventually overturns the existing dominant technology or status quo product in the market" (Wikipedia, http://en.wikipedia.org/wiki/Disruptive_innovation); note the table of examples.

8. Target Analysis Group (http://www.targetanalysis.com), now a part of Blackbaud, conducts an annual survey of nonprofit members of the NGO-CIO listserv. This is the 2005 and 2007 average of the survey.

9. See Jim Collins, *Built to Last* (HarperCollins, 1995), pp. 146–147.

# INDEX